I0823025

THE WAGE STANDARD

THE WAGE STANDARD

What's Wrong in the Labor Market and How to Fix It

Arindrajit Dube

DUTTON

An imprint of Penguin Random House LLC
1745 Broadway, New York, NY 10019
penguinrandomhouse.com

Figures / charts / graphs all courtesy of the author

Book design by Silverglass Studios

Library of Congress Cataloging-in-Publication Data has been applied for.

ISBN 9780593471418 (hardcover)
ISBN 9780593471418 (ebook)

Printed in the United States of America
1st Printing

The authorized representative in the EU for product safety and compliance is Penguin Random House Ireland, Morrison Chambers, 32 Nassau Street, Dublin D02 YH68, Ireland, https://eu-contact.penguin.ie.

Dedicated to the memory of Frank Morley,
the contract custodian of Littauer Hall, and a member
of the Harvard Living Wage Campaign

Contents

THE WAGE STANDARD

CHAPTER 1

A Raise Deferred

Stalled Pay and the Road to Renewal

If you're like most working Americans, I have some good news: You probably deserve a raise!

Now, you very well may share this sentiment—after all, most of us believe we're doing a decent job. But here's the kicker: In this case, chances are, you're right. You might wonder how I could possibly know that, since we've likely never met. I've never been to your workplace, and we've never shared a meal or even a coffee. So how can I be so sure?

Well, it has everything to do with my job. I study how people get paid, and why they earn what they earn. My work involves poring over mountains of data, analyzing how companies set wages, and examining the ripple effects of those decisions on employees, customers, and companies themselves. I've researched what happens when businesses compete to attract talent and what unfolds when governments step in to establish pay standards. A few years ago, I even advised the United Kingdom's government on setting its minimum wage policy. These experiences have given me a unique perspective on how companies—your employer included—figure out what to pay.

Here's the truth: Over the past half century, many working- and middle-class Americans have received paychecks smaller than they should be, even as our society has grown more prosperous. In this book, I aim to show you why—and, more importantly, how—we can change the labor market to work better for us all.

The Wage Standard tells the story of how we got here, the choices that led to this situation, and the steps we can take to give America a raise. Let's start with a thought experiment. Imagine we were time-traveling anthropologists transported back to 1980 to study the American economy. What would seem familiar? What would feel completely different?

Life in 1980 was, in many ways, a world apart from our own. If you wanted to buy a TV, you might head to a department store like Sears, where a 19-inch color RCA television would cost the equivalent of $1,700 today (as in 2023 dollars, after adjusting for inflation).[1] These TVs were clunky and expensive, and they required manual adjustments for a decent picture. On your way home, you might drive to a supermarket called Alpha Beta—yes, that was a real chain—in a car without keyless ignition, built-in navigation, or even airbags, likely getting around sixteen miles per gallon. Inside the store, you'd find few pre-prepared meals, no exotic fruits out of season, and hardly any imported food products.

Fast-forward to today, and the differences are staggering, but the most notable is economic: America has become a far wealthier society than we were forty-five years ago. One way to measure this progress is by looking at how much American workers produce from an hour of work. After accounting for inflation in a manner consistent with how pay is measured, and subtracting the portion of output needed to replenish machinery, buildings, and so on, American workers' overall hourly productivity rose by *73 percent* between 1980 and 2019.[2] That statistic alone shows how much wealthier our society has become: We can produce over 1.7x as many goods and services in an hour as we did forty years ago. To put this in perspective, a 73 percent gap in current overall income is roughly the difference between America and countries like Estonia or Poland.[3]

But how have wages grown since 1980? If everyone's wages had risen in step with overall productivity—and if the shares of income going to labor and capital had stayed the same—then real (inflation-adjusted) wages could have grown by as much as 73 percent between 1980 and 2019.[4] But is that what actually happened? Or did wages evolve in a way that diverted much of the productivity gains to top earners and business owners rather than to most workers?

During our hypothetical trip back in time, imagine asking the employees at Alpha Beta how much they were making. To find out what their wages looked like—and how they've changed—we can turn to the Current Population Survey (CPS), a monthly federal survey based on household interviews. According to the CPS, the average hourly wage for retail workers in 1980 was about $14.60 in today's dollars. Fast-forward four decades: If we repeated the survey in 2019, just before the pandemic, we'd find that their average pay had risen to only about $17.40, a 19 percent increase in the real (or inflation-adjusted) wage.[5]

In other words, while the broader economy has changed in dramatic, fundamental ways—becoming much richer overall—wages for many workers have remained much more suppressed. Even as economy-wide productivity climbed by *73 percent*, the purchasing power of frontline retail workers grew much less—only by around *19 percent*. That's a striking—and sobering—gap, reminding us that economic growth alone doesn't guarantee broad-based prosperity.

Measuring Inequalities

Was there something peculiar about retail jobs that could explain why wages at the checkout counter diverged so sharply from overall productivity gains? Not really. In fact, wages for middle- and low-income workers across many industries failed to keep pace with the growth in economy-wide productivity. To get a clearer view, we can again turn to CPS data and examine wage trends across the distribution.

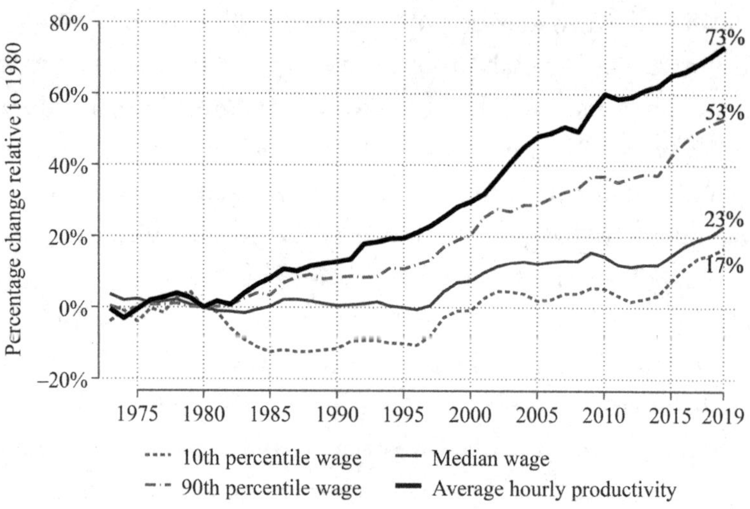

FIGURE 1.1 REAL HOURLY WAGES BY PERCENTILE AND OVERALL PRODUCTIVITY SINCE 1973[6]

For context, the 10th percentile wage is what 10 percent of workers earn less than, while the 90th percentile wage is what 90 percent of workers earn less than. If economic gains are broadly shared, these percentiles would grow at similar rates. But if gains are concentrated at the top, we will see widening gaps. And keep in mind that a *real wage* growth of zero means nominal wages rose just enough to match inflation. (The glossary in appendix A goes more deeply into how *real wages* are constructed.)

Between 1980 and 2019, real wages at the 90th percentile rose by *53 percent*—an impressive gain, though still below the growth in overall productivity. But the picture looks far worse for workers at the middle and bottom. Over the same period, median wages rose by just *23 percent*, while wages at the 10th percentile grew only *17 percent*. These modest gains resemble the sluggish growth seen in retail wages and fall well short of both productivity growth and the pay increases at the top. In short, while top earners surged ahead, workers at the bottom barely kept up with the rising cost of living until very recently. As recently as 2014, real wages at the 10th percentile were still hovering near their 1980 level.

The divergence in wages began in the early 1980s, when pay at the bottom actually fell in real terms. Strikingly, the median hourly wage was virtually stagnant between 1980 and 1997, even as hourly productivity increased by 23 percent during that period. Wages for the middle and lower percentiles only ticked upward during select years, such as the late 1990s and late 2010s, driven by tight labor markets and supportive economic policies—topics we'll explore in this book. Even with those sporadic gains, by 2019, average wages for the bottom 90 percent of earners were just *29 percent* higher than in 1980, while productivity had grown by 73 percent.[7] As the economist Lawrence Mishel has pointed out, this disconnect meant that most workers' pay lagged well behind their potential during the post-1980 era.[8]

A big reason behind this gap between median wages and overall productivity is that wages in America have become more unequal over the last half century. While average (mean) wages grew by 42 percent over this period, both the median wage and the 10th percentile wage trailed well behind.[9] This happens because average wage growth is pulled upward by large gains at the top, whereas the median wage reflects what's happening at the middle. A second factor is the declining share of income going to labor, which has fallen, especially since 2000. As wages claim a smaller slice of the economic pie, it boosts the share going to capital owners, further dampening the gains most workers see in their paychecks. All in all, less than 10 percent of salary earners saw their wages keep pace with productivity growth.

You may wonder whether these figures depend on how we measure inflation. In short, yes, different inflation measures can shift the wage numbers somewhat. Yet because I used the same measure to adjust both wages and productivity, the key comparisons still hold, and the overall story remains much the same.[10] The gap between middle- and low-income wages relative to overall productivity persists, as does the disparity between top and bottom wages. No matter which inflation measure you use, it's clear that since 1980, most Americans—particularly those near the bottom—have gained relatively little from the nation's growing prosperity. Many even saw their real wages decline in the 1980s and early 1990s.

Household surveys don't allow us to peer into the upper echelons of earners—like those in the top 1 percent—because of issues like limited sample sizes, confidentiality constraints, and low response rates to surveys from high-income households. To fill that gap, researchers use administrative data (for example, from the Social Security Administration) that covers nearly all U.S. earners. Analyses of these more comprehensive data confirm that the concentration of earnings at the top is even more extreme than household surveys suggest. Real annual earnings for the bottom 90 percent rose by 40 percent between 1980 and 2019, whereas for the top 1 percent they soared, increasing by 169 percent.[11] Looking further up the pay ladder only reinforces how dramatically inequality has climbed since the 1980s.

As its title suggests, *The Wage Standard* focuses on money that workers earn. For most households—especially those below the top tier—wages also constitute the largest share of their *total* income. Nevertheless, once we factor in other income sources such as business earnings, investments, and government transfers, additional trends and complexities appear that wage data alone can't show. There is also the role of taxes: In theory, a progressive tax system reduces inequality, but how well it has done so in recent decades is another question.

Using data from both surveys and federal tax records, analysis by the Congressional Budget Office (CBO) reveals that pre-tax income in the United States has become significantly more unequal since 1980. Pre-tax income includes wages, business and capital income, and social insurance benefits like Social Security and unemployment insurance. Between 1980 and 2019, incomes for the bottom fifth of households rose by *45 percent*, middle-income households saw a *34 percent* increase, and incomes for the top fifth surged by *111 percent.* Meanwhile, the top 1 percent experienced a staggering *232 percent* increase, clearly showing that the highest earners have pulled far ahead.[12]

What happens when we factor in government programs such as food stamps, welfare, and the Earned Income Tax Credit, and then subtract federal taxes? Since these programs primarily benefit lower-income households and taxes are applied progressively, incomes at the bottom rise more when we take these programs into consideration. Yet even with these adjustments, inequality remains significant and has continued to grow. According to the CBO, between 1980 and 2019, post-tax income for the bottom fifth of households rose by 89 percent, middle-income households saw a 51 percent increase, and the top fifth experienced a 119 percent gain. At the very top, the post-tax income of the top 1 percent climbed by an extraordinary 248 percent, widening the gap between them and the rest of the population.[13]

There is some debate among scholars over the precise increase in household income inequality since 1980. The CBO estimates focus on "fiscal income," which includes wages, business income, capital gains, Social Security, and unemployment benefits, among other sources. However, economists Gerald Auten and David Splinter claim that these official figures miss a substantial amount of hidden income—unreported to the IRS—collected by non-wealthy taxpayers. This leads them to conclude that the rise in inequality has been less dramatic than it appears in official data.[14]

In contrast, Thomas Piketty, Emmanuel Saez, and Gabriel Zucman argue that it's the rich who have increasingly underreported income, especially from pass-through businesses and funds sitting in offshore accounts. They contend that the wealthiest households are responsible for the bulk of unreported income, leading them to estimate a *greater* rise in inequality than both the CBO and Auten-Splinter.[15]

My own reading of the evidence is closer to Piketty, Saez, and Zucman. But whatever the exact numbers, there is little doubt that U.S. income inequality has risen markedly since 1980. As the Nobel laureate Daron Acemoglu remarked, technical disputes shouldn't obscure the bigger picture: The U.S. economy has been malfunctioning for over four decades.[16] Another laureate, Paul Krugman, famously dubbed this era the "Great Divergence," reflecting the widening chasm between the rich and everyone else.[17]

Here is the bigger point. While early twentieth-century inequality was largely driven by asset ownership and inherited wealth, today's gap is powered by labor income. In their 2003 landmark study, Piketty and Saez put it succinctly: "[T]he working rich have replaced the rentiers at the top of the income distribution."[18] And no one seriously disputes that *wage* inequality has soared over the past forty-five years.

To understand why *incomes* at the top—whether for business owners or highly paid executives—have skyrocketed while most American workers' pay has lagged behind productivity growth, we need a closer look at how *wages* are set. Government programs may have softened some of the blow, but the underlying story remains much the same: The market wages of ordinary Americans have not kept pace with the country's rising prosperity.

Ultimately, wages lie at the heart of the divide between the rich and the rest. This book sets out to examine how pay is determined and why they've diverged so sharply.

A Broader Look Across the World

We live in a globally connected world—trade and investment flow across borders, and major technological advancements spread rapidly from one country to another. This interconnectedness may lead some to assume that rising wage inequality in the United States is part of a universal trend. But the numbers tell a different story. Inequality in wages and incomes has grown more sharply in America than in most comparable economies.

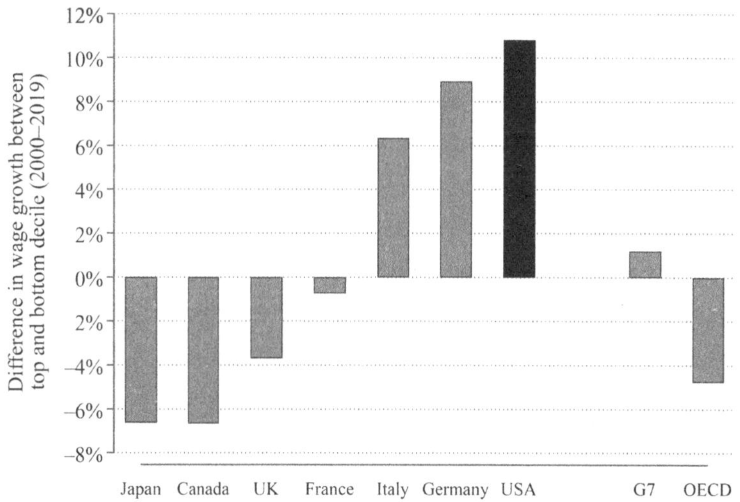

FIGURE 1.2 **DIFFERENCE IN WAGE GROWTH BETWEEN THE TOP AND BOTTOM DECILES OF WAGES (2000–2019)**[19]

Figure 1.2 presents data from the Organization for Economic Cooperation and Development (OECD), tracking wage gaps between the top 10 percent and bottom 10 percent (deciles) of full-time workers across thirty-eight high- and middle-income countries. While the OECD's older data is spotty for the 1980s and 1990s, from 2000 onward we have a solid record.

The figure shows the difference in wage growth between the top and bottom deciles from 2000 to 2019. Larger numbers mean the top decile's pay grew faster than the bottom decile's. In America, top-decile wage growth outpaced bottom-decile growth by around 11 percentage points—consistent with the pattern of rising inequality that we documented in the first pages of this chapter. Yet in the G7 countries overall (Canada, France, Germany, Italy, Japan, the United

Kingdom, and the United States), wage growth for the bottom decile lagged the top decile by only 1 percentage point. And across all OECD countries with complete data, the bottom outgrew the top by 5 percentage points. America not only started out more unequal—with a top-to-bottom decile wage ratio of 4.5 in 2000 compared to 3.3 for the G7 average—but it has also become more unequal over time.

Did it have to unfold this way? Or was there a time when the fruits of economic growth were more equally shared with workers in this country?

To better understand the rise in wage inequality and the gap between productivity and the wages of most workers, we need to look further back. The arc of this story traces back to the early twentieth century, where a series of political and economic upheavals led to a tentative balance between labor and capital.

Before the Divergence

The household survey behind figure 1.1 began collecting hourly earnings data only in the 1970s, which complicates comparisons with earlier decades. Fortunately, other sources help us extend wage trends further back—especially for workers around the middle of the pay scale—and compare them to overall productivity growth.

One key source is the government's monthly establishment survey, which collects data from businesses on the wages of non-managerial employees (about 80 percent of the private workforce). From 1973 to 2019, these average wages closely tracked the median wage, allowing us to use them as a stand-in for earlier years. Before 1964, the only data on non-managerial wages came from manufacturing, but those wages rose at about the same pace as in other sectors around that time. Combining these sources lets us trace average non-managerial wages back to 1948.

This longer timeline reveals a stark contrast between two periods.

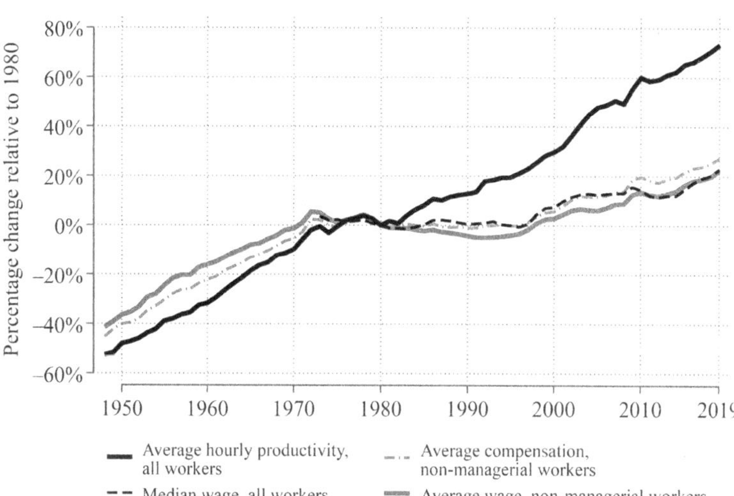

FIGURE 1.3 **AVERAGE REAL HOURLY WAGE OF NON-MANAGERIAL WORKERS AND PRODUCTIVITY SINCE 1948**[20]

From 1948 to 1979, wages and productivity rose more or less in tandem: After inflation, non-managerial wages rose by about 1.8 percent annually, not too far off from productivity's 2.5 percent growth. In contrast, between 1980 and 2019, non-managerial wages grew at roughly 0.5 percent per year, lagging far behind productivity growth of about 1.4 percent. Wage growth was around 73 percent of productivity growth in the earlier period, while it was only 37 percent in the latter.

But could workers simply be getting more of their total compensation through nonwage benefits like health insurance or retirement plans? As it turns out, this changes things only marginally. Figure 1.3 also tracks "compensation," which includes these benefits. Before 1980, total compensation actually kept pace with productivity even more closely than wages alone.[21] But after 1980, it began to lag almost as much as wages. The upshot is clear: Whether measured by wages alone or by wages plus benefits, typical American workers have not kept pace with the economy's growing prosperity since the 1980s. As a result, America has grown more unequal: From 1951 to 1980, annual earnings for the bottom 90 percent and the top 1 percent rose more similarly, but since 1980 the gap has widened sharply.[22]

Finding the Culprits

When I was in graduate school, my PhD adviser Richard Freeman liked to say that empirical economists are like detectives at a crime scene. First, we document the scene as precisely as possible; then we track down suspects, weigh the evidence, and figure out who's responsible. In our case, the "crime scene" is the growing gap between overall economic prosperity and what ordinary Americans bring home in their paychecks. So we have to ask: Why did this happen, and was it inevitable?

As with most major shifts in the economy, more than one factor underpins this Great Divergence. We can start with the usual suspects. Many economists point to technological change that has hollowed out routine jobs, especially in manufacturing. Work by Daron Acemoglu and David Autor shows how automation and shifts in skill demand lowered pay for non-college-educated workers.[23] Educational shortcomings, highlighted by Lawrence Katz and Claudia Goldin, have also played a role: America's higher-education system hasn't produced enough college graduates compared to some peer nations, adding to challenges.[24] And job losses from trade matter, too. China's entry into the World Trade Organization in 2000 and the earlier North American Free Trade Agreement (NAFTA) both hit regions heavily exposed to import competition, eroding many traditional, stable, well-paying jobs.[25]

Technology and globalization help explain how we got here—but they aren't destiny. Too often, we're told that inequality in market incomes is inevitable and that the best we can do is "compensate the losers" with government transfers. Yet, as we've already seen, other countries faced similar pressures from technology and trade without experiencing the same surge in wage inequality. Even Canada—our next-door neighbor with many similar economic structures—saw far less divergence between the top and the bottom.[26] Market forces are important, but they are not irresistible.

This book offers a different explanation, focusing on the choices we have made as a society. These choices include those undertaken by major employers who have shaped the terrain of wage-setting here in America—leading to decades-long wage stagnation, particularly for those without a college degree. This is a story where corporate pay strategies are shaped by the crosscurrents of historical upheavals in union organizing, labor market structures that determine competition, macroeconomic policies that determine availability of jobs, and pay regulations such as minimum wages. While technology and globalization undoubtedly factor in, their impact is filtered through institutions and corporate decisions.

From the late 1930s through the 1940s, America enacted policies and built institutions that helped narrow pay differentials—producing a major reduction in wage inequality that economists Claudia Goldin and Robert Margo later termed the "Great Compression." For decades after World War II, typical workers—blue- and white-collar alike—moved ahead in step with the broader economy. The story of how this arrangement came to be is a fascinating one, involving changes in wage-setting practices at some of the country's most iconic companies—like General Motors (GM)—and driven by social movements and union organizing, particularly by the United Auto Workers (UAW). Technological change, like electrification, did shape this era, too, but it was mediated by institutions and history.

If GM and the UAW sound familiar from recent headlines, it's because the historical arc I explore in this book is still unfolding today. Fast-forwarding from the late 1940s through the early 1980s, earnings of most American workers grew in unison. Both blue- and white-collar workers benefited from the economy's growth during this time. This social compact forged through the upheavals of the twentieth century—often referred to as the "Treaty of Detroit" after a landmark 1950 agreement between General Motors and the UAW—laid the foundation for this shared prosperity.

Then came the 1980s and 1990s, which saw the erosion of what I call the *wage standard*: the idea that there is a societally acceptable range of pay for most jobs. Contrary to some economic narratives, the job market is not a well-oiled machine that seamlessly matches the right workers with the right companies at a pay rate determined solely by impersonal market forces. Don't get me wrong: Supply and demand definitely matter when it comes to wage formation. But they matter in an environment teeming with all sorts of different business strategies, pay norms, institutional forces, and macroeconomic environments. These other factors mean that if you want to make sense of what happened to job quality and inequality, the hidden explanations involve choices made by people rather than inescapable economic forces. As I will keep coming back to throughout the book, major American employers, for example Walmart and General Motors, have considerable discretion when it comes to setting wages. There are a lot of differences among wage policies chosen by employers—with similar workers often getting very different pay at different companies. And when contexts shift, wage policies change, too, moving the balance between good and bad jobs.

Here's an intriguing fact: In 1980, large employers generally paid substantially higher wages than smaller companies, offering even non-college-educated workers a solid path into the middle class. By the 2010s, however, that large-employer advantage had largely disappeared for blue-collar workers.

One reason large employers used to pay more was to uphold a sense of fairness and internal equity. Profitable companies shared their wealth broadly (a practice economists call *rent-sharing*), especially when unions were strong enough to influence wages—even in nonunion firms. Norms also prevented pay scales from drifting too far apart; it would have been unseemly for a leading employer to lavish pay on white-collar staff while offering paltry wages to service workers. These fairness norms didn't appear out of thin air: They were forged through conflict and upheaval in the first half of the twentieth century. Once established, they helped keep wage disparities in check throughout the post–World War II era, buoyed by strong unions, wage regulations, tax policy, and a commitment to full employment. CEOs certainly outearned janitors, but the accepted degree of inequality within a single workplace was limited by these shared notions of fairness.

Those norms crumbled in the 1980s and 1990s. Companies began sharing far fewer rents with blue-collar workers, partly because newcomers like Walmart had no historical constraints shaping their pay policies. Meanwhile, older corporations adopted cost-cutting strategies—often championed by business schools—that further undercut rent-sharing.

Few figures illustrate these seismic shifts in corporate norms as vividly as Jack Welch. As CEO of General Electric from 1981 to 2001, Welch championed relentless cost-cutting and placed an unwavering emphasis on shareholder returns. Dubbed "Neutron Jack" for his willingness to shed thousands of jobs, Welch also popularized "rank-and-yank" performance reviews, which forced out the lowest-rated employees. His model became a blueprint for other big corporations.[27] By the 1990s, many firms had embraced Welch's brand of aggressive management, often at the expense of workforce stability and pay equity. Where companies once aimed for long-term loyalty and broadly shared gains, they now focused on short-term profitability, amplifying the breakdown of the wage standard.

Another way to bypass internal equity norms was to reclassify who counted as part of a company. If a company like Apple employed its own janitors, it might feel obliged to pay them in line with corporate fairness standards. But outsourcing those roles to contractors put those wages "out of sight, out of mind," and service contractors competing on cost could drive wages ever lower.[28] Outsourcing thus became a potent tool for dismantling pay norms.

It's crucial to recognize that none of these shifts were inevitable. As this book will show, the past four decades have been molded by a series of policy and managerial choices—by corporate leaders, public officials, and by us, wearing various hats as managers, investors, consumers, voters, activists, and workers deciding whether (and how) to speak up. The erosion of pay norms wasn't fated; it was chosen.

Why Not Quit?

You might wonder whether the central tenet of this book—that employers have real discretion in setting wages—goes against standard economic theory. After all, Econ 101 teaches that in a competitive labor market, wages are determined by supply and demand. If General Electric under Jack Welch or Walmart under Sam Walton offered low pay, why wouldn't workers just quit for better jobs elsewhere, forcing employers to raise wages to the "market rate"? In a perfectly competitive market, people with similar qualifications should earn similar pay, no matter where they work, and the market wage should reflect a worker's productive value.

In reality, labor markets don't behave that neatly. They're often riddled with power imbalances that favor employers. Most of the time, the ability of workers to walk away from a bad job and find a better one is limited in important ways. Indeed, the freedom to quit a bad job is one of the best indicators of how competitive a labor market really is. By this standard, the U.S. labor market has been far less competitive than the textbook models imply they should be—especially over the last forty-five years. Employers have considerable latitude in setting wages, exercising what economists call *monopsony power*—the labor market counterpart to monopoly. While a monopoly describes a single seller, a monopsony describes a situation in which there is a dominant buyer. In practice, it's rare to have only one buyer, but many employers do have enough market power to pay less than a theoretical "competitive" wage without prompting a massive worker exodus.

In essence, a hands-off labor market is better understood as monopsonistic than perfectly competitive. In this world, employers aren't mere wage-takers: They *choose* what type of wage policies to pursue. A growing body of research from the past decade has provided compelling evidence for this view. In the next chapter, I'll take a closer look at the concept of monopsony, laying out the most persuasive findings that will help us understand how the wage standard is shaped by competing forces.

Recognizing employer-side power unlocks mysteries about why wages for so many workers have failed to keep pace with productivity and why inequality has soared. Historically, various mechanisms held monopsony power in check. These countervailing forces include policies such as minimum wages. But they also include wage norms and public pressures that enforce them, labor unions, and policies that run the labor market hot and help boost worker leverage.

As I'll show, the weakening of such countervailing power was a key part of how corporate America restructured the workplace in the 1980s, reshaping the fortunes of workers. Understanding these restructurings is vital for explaining what happened to job quality over the past forty-five years. But in the magical textbook realm of perfect competition, it's hard to talk about how GM jobs stopped being "good jobs" in the 1990s, or why they improved more recently. It's equally puzzling to account for how Walmart's low-wage model reshaped the retail sector, driving wages and benefits lower both directly and indirectly by pressuring rivals and suppliers. Or to make sense of how business schools helped propagate Jack Welch–style management strategies and drive down pay across shop floors. Yet these are essential parts of the story, and leaving them out would leave our understanding incomplete.

A Hopeful Message

The Wage Standard is a deep dive into what broke the labor market for so many workers in America. But this book isn't all gloom and doom. It's also a story about how we can successfully rebuild the standard *right now.* Drawing on more than two decades of research and public engagement, I begin a conversation about how to raise wages for workers in America. While paychecks have been slow to grow for many workers, there's a growing desire for changes that help working people thrive. More and more, we're asking: What would an economy look like where workers have real power and voice?

A big reveal in this book is that the wage standard is *already* being rebuilt. Here is a fact that may surprise you. In the final years of the 2010s, and especially since 2020, the decades-long rise in wage inequality began to reverse. Measured by the gap between the 90th to 10th percentile wage, inequality declined by about 8 percent between 2019 and 2024. Combined with a smaller drop in the late 2010s, this amounts to a 10 percent reduction—wiping out nearly one-third of the increase in wage inequality that accumulated between 1980 and 2013. To a large extent, this turnaround happened because tight labor markets forced employers to compete for workers, curbing employer power and lifting pay at the lower end. In other words, when the labor market runs hot, wages in the middle and the bottom see real gains. The pursuit of full employment meaningfully disrupted wage inequality for the first time in decades. The gains remain fragile but show that change is possible.

Rebuilding the wage standard isn't just about macro-level fixes. Public outcry and worker activism in the 2010s pushed major employers like Amazon to adopt higher internal pay floors, prompting companies such as Walmart and Bank of America to follow suit by raising entry-level wages to between $14 and $25 an hour. In 2023, a successful strike by the United Auto Workers compelled major automakers to raise pay, and those gains have begun to spill over to nonunion shops as well. These examples remind us that social movements and public pressure can unite businesses and activists alike to revive fair-wage norms. Meanwhile, antitrust enforcement has turned its attention to employer-side monopsony power, opening yet another route to strengthen worker leverage.

Between broad policies that influence the entire labor market and the individual choices of specific firms lies a *meso-economic* realm where key policy tools reside. For instance, the ongoing decline in the real federal minimum wage—stagnant since 2010, the longest stretch on record—has worsened inequality and hit living standards hard. However, at least thirty states have enacted higher minimum wages, including traditionally conservative or swing states like Nebraska, Florida, and Arizona, where ballot initiatives reflected voters' insistence on better pay. Research shows that these state-level policies over the past decade have contributed to reversing some of the decades-long increase in inequality.

The academic debate on minimum wages has often been heated, sometimes leaving nonexperts confused. This book provides a guided tour of that terrain, offering clear, up-to-date evidence on how minimum wages affect pay, jobs, inequality, and other key outcomes. In recent years, countries like the UK and Germany have adopted more ambitious minimum wage policies with encouraging results, paving the way for thoughtful reforms that help low-wage workers without causing many of the feared downsides.

These are just glimpses of the ways we can build broader standards. Minimum wages help at the bottom of the pay scale, but what about the middle? We will explore the landscape of sectoral standards and bargaining—widely used in other advanced economies—that can shelter workers from wage inequality and stagnation. Australia, for instance, uses wage boards to set minimum pay rates across various occupations. Following that lead, some American states like Minnesota and California have started to experiment with sectoral wage boards, pointing to new ways of raising pay across large segments of the labor market. This approach also offers a path to revitalizing the labor movement by moving beyond the traditional company-by-company organizing model.

Where there is political will, I have a hopeful message—rooted in data—that shows how public engagement and persistence can improve the lives of American workers in the here and now. Despite the challenges of the pandemic and economic turbulence, the past decade has shown that meaningful progress in the labor market is possible. Let's learn from these successes and harness our policy tools to rebuild the wage standard that underpins broadly shared prosperity.

CHAPTER 2

Monopsony!

A Free Labor Market, but Without Standards

The Shift Project was started in 2016 by sociologists Kristen Harknett and Danny Schneider to shed light on how different companies pay their workers. It's not easy to get public information on company pay practices, as they tend to guard this information jealously. So, to get at this question, the Shift Project researchers did something clever. They used Facebook and Instagram to target ads toward users who are currently working for a particular company and offered them a small incentive to participate in a survey. By clicking on these ads, workers could report their wages, describe how they were treated, and share other job-related details. Thousands of respondents spanning dozens of companies participated, giving the Shift Project a broad database on pay distribution at over sixty-six major American employers. These data were then shared via an interactive website codeveloped with the Economic Policy Institute, allowing users to compare company size, revenue, CEO pay, and worker wages.

A quick browse of the website reveals striking pay variations even among companies that appear quite similar. For instance, FedEx and UPS each employ around half a million people, and in 2021, each worker generated roughly $150,000 in annual revenue.[1] Despite these parallels, Shift Project survey data from 2021 showed that about 63 percent of UPS workers earned over $20 per hour, compared to only

40 percent of FedEx workers. In other words, two similarly matched companies can arrive at very different wage policies.

This isn't an isolated case. This pattern surfaces in the retail sector as well. Walmart, for example, had higher revenue per worker than Target in 2021, yet its wages were noticeably lower. While 51 percent of Walmart's workforce reported earning under $15 an hour, only 3 percent of Target's workers did—a gap that translates to roughly a 25 percent higher average wage at Target than at Walmart. These pay differences are consistent with Walmart's reputation as a relatively low-wage employer, and with other data. For example, on Glassdoor—a website where workers rank their employers on job satisfaction—Walmart's rating trailed those of Target and Costco.

Such disparities raise big questions. If a stingy boss pays less than competitors, why wouldn't workers just quit? Isn't that how markets work—by fostering competition? Can companies really choose between a high-wage and low-wage strategy in a modern, dynamic economy?

Economists have grappled with these questions for over a century. In the idealized world of perfect competition, workers are free to move between jobs, and employers must offer competitive wages to retain talent. However, in the real world, where opportunities for workers are often more limited, employers have a say over wages, which—as you may remember from the previous chapter—economists refer to as *monopsony* power. You're probably more familiar with the term "monopoly," which you may recognize from the board game, where players try to accumulate properties, charge rent, and drive competitors out of business. "Monopoly" refers to the power a company has to set prices for goods or services due to a lack of competition. Monopsony is similar but applies to the buying side, and in this case, it refers to companies' power in the labor market: their ability to set wages when hiring workers due to a lack of alternative employment options.

The idea that employers hold such wage-setting power isn't new. In her 1933 book on imperfect competition, the British economist

Joan Robinson—sometimes described as the most prominent economist never to win a Nobel Prize—coined the term "monopsony" to capture this idea. But even before that, the eighteenth-century economist Adam Smith famously described a labor market rigged in favor of employers, warning that employers are "always and everywhere in a sort of tacit, but constant and uniform combination, not to raise the wages of labor above their actual rate."[2] He observed that this collusion among employers was so ingrained that it often went unnoticed. Today, rather than literal meetings in smoke-filled rooms, it's often market positioning and wage surveys that allow companies to respond to each other's pay policies and coordinate on wage levels. But even when employers are not engaging in any collusion—explicit or implicit—here is the key point: When employees face limited job options, employers can wield outsize wage-setting power.

In this chapter, we'll explore how economists' perspectives on wage-setting and employer influence have evolved over time. In many ways, the economics of wages has followed an arc. Early on, the focus was more on the institutional details of wage-setting and company pay policies. Then the emphasis shifted toward human capital theory, which cast wages as merely a function of skills—be it education, training, or experience. In recent years, though, renewed attention has been paid to employer wage policies as deliberate, consequential choices—a viewpoint spurred by growing recognition of how monopsony power shapes the labor market. Much of this shift was driven by improved data and empirical methods, which have allowed economists to more precisely gauge how companies set wages and exercise their power. Notably, a key figure in bringing monopsony to the fore was another British economist, Alan Manning, who studied at Cambridge when Joan Robinson—older and holding court with her trademark long cigarette holder—was still there to inspire new debates.

Against this backdrop, it's instructive to jump back to the mid-twentieth century to see what was happening in the labor market then and how economists of that era confronted (or occasionally overlooked) the influence of firm-level wage-setting.

From Institutionalist Economics to the Human Capital Revolution

In the early 1950s, a Harvard economist named Sumner Slichter decided to roll up his sleeves and visit fifteen factories in the Boston area. He wanted to learn exactly how much people made—janitors, machinists, electricians, carpenters—and he discovered startling disparities. His findings were eye-opening: For janitors alone, wages varied by more than 50 percent between the highest- and lowest-paying plants, and for machinists, carpenters, and electricians, the gap hovered around 40 to 42 percent. He also noticed that companies paying well for high-skill positions tended to pay well for low-skill jobs, too.[3]

Around the same time, Richard Lester at Princeton was examining a Bureau of Labor Statistics survey of workers in Denver and Atlanta. He saw a similar "range of indeterminacy": Within a certain band, the same skill set could translate to noticeably different pay, depending on which workplace you landed in. To Lester and other institutionalist economists, that spelled trouble for the idea of "the competitive wage." If there was a single going rate for each occupation, then big wage variations shouldn't exist.

Not everyone was convinced. Skeptics countered that maybe those "low-paying" plants simply hired less-skilled workers, so skill differences—rather than the plants themselves—were driving the wage gaps. By the 1960s, many economists had begun to shift toward theories of human capital—how education and experience shape skills, and thus pay. The famed "Mincer earnings function" (created by economist Jacob Mincer) put schooling and work experience front and center in explaining wages. (See appendix B for more of a deeper dive.) With newly available household-level data sources like the

Census and the Current Population Survey (CPS), labor economists could conduct large-scale statistical analyses. It was far simpler to measure a worker's education than to pinpoint a firm's pay policy.

Of course, the Mincer equation usually never explained more than about one-third of the variation in wages. The rest sat in the "error term." It included all the unmeasured factors that might influence pay, such as a company's pay strategy or local hiring practices. Yet, because researchers had limited information on each worker's employer, firm-level effects got short shrift in the mainstream.

A handful of economists resisted this new consensus during the 1970s. A group of scholars—like Michael Piore, Peter Doeringer, David Gordon, Richard Edwards, and Michael Reich—argued for "dual labor market" or "segmented labor market" theories. They contended that workers were split between a stable, higher-paying primary market and a precarious, lower-paying secondary one, driven by institutions and market structures rather than strictly by individual skill.[4] But with no large-scale data on firms' internal pay decisions, these theories had difficulty dislodging the new orthodoxy.

Within mainstream economics, Alan Krueger and Lawrence Summers did important work in the 1980s showing how different *industries* paid seemingly similar workers differently.[5] The logic was straightforward: If, say, the tire industry consistently paid more than the textile industry for similar workers, maybe something about the company or industry itself—profits, productivity, or corporate culture—mattered. Their 1980s research used the best available household data (like the CPS) to track workers who switched industries. If the same person switched from a low-paying industry to a higher-paying one, and got a wage bump, that suggested the difference wasn't about hidden traits of the worker. Robert Gibbons and Lawrence Katz took it one step further, looking at displaced workers forced to find new jobs because of plant closures. Their approach helped rule out the idea that "superstar employees" self-selected into high-paying industries.

Indeed, they still found significant pay jumps when people changed industries.[6]

Although these studies were compelling, they often relied on small samples, and some findings proved sensitive to methodological assumptions. By the mid-1990s, interest in industry wage premiums had waned, and most economists returned to focusing on education, experience, and other individual traits to explain earnings.

Behind the scenes, though, the role of the firm was quietly reemerging. Starting in the 1990s, European governments began granting researchers access to matched employer-employee data from tax records. The idea was revolutionary: Instead of guessing whether skill differences explain wage gaps, you could watch actual pay changes when people moved from one employer to another.

Eventually, American researchers got access to similar administrative data from unemployment insurance, Social Security, and income tax records. As computing power surged, it became feasible to analyze hundreds of millions of pay records, scanning entire career paths in the process.

For modern labor economists, these developments were game changers. We could finally see how wages, profits, productivity, and hiring decisions interact—and measure the extent of sway employers hold in setting wages. We finally had the data and the technology to revisit the questions being studied by Slichter, Lester, and others more than fifty years earlier and provide evidence that could convince the critics. And this wasn't just an intellectual exercise: It would help make sense of changes in corporate strategies and pay practices affecting American workers over the past forty-five years.

It's *Where* You Are, Not Just *Who* You Are

Between 2015 and 2017, two individuals we'll call Marta and Petra both worked about forty hours a week at a corner store in Portland, Oregon. Their starting wages were around $12.50, and by mid-2017, both were making roughly $14 per hour. In other words, they had similar job roles and work histories.

Come September 2017, they each found new jobs—Marta with Walmart at $15.25 per hour, and Petra with Target at $16. These numbers mirror the data gathered by the Shift Project, showing that Target typically pays higher wages than Walmart. Although both benefited from a pay bump, Petra ended up earning about 5 percent more simply because of where she landed.

OK, so Marta and Petra are fictional names, and the specific employers here are meant to be illustrative. However, they're based on statistical composites drawn from real administrative data provided by the Oregon Employment Department, containing a near universe of worker-level employment history. My colleagues (Suresh Naidu, Ihsaan Bassier) and I used this data for a 2022 study, taking advantage of details on both earnings and hours worked to calculate precise hourly wages—an invaluable lens into how wages are actually determined.[7]

Marta and Petra's story reflects actual patterns in the retail sector during that time. Our research found that if one company's average wages were 25 percent higher than another's, workers with similar profiles still faced about a 5 percent pay difference, driven purely by company-specific pay policies. In other words, roughly one-fifth of the wage gap between two employers (5 of those 25 percentage points) could be traced back to a pure "company pay premium."[8]

So what does that tell us? Most importantly, it challenges the notion that wages are determined solely by market forces and individual skills. If the labor market were truly as competitive as some economics textbooks suggest—where pay is simply set by supply and demand—then Marta and Petra would be paid exactly what their work contributes to their employer. In economic terms, they would earn their "marginal product." And if one employer tried to pay them less than that, a rival would quickly step in with a better offer.

But that's not what happened. At the corner store, Marta and

Petra earned almost identical wages. Once they moved on to Walmart and Target, Petra earned more—not because she had greater skills than Marta but because Target simply paid more. This highlights the importance of what economists call the "firm pay premium": the idea that part of the wage gap between similar workers comes down to the pay policies of the companies they work for.

These findings on the importance of company pay policies hold up in a large body of research that has blossomed with the advent of similar administrative datasets, both in America and abroad.[9] For example, using data on annual earnings from the Social Security Administration over the 1980 and 2013 period, the Census Bureau's Jae Song and a team of economists including from Stanford and UCLA quantified the role of the workplace in explaining pay in a landmark 2018 study.[10]

Their work confirmed that pay policies vary considerably across companies and that differences in company pay premia explained around 20 percent of pay differences in what people earned across America—similar to what we found in Oregon.[11] Their research also showed that two-thirds of the rise in U.S. wage inequality between 1980 and 2013 came from growing pay gaps *between* employers, rather than from each employer becoming more unequal internally. This pattern reflects "sorting": White-collar workers increasingly cluster in higher-paying firms, while blue-collar workers end up in firms that pay less in general—regardless of the tasks they perform.

One key factor in this sorting is that higher-wage employers have been outsourcing more service work to outside contractors paying low wages. Numerous studies, including my own work with Ethan Kaplan, show how outsourcing janitors, security guards, and cafeteria staff reduces pay and benefits for these workers.[12] The same pattern extends beyond service roles: Sociologists Nathan Wilmers and Clem Aeppli found that production and clerical jobs are increasingly located in low-premium firms, while higher-premium firms concentrate on managerial and professional roles. Over time, this trend has deepened wage inequality.[13]

Simply put, our workforce has become more divided, in how different types of workers are spread across employers. Good employers, paying a premium, are increasingly composed of higher-tier workers, while lower- and middle-tier workers are increasingly employed by companies pursuing less generous business models.

Employer pay policies also explain why unfortunate timing can have long-lasting effects. Research by Till von Wachter and others shows that graduating into a recession leads to an initial earnings hit of 10 to 15 percent, which can persist for up to fifteen years—often because these graduates begin their careers at lower-paying firms.[14]

Why does this happen? During recessions, high-paying firms cut back on hiring, forcing new entrants into lower-wage jobs. While some workers eventually move to better-paying firms, the initial setback often leaves a lasting impact on their lifetime earnings.

Consider millennials who graduated amid the 2008 financial crisis. Many spent their twenties in low-wage positions, not because they lacked ability but because they entered the job market at a time when higher-paying firms weren't hiring. In contrast, those who graduated just before the downturn or during the tighter labor markets of the late 2010s often fared better, largely because of where they secured their first jobs.

Ultimately, Marta and Petra's story illustrates a bigger truth: *Your pay is not just about who you are—it's also about where you work.* In a world with frictions, where market forces leave plenty of puddles of good and bad jobs in their wake, luck matters. And in such a market, an employer's wage policy—how much it chooses to pay—makes a real difference in workers' lives.

"Release Your Job": The Power of Quits

So, what determines the extent of employers' wage-setting power? It boils down to how easily—borrowing Beyoncé's phrase—you can "release your job" when pay isn't good enough. But how simple is it for someone like Marta to quit Walmart if she's dissatisfied with her wage?

To answer this question, my collaborators Suresh Naidu and Adam Reich and I surveyed about ten thousand Walmart workers in 2019 using a Facebook-based strategy, similar to the Shift Project.[15] As we saw previously, Walmart, the nation's largest private employer, has long been associated with low pay. In 2019, its voluntary company-wide minimum wage stood at $11 per hour, lagging behind competitors like Target and Costco. If low-paying jobs were truly easy to replace, one would expect Walmart jobs to be among the easier to quit and move on from. Or market pressure would already have pushed Walmart wages up to match those competitors.

To make an apples-to-apples comparison, here I focus on roughly six hundred workers earning exactly $11 in states where that wage was legal (i.e., the state minimum wage was below $11). We asked these workers how easy it would be to find a new job at least as good as their current one. The results were striking. Only 36 percent said it would be "very easy" or "somewhat easy" to get a comparable job—meaning nearly two-thirds felt it wouldn't be easy at all. Even in higher-wage northeastern states, where $11 was relatively low, 42 percent still said that replacing their $11/hour Walmart job wouldn't be simple. The common belief that low-paying jobs are easy to leave and replace just doesn't match the reality many workers face—even at Walmart.[16] And this was in 2019, when jobs were relatively easy to find.

The *Quit Elasticity*

We can get a better sense of how hard it is for workers to quit by looking at how pay affects the chances of leaving a job. To see this in action, let's take another look at Marta and Petra. Marta ended up at

Walmart, earning 75 cents less per hour than Petra, who got a job at Target. If we track how long they each stick with their jobs, it can tell us a lot about how competitive the job market really is. In a truly competitive labor market, Marta would quickly jump ship for a better opportunity. But if she sticks around almost as long as Petra, that suggests the market is more "monopsonistic"—Walmart can pay less without losing all of its workforce.

Why would this matter? In a hypercompetitive world, a 5 percent lower wage than competitors should send workers running for the exits, pushing employers to raise pay closer to workers' productivity. But real-world evidence suggests this is rarely the case.

Based on our data, Marta's 5 percent lower wage at Walmart would nudge her monthly quit rate up a bit to 7 percent, compared to Petra's 6.5 percent at Target.[17] That's a difference, but nowhere near the mass departures predicted by a textbook competitive model. On average, Marta might stay at Walmart for about fourteen months, compared to Petra's fifteen months at Target—a modest gap. For labor economists, this simple comparison says a lot about what's really going on in the market. Companies that pay less do face higher turnover, but not massively so.

It might seem bland at first glance, but this sensitivity of quits to wage changes is a spicy measure of labor market power. Economists often use *elasticities* to put a single number on how responsive one thing (like quits) is to changes in another (like wages). The *quit elasticity* answers "If a firm changes wages by 1 percent, by how many percent do quits go up or down?" In other words:

$$Quit\ Elasticity = \frac{\%\ Change\ in\ quits}{\%\ Change\ in\ wages}$$

A large (negative) elasticity, say –10, would mean most workers bolt at the slightest pay cut—classic high competition. A smaller magnitude, like –1, indicates a fair amount of monopsony power:

Workers aren't as quick to quit, so companies can keep wages lower without losing everyone.

Let's apply this to our data. A 5 percent lower wage boosted the monthly quit rate from 6.5 percent to 7.0 percent, a jump of roughly 7 percent. Dividing 7 by 5 gives a quit elasticity of –1.4. That's miles away from the hypercompetitive model and indicates that retailers like Walmart or Target have notable wage-setting power. This is what we found in our data on low-wage industries like retail and food services. When we expanded our analysis to include workers across the economy, we found a general quit elasticity of around –2. Figure 2.1 illustrates the underlying calculations: If a company pays 10 percent less than a competitor, quits will be about 20 percent higher. Employers can opt for a lower pay position without hemorrhaging workers.

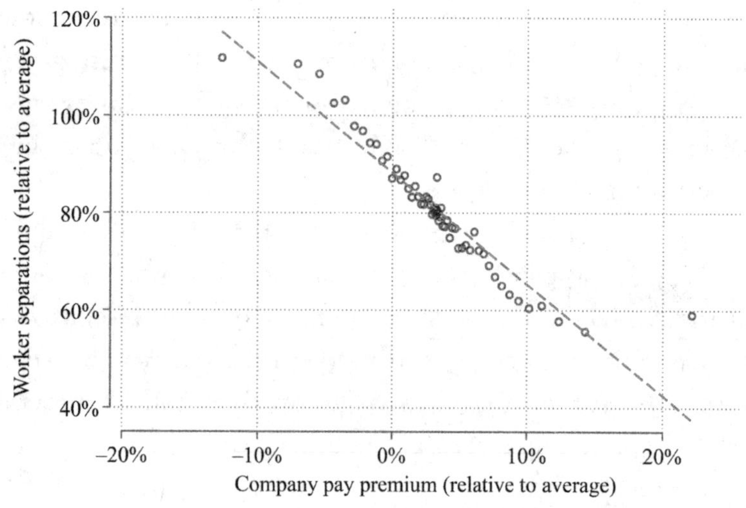

FIGURE 2.1 **COMPANY PAY POLICY AND WORKER QUIT RATES**[18]

In case you are wondering, monopsony is not just a rural or small-town story. We found that the labor market in the Portland metro area to be a little bit more competitive than the rest of the state. But it was still well below anything close to the competitive ideal—

proving monopsony power exists even in big cities with more employers to choose from.[19]

So far, we've focused on quits. But wage changes also affect how easily a firm can recruit new workers. The *elasticity of labor supply* to a firm combines the recruitment and separation elasticities (by adding up their magnitudes), showing how much the overall workforce expands or shrinks if a firm offers higher or lower wages.

Now, for various data-related reasons, estimating recruitment elasticities is more challenging, though recent studies have begun to make headway.[20] Still, economist Alan Manning (arguably the dean of monopsony scholars) has very helpfully shown that, under certain assumptions, the recruitment elasticity tends to be similar in magnitude, but opposite in sign to the quit elasticity. The reasoning is straightforward: Many new hires at one firm are workers quitting another. As a result, when you add the quit and recruit elasticities together, the total labor supply elasticity ends up being roughly *twice the quit elasticity, but with the opposite sign.* So in our Oregon case, a quit elasticity of –2 implies a labor supply elasticity of about 4—far below what you'd expect in a highly competitive, frictionless labor market.

Once you do the math, this range of labor supply elasticity suggests that firms can get away with paying only about 80 percent of what workers would earn in a truly competitive market. (If you want to dig deeper, check out "Five Equations That Explain How Wages Are Set in the Labor Market" in appendix B.) The other 20 percent goes to companies as higher profits or covers turnover and recruitment costs. Monopsony explains why less productive companies can survive in the market, paying lower wages than better-paying competitors. Yes, they will have higher turnover, but not inordinately so. Monopsony also helps explain why wages can vary across employers with similar productivity: Some adopt a *low-wage, high-turnover* approach, while others aim for *higher wages and lower turnover.* Both can be profitable, but one is clearly more worker friendly.

Ultimately, seeing how little wage differences affect quits tells us that labor markets aren't as fluid as many free-market adherents might predict. That's why the quit elasticity—and the broader notion of monopsony power—is vital for explaining how wages are set in the real world and why some jobs simply pay better than others, even when the workers are equally qualified.

The Burgeoning Evidence on Monopsony Power

The evidence on monopsony from tracking workers like Marta and Petra at their jobs matches a fast-growing, and exciting, literature that has now documented labor market power using a host of empirical strategies and data sets, and from very different types of labor markets. Here are some of the key studies and findings from actual (or "natural") experiments that illuminate just how pervasive monopsony can be.

Market power in an online gig world

In 2018, I teamed up with Suresh Naidu and Jeff Jacobs from Columbia University, along with Siddharth Suri from Microsoft Research, to measure market power on Amazon Mechanical Turk (or MTurk).[21] This is an online platform where "Turkers" do small digital tasks—tagging images or transcribing audio—for pay. Many people assumed MTurk was highly competitive: It's easy to see all available gigs, and there are no regulations on hours and pay. That should, in theory, give workers a lot of freedom to pick higher-paying tasks.

Our goal was to obtain "gold standard" evidence on market power using a randomized *field experiment.* We initially posted fifty-five hundred short tasks. Once people completed a quick survey and screening step (identifying markings in old census records), we offered them a follow-up micro-task at a randomly assigned rate ranging from $0.05 to $0.15. Workers could accept or reject the offer. If the market were truly competitive, we'd expect the low-end $0.05 offers to be rejected in droves while higher-paying tasks would be mobbed with takers.

Instead, we found that 79 percent accepted the task when it paid $0.15—but a surprisingly high 73 percent accepted even at $0.05. In other words, paying just one-third as much barely reduced acceptance. Put in terms of elasticities, we found an acceptance (or labor supply) elasticity of slightly smaller than 0.1: meaning a 10 percent higher wage increases workers' willingness to accept the task by less than 1 percent—a very small amount. Even in this online platform where workers and employers could be matched to tasks instantaneously, employers apparently had wide latitude in setting pay.[22]

Evidence from Uber

You might wonder, "Does this really tell us about regular, offline jobs?" After all, real-world wages and job-switching patterns—like those of Marta and Petra—may be very different than the online gig economy. But "field experiments" in other settings also show that different types of employers demonstrate significant monopsony power.

A 2022 study by Sydnee Caldwell and Emily Oehlsen, done with Uber, is a great example. They randomly offered some Uber drivers 10 to 50 percent higher earnings for a week, then measured whether these drivers quit working for a competitor (like Lyft). They found an elasticity similar to ours in Oregon: about –2, indicating notable employer wage-setting power.[23]

Mind the gap . . . in wages

Another fascinating study comes from economist Nikhil Datta in the UK. He focused on a single large employer (nicknamed "the Company") that provides services to municipalities, some of which passed "Living Wage" laws during 2010–2018. These laws forced only this Company, and not its competitors, to raise wages in certain places at certain times. This scenario was like a *natural experiment*: *One* company suddenly had to pay more, but only at certain locations. Datta could compare what happened to quits and hiring across affected and unaffected worksites to arrive at a causal estimate.

He found that a 10 percent wage boost cut quits by around 16 percent, which aligns neatly with the Oregon and Uber findings. Because he also had data on job applications and how quickly vacancies were filled, Datta could pin down the recruitment side of things. Combining quits and hires, he calculated an overall labor supply elasticity of around 4.6—in other words, wages in this market can be marked down by almost 20 percent from what a truly competitive scenario would suggest.[24]

Experimental evidence from Mexico

Monopsony power even shows up in public sector hiring programs. In Mexico, a government project recruited community development agents by randomly varying wages in different areas. Researchers Ernesto Dal Bó, Federico Finan, and Martín Rossi studied this real-world experiment and found that offering a 33 percent higher wage grew the applicant pool by 26 percent and acceptance rates by 35 percent—much smaller than a textbook competitive market would predict. Overall, they estimated a labor supply elasticity of about 2.2, implying employers could be paying wages around 30 percent below what we'd see in a frictionless labor market.[25]

Putting it all together

These examples give just a taste of the new research that is coming out on monopsony power. We'll see more later in the book—including what happened to quit rates when big companies like Amazon suddenly raised wages. But how does all of this evidence stack up? In a 2021 meta-analysis, Anna Sokolova and Todd Sorensen reviewed estimates from fifty-three published studies. For over eleven hundred directly measured estimates, the average labor supply elasticity to a single firm was around 4.8. They concluded that "overall, the literature provides strong evidence for monopsonistic competition and implies sizable markdowns in wages."[26]

In simpler terms: Across the board—whether it's retail workers in Oregon, rideshare drivers in major cities, municipal contractors in the UK, or even gig workers on MTurk—employers can often pay less without losing significantly from their workforce. The real-world job market is far from the theoretical ideal of constant, fierce bidding for every worker's time. Instead, many companies enjoy the kind of market power that lets them set wages below the competitive rate.

The Source of Labor Market Power

Monopsony by artifice

At this point, you may be wondering: What gives employers such power to set wages in the modern-day economy? The most pernicious—though as we will see, not the most prevalent—example is what I would call "monopsony by artifice." These are employer practices that explicitly create artificial barriers to worker mobility, using legal or illegal means. One of the most blatant forms is outright collusion between employers. While it may seem rare, it happens more often than we might expect—just as Adam Smith warned centuries ago.

A particularly egregious example comes from the use of illegal no-poaching agreements among Silicon Valley tech companies including Adobe, Apple, eBay, Google, Intel, Intuit, Lucasfilm, and Pixar. Recruiters were informed about which potential hires were off-limits based on their current place of employment. Some agreements specifically added other restraints like prohibiting any bidding wars over hires. Making this work was not difficult. First, prospective hires usually disclose their current jobs; though it is easy to use platforms like LinkedIn to figure that information out in any case. Then, if one of these colluding firms violated the agreement by hiring "the wrong person," the counterparty typically contacted a senior manager and complained.

Following a whistleblower's disclosure, the Department of Justice (DOJ) launched an investigation in 2009, uncovering compelling evidence of this type of collusive enforcement. In one memorable instance from 2005, Apple's CEO Steve Jobs, annoyed by Google's attempt to poach an Apple employee, sent an email to Google's CEO Eric Schmidt, stating, "I would be very pleased if your recruiting department would stop doing this." Schmidt responded, "Apologies again on this . . . on this specific case the sourcer who contacted this Apple employee should not have and will be terminated within the hour." Jobs replied with a simple ":)".

The DOJ investigation led to the unraveling of the no-poaching agreements, along with civil class-action lawsuits that led to settlements in 2015 and 2018. While the DOJ did not charge these companies in criminal prosecution (in spite of its legal authority to do so), its 2016 guidance to human resource departments clarified that in the future it would do so. Interestingly, research by Matthew Gibson used the timing of the collapse of the no-poaching agreements to compare wages at the colluding firms to those at similar companies that were not part of the scheme. Gibson found that the no-poaching agreements had reduced salaries at the colluding firms by about 6 percent and had led to lower bonuses and decreased job satisfaction.[27]

Another notable example comes from the widespread use of no-poaching agreements in franchise businesses. In a 2021 study, Orley Ashenfelter and Alan Krueger revealed that a surprisingly large share of franchise agreements—from McDonald's to Jiffy Lube to H&R Block—included no-poaching clauses. These clauses prevented franchisees from hiring workers who had recently been employed by other franchises within the same chain. The share of major franchises with these no-poaching agreements increased from 36 percent in 1996 to 53 percent by 2016.[28] Economically, these agreements seem to be little more than an attempt by franchises to "combine" forces and gain more leverage over their workers, not unlike the Silicon Valley example. What's more, this practice remained largely unnoticed until recent times when workers at McDonald's and Carl's Jr. began suing their employers for including such clauses.

The legality of within-franchise no-poaching agreements remains murky. However, the study by Ashenfelter and Krueger was a landmark moment in bringing these practices into the light. The State of Washington, for instance, filed antitrust lawsuits against many of these companies, leading over one hundred franchise chains to remove no-poach clauses from their contracts by 2019—a remarkable outcome for a paper that hadn't yet been officially published in a peer-reviewed journal at the time (though it was later).

Another troubling development has been the proliferation of noncompete clauses, which prevents workers from leaving their jobs to work for competitors. Historically, noncompetes were meant to protect trade secrets, ensuring that employees wouldn't take sensitive information to rival firms. However, in recent decades, the use of these clauses has expanded significantly. Research from 2014 shows that one in five employees—around 30 million American workers—were bound by noncompete agreements.[29] What's concerning is that many of these noncompetes exist in settings where trade secrets aren't a factor, such as fast-food restaurants, summer camps, and repair services. One infamous example is the case of Jimmy John's, a sandwich chain that used noncompetes for its employees in Massachusetts.

Public outcry, particularly following reports from various agencies during the Obama administration, has led to a pushback against the widespread use of noncompetes. Since 2016, dozens of bills at the state and federal levels have sought to ban or rein in noncompete agreements—many successfully. These bans have had tangible effects. For instance, after Hawaii banned noncompetes for tech workers and Oregon did the same for all hourly workers, studies showed an increase in worker mobility as well as wages.[30]

In 2023, the Biden administration's Federal Trade Commission (FTC) under Lina Khan took a bold step by announcing a rule to ban most noncompete agreements across the United States. The rule, which applies to the majority of workers, would make it illegal for employers to enforce noncompete clauses and would require them to rescind any existing agreements. This move aimed to boost worker mobility and raise wages by eliminating a practice that often limits job switching. However, employers challenged the rule in court, leaving its future uncertain.

Overall, public outcry around anticompetitive behavior has exposed some of the worst practices. However, more work remains to be done, as vigilance is critical to rein in the efforts by employers to hold down wages through the combinations Adam Smith warned us about.

The triumvirate of endemic monopsony

While wage-fixing scandals and no-poach agreements make for dramatic headlines—and certainly do matter—they are not the only reasons why employers often hold wage-setting power. More fundamental features of labor markets ensure that even if we banned every anticompetitive practice tomorrow, real-world labor markets would still fall short of the hypercompetitive ideal found in Econ 101. These deeper forces are what I call the triumvirate of endemic monopsony: concentration, search frictions, and job differentiation.

Concentration occurs when there simply aren't that many employers hiring for the type of work you're qualified to do. This often happens if your job is highly specialized or if you live in a small town where just a few businesses dominate your industry. In some ski towns, for instance, the local resort has long been the only major employer in sight. But historically, even if a particular town had only one resort, workers could still find competing opportunities at other resorts in the region. This gave ski instructors, ski patrollers, and seasonal workers some freedom to shop around for better pay or conditions—like a roaming band of snow-seeking professionals.

However, beginning in the 1990s, a wave of consolidation dramatically shrank this pool of potential employers. Major players like Vail Resorts, Alterra Mountain Company, and Powdr acquired numerous ski resorts across the country, turning once-competing resorts into parts of a single corporate portfolio. Not surprisingly, this increased concentration reduced overall competition among resorts to hire and retain talented workers, exerting downward pressure on wages.

In more than a few ski towns, this situation has fueled employee dissatisfaction, culminating in labor disputes and fresh pushes for unionization. For instance, in 2024, a two-week strike by ski patrollers at the Vail-owned Park City Mountain Resort in Utah culminated in raises and a starting wage of $23.[31] That victory notwithstanding, the fundamental change is clear: Where once a ski patroller or instructor could pit multiple, independent resorts against each other to negotiate better wages, they now face a concentrated employer landscape that can more easily set pay rates on its own terms.

Ski towns are hardly alone in facing the ills of labor market concentration. Recent research by University of Pennsylvania economist Ioana Marinescu and her coauthors shows that many labor markets—defined by occupation and geography—are concentrated, meaning there are fewer competing employers than one might expect. In fact, the average labor market in America is about as concentrated as having just *three* equally sized employers. This isn't just a problem in the classic "factory town"; it can happen in suburban health care, IT hubs, and beyond. The data show that in these concentrated markets, wages are noticeably lower for the same kind of work.[32]

Concentration alone, however, does not explain every instance of monopsony power, especially in larger urban areas like Portland.

Here other factors—more fundamental to the work process—come into play. Most crucially, this includes the idea of *search frictions*, which refers to the practical hurdles of finding, applying for, and landing a better job. Transportation constraints create real barriers. Additionally, there's also the challenges inherent in the job search process. This process can be exhausting, stressful, and time-consuming: You send résumés, juggle interviews, and possibly face rejections—all while still working. Faced with the mental strain and emotional energy required to maintain a job search while managing the demands of their current position—the very job they're hoping to leave—many workers simply decide to settle for less. In the physical world, frictions caused by a rough surface prevent water from flowing smoothly, creating puddles. Similarly, in the economy, these frictions in job transitions prevent workers from easily moving to better-paying companies that may be interested in hiring them. The resulting "puddles" give employers monopsony power, even in dense metropolitan labor markets.

Of course, the costliness of job searching doesn't mean workers in bad jobs don't search at all. Evidence suggests that when an employer pays 10 percent less than its competitors, workers spend about 5 percent more time looking for other jobs.[33] This is part of why Marta left her job a month earlier than Petra. But even with that, employers still retain significant latitude in setting wages. Interestingly, recent evidence shows that one reason workers at low-wage employers don't search more aggressively is that they often underestimate how much better other job opportunities might be.[34] This creates a vicious cycle where proliferation of poorly paid jobs creates its own supply of workers willing to fill it.

Job differentiation, the final pillar of endemic monopsony, captures how the same position can be perceived differently by different people. Commute time is a classic example. If I live five minutes from the worksite, while you live an hour away, we're not really looking at "the same job." A recent study by Nikhil Datta shows that commute-time differences make workers value the same job very differently, creating local monopsony power in UK labor markets.[35] In rural areas especially, driving distances or weak transit options can make a job far more valuable to one person than another, even if the wage is identical. But it's not just commuting—we also see differences arising from personal preferences. One person might love the boss's style or the team's vibe, while another might dread the same environment. Just as brand loyalty in cereals can give a single company like General Mills—the maker of Cheerios—some pricing power, so can a worker's personal attachments or convenience factors give an employer wage-setting clout.

Taken together, these three forces help explain why many workers lack strong alternatives. High labor market concentration means fewer employers are hiring for similar jobs in a given area—limiting the number of viable opportunities a worker can turn to. Search frictions make it hard and costly to find and transition into a new job. And job differentiation means workers don't view all roles as interchangeable; a position that looks similar on paper may not be a good fit in practice.

Each of these forces limits workers' job alternatives and gives employers more power to keep pay below competitive levels, even without collusion or illegal tactics. By understanding this triumvirate of monopsony power—concentration, friction, and differentiation—we see why simply banning anticompetitive agreements isn't enough to make labor markets behave like textbook models: Workers aren't always one step from the exit, and often there's no clearly better exit to take.

So What Does Monopsony Have to Do with Our Troubles Today?

We covered a lot of theory and numbers showing employers often wield considerable power in setting wages. But what does all of this tell us about why wages for so many Americans have stagnated or fallen behind over recent decades?

Monopsony teaches us that the economy doesn't naturally settle on a single, inevitable outcome. What ultimately determines wages are the pressures that employers face when determining pay. Historically, forces like labor unions, tight labor markets, minimum wage laws, and societal wage norms worked together to counteract employer monopsony power. The erosion of these checks and balances over the past forty-five years is a key reason why wage standards have weakened.

Monopsony can also shed light on perplexing labor market phenomena—like the reluctance of employers to raise wages even when they're desperate to fill vacancies. One reason is that higher pay for new hires often forces employers to boost wages for current employees, a cost they're keen to avoid. Monopsonistic employers, in essence, remain "hungry for labor," but unwilling to pay what the market would otherwise require.[36]

We saw this dynamic on full display after the Covid-19 lockdowns, particularly in low-wage industries like hospitality. Take John Horne, owner of Anna Maria Oyster Bar in Florida, who, in a 2021 interview with CNN, lamented not being able to hire enough staff despite offering $13 to $18 per hour for kitchen workers.[37] Horne relied on hiring bonuses to attract new employees. He resorted to sign-on bonuses for new hires—common at the time—as a way to sidestep the broader wage increases that could draw more workers into the industry overall, though its effectiveness was questionable.[38] (Horne also voiced concerns about raising the minimum wage, which could potentially draw more workers into the industry as a whole, but also increase costs across the board.) Despite widespread complaints of "labor shortages," many employers remained slow to raise wages substantively, even as vacancies and quit rates stayed high. Such behavior is hard to reconcile with a perfectly competitive model, where supply shortages would trigger immediate wage hikes.

The reluctance to raise wages in monopsonistic markets also means that many companies deliberately hire fewer workers than they would in a fully competitive market. The profit-maximizing wage for these employers is too low to attract all the workers who would take jobs at a competitive pay rate. As we'll see, this has surprising implications for policies like minimum wages and broader wage standards, which may not lead to fewer jobs, contrary to conventional wisdom.

Understanding these dynamics is critical to unpacking how macroeconomic forces and policy decisions shape wages and inequality. For example, the post-pandemic experience highlighted that it takes a very tight labor market to even come close to the competition predicted in the textbooks. More generally, we will discover in the next chapter that right macroeconomic policies—like those that promote tight labor markets—have proven essential in curtailing monopsony power and raising wages. These policies help level the playing field, ensuring that workers see more of the value they generate.

In short, the framework we've developed in this chapter will help unlock some of the mysteries of how the labor market works—and, more importantly, chart a path toward a fairer, more inclusive economy.

CHAPTER 3

Tales of Market Tightness

How a Full-Employment Economy Creates Broad-Based Prosperity

The Federal Reserve (or "the Fed") is a public-private partnership that oversees the nation's financial institutions and serves as the central bank of America. Members of the Fed's board of governors are appointed by the president, but the Fed is usually thought of as an independent, technocratic organization. The Fed is responsible for an important job: to help manage America's macro-economy in partnership with the federal government. While Congress and the president craft fiscal policy (federal spending and borrowing), the Fed oversees monetary policy. Now, the details of the Fed's activities can seem (and sometimes really are!) complex. But its most important role boils down to setting one number: the federal funds rate. This is the short-term interest rate at which banks lend to one another, but it also heavily influences longer-term interest rates that affect borrowing costs for businesses and households alike. The Fed touches the household finances of most Americans, directly or indirectly, even those who have never heard of it. For example, if you have a home mortgage, the interest rate for your monthly mortgage is strongly influenced by the federal funds rate. The basic idea is that when the Fed sets the rate low, it helps stimulate the economy—as families and businesses take out loans to make home improvements and business investments. When it sets the rate high, the economy cools down or contracts.

So how does the Fed decide on the sweet spot when it comes to setting the federal funds rate? Here, it is important to understand that, by law, the Fed has a dual mandate: *price stability* and *maximum employment*. Price stability means a sufficiently low inflation rate, which since the 1990s has meant a target of 2 percent annual increase in prices. Now, to be clear, there is nothing magical about 2 percent, except that it represents a relatively low level of inflation, which is what the Fed wants to ensure. And the public broadly supports keeping inflation low, although a 3 percent inflation rate may have been just as good a target. But, leaving aside the exact target for inflation, let us turn to the other side of the Fed's dual mandate: What is maximum (or full) employment?

In principle, full employment means creating as many jobs as possible without sacrificing price stability. If the Federal Reserve sets interest rates too high, raising the cost of borrowing for businesses and households, the economy will likely generate too few jobs, even if inflation remains under control. This represents a squandered opportunity for economic and human potential. On the other hand, setting interest rates too low—or keeping them low for too long—risks overstimulating the economy, potentially pushing inflation above the Fed's target.

The trade-off between jobs and inflation is often described by the "Phillips curve," a concept developed by New Zealand economist A. W. Phillips in the 1950s, which shows a negative relationship between inflation and unemployment.[1] However, the Phillips curve has not always been dependably predictive, and other factors can drive inflation independent of employment levels. For example, global supply-and-demand shocks, like those affecting oil or food prices, can influence inflation in ways unrelated to the Fed's actions. A case in point is the 2021 Russian invasion of Ukraine, which caused a spike in global crude oil and wheat prices—both major Ukrainian exports. This led to increased inflation entirely outside the realm of influence of U.S. monetary policy. Nevertheless, there are times when the Fed faces a genuine trade-off between pursuing price stability and maximizing employment.

In practice, maximum employment is hard to measure. To begin with, not every working-age adult is likely to work, even if jobs are plentiful. For example, some people may simply not be interested in a job because they have health issues or are taking care of children or other family members. One solution would be to ask how many people who say they are actively looking for a job actually have one. This is the approach taken by the official unemployment rate measure. Now, to be sure, this approach has flaws. For example, it is well known that periods of low unemployment rate also bring in new entrants to the labor force who were not looking for jobs before. So, the true number of potential workers may be more than the ranks of the officially unemployed (those who are actively looking for a job). But even if we were to take the unemployment rate as the relevant measure, what is the unemployment rate consistent with price stability? 4 percent? 2 percent? 0 percent?

This is a difficult question to answer definitively, but economists have made good attempts at getting estimates. These estimates have different names reflecting somewhat different conceptual or methodological approaches. They include "non-accelerating inflation rate of unemployment" (abbreviated as NAIRU), or the "natural rate of unemployment." The basic idea is that this level is as low as the official unemployment can go without igniting an inflationary spiral. Defining this level is not an exact science, and a lot of assumptions are needed to arrive at such an estimate, especially when the economy is in flux.

Despite these caveats, one of the more widely used estimates of the unemployment rate associated with full or maximum employment comes from the Congressional Budget Office (CBO), which calculates a version of NAIRU under a different name. For simplicity, we'll refer to this estimate as U★ (*U-star*). It's instructive to compare how the actual unemployment rate has tracked against U★ over the past seven decades. The gap between these two measures is plotted in Figure 3.1, and this is where the story gets interesting.

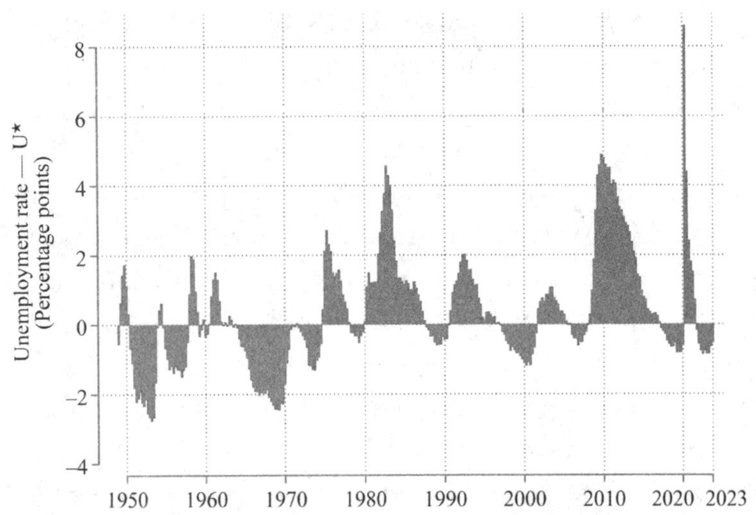

FIGURE 3.1 **EXCESSIVE UNEMPLOYMENT: GAP BETWEEN ACTUAL UNEMPLOYMENT AND U***

Between 1949 and 1979, the actual unemployment rate was above the CBO's estimate of U★ in 39 of the 124 quarters—about 31 percent of the time. While we can debate whether this truly constituted full employment, it's a reasonable first approximation. In contrast, from 1980 through 2023, the actual unemployment rate was above U★ a staggering 64 percent of the time.

But there's more. When the unemployment rate exceeded U★ in the earlier period, it did so by an average of around 1 percentage point. After 1979, when the unemployment rate was above U★, the gap averaged 1.7 points—a considerably larger difference than before.[2] In other words, not only did the share of time spent outside of "full employment" nearly double after 1979, but when we did stray from full employment, we were even further away than we used to be.

Now you may be wondering if these conclusions stem from particularities of the CBO measure of U*. There are valid reasons to believe the CBO's estimate of U* might be too high, and alternative measures sometimes suggest a lower U*. However, the central takeaway from this analysis remains remarkably consistent, no matter which U* is used. For instance, consider how often the unemployment rate exceeded 5 percent. Between 1949 and 1979, this happened about 56 percent of the time, whereas from 1980 to 2023, it occurred 68 percent of the time. You can use different thresholds, but the conclusions remain the same: Since 1980, we've spent significantly more time in periods of high unemployment than we did between 1949 and 1979. Full employment became an elusive goal starting in the 1980s, and this trend persisted for decades. It's only since around 2017 that we've once again seen a sustained period of low unemployment—punctuated by the sharp but short-lived spike during the pandemic recession.

Why does this matter? The most obvious reason is that when unemployment rates are excessively high, we waste a tremendous amount of human potential, which takes a severe toll on workers and their families. As we will see, the slow recovery after the 2008 financial crisis left deep scars on those who lost their jobs during the downturn. Pursuing a policy of full employment is crucial to ensure that workers aren't left permanently behind due to the scourge of joblessness.

But full employment is not just about the *quantity* of jobs; it is also about job *quality*. It turns out that in theory, full employment—or, more generally, a tight labor market—can be an elixir that cures many ailments of a labor market marred by employer-side monopsony power. In economics, we refer to the job market as being *tight* when it's relatively easy for workers to find a job and tough for employers to fill a vacancy. In everyday language, the word "tight" might evoke something uncomfortable or restrictive, and for employers struggling to hire, that's often how it feels! But from a job seeker's perspective, a tight labor market is typically a very good thing. If the theory holds, policies that push us toward full employment could unlock the full potential of a dynamic labor market and help drive us toward shared prosperity.

But does it? Does a tight labor market actually boost workers' bargaining power and create broad-based prosperity? What does the data show? Ironically, the period when we had something closer to full employment in America—between 1949 and 1973—is precisely when data on this issue is scarce. For example, we can't easily track worker movements across jobs during the fifties, sixties, or seventies using survey or administrative data. But don't despair—not all is lost! Thankfully, we had several episodes of tight labor markets in the past five decades that do help us answer this question. And America is not one single labor market; there are many subeconomies with their own rhythms. Some local areas may boom while others struggle, and vice versa. This provides plenty of data to examine how we all fare in a full employment economy. In fact, as we will see, the most striking evidence comes from a much more recent period—the labor market recovery in the aftermath of the pandemic that showed the equalizing potential of policies that prioritize full employment.

But before delving into the data, let's start with the basics. At a conceptual level, why would labor market tightness help resolve some of the key issues that plague insufficiently competitive markets and keep wages down? And what does it have to do with inequality?

A Theory of Tightness and the Job Ladder

In 2010, the Nobel Prize in Economic Sciences was awarded to Peter Diamond, Dale Mortensen, and Christopher Pissarides for their work on search and matching in the labor market. The work by this trio culminated in a class of mathematical models that is known in the profession as Diamond-Mortensen-Pissarides, or DMP for short.

A key aspect of this work is that in a world with search frictions, markets fail to clear, so there are both vacant job openings and unemployed workers who remain unmatched. Another important implication of frictions in the labor market—which we have already seen—is that similar workers may get paid different wages.

But what determines the average level of wages in the market? A key contribution of the DMP framework was to show that this was driven by the overall labor market *tightness*, which in their model boils down to the ratio of the number of vacant job openings to the number of unemployed workers. If there were twice as many vacant jobs as unemployed workers, that would be a very tight labor market where workers have a lot of leverage. If there were only half as many vacant jobs as unemployed workers, that would be a slack (as in, not tight) labor market; and now it is the employers who have a lot of leverage. In the model, more vacancies per unemployed worker allows unemployed workers to exit joblessness faster, making them better off. In turn, this raises workers' fallback position (i.e., what happens if they lose their job), which helps them negotiate better wages with prospective employers. A tight labor market makes employers' lives more difficult as filling job openings becomes more costly. But it makes it easier for workers to find more and better jobs.

DMP is a very popular framework in economics, and it paints an informative picture of what a tight labor market looks like. However, it is incomplete. DMP's focus is on how workers without jobs find one. But it leaves out an equally important element: the role of workers *changing* jobs, or the "job ladder." In DMP, all the hiring is from the ranks of the unemployed, so there is no scope to measure workers who quit bad jobs and take better ones. But as we saw with the example of Marta and Petra, employers actively competing to poach from one another is a critical part of competition. Offering a higher wage reduces the number of workers who quit to take a better job by making the job more attractive compared to possible outside offers.

That is why a tight labor market also means a lot more movement of workers from job to job—in particular, moves up the job ladder from worse to better positions.[3]

There are two related measures that capture how a tight labor market is related to job switching. The first is the job-to-job separation (or "job-hopping") rate: the rate at which workers transition from one job to another without an intervening spell of unemployment. In a tight labor market, job offers are plentiful. This means workers are more likely to find an offer that is better than their current compensation, and hence more likely to change jobs. The job-hopping rate is a strong barometer of labor market tightness and wage growth. In practice, this job-hopping rate is closely related to the quit rate, since most voluntary quits result in job-to-job transitions.

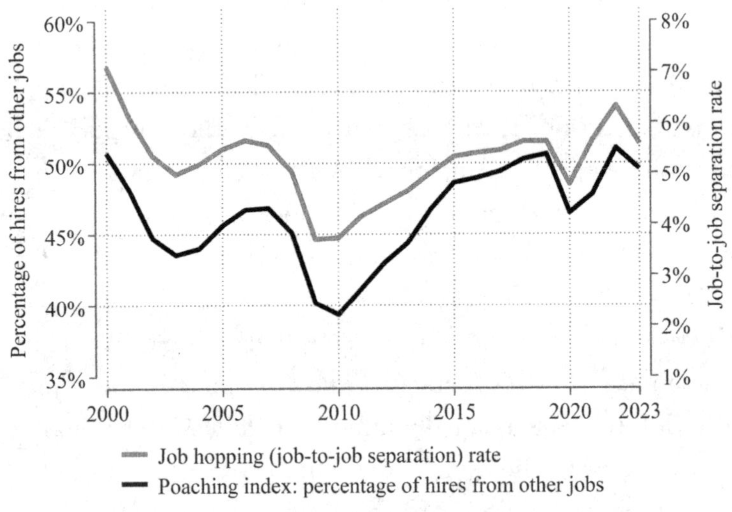

FIGURE 3.2 JOB-HOPPING RATE AND THE POACHING INDEX[4]

The second measure is the poaching index, or the share of all new hires who are recruited from other jobs (as opposed to from the ranks of the jobless). Hiring someone who is currently without a job is generally a cheaper bet for employers, since these individuals tend to have lower reservation wages (the lowest wage offer they would accept). In contrast, recruiting someone from another job is typically more costly, since their current pay serves as a benchmark for any new job.

Therefore, a higher poaching index (i.e., a larger share of new recruits from other jobs) signals more competition among employers. As a practical matter, the poaching index and the job-hopping rate are closely correlated, since they both measure the importance of active competition among employers to recruit and retain workers. Figure 3.2 illustrates how these measures have evolved since 2000, with both indicators showing rather weak levels of competition between 2001 and 2015, reaching a low point in the aftermath of the Great Recession.

All of this means that accounting for job changes is an important part of the story of how a tight labor market helps workers. Importantly, these job-to-job changes are not like a game of musical chairs with workers moving between similar jobs. Rather, it is predominantly workers moving from *worse* to *better* jobs, or climbing the rungs of the job ladder. This represents a *reallocation* of workers toward better, typically more productive, employers. And because it accelerates movement out of the worst-paying jobs, we expect a higher level of tightness to compress wage differences (or reduce inequality) besides raising the average wage.

Can we measure this reallocation empirically? One way to get at this is to see *where* job-hopping rises during a tight labor market: In particular, do they rise more in jobs that pay worse? In my work with Ihsaan Bassier and Suresh Naidu using the data from Oregon, we looked at how the sensitivity of quits—proxied by job-to-job transitions—to firm wage policies varies over the business cycle (remember the quit elasticity?). We found that as labor markets tighten, quits rise most from the lowest-paying jobs: evidence that monopsony power weakens in expansions. The magnitude of the quit elasticity was around –2.0 during the Great Recession and its aftermath, when the market was very slack; and it was around –2.5 in the period of early recovery when the market tightened.[5] To put it differently, during a tight labor market, workers' quits become more sensitive to jobs paying low wages as other, better-paying jobs become easier to find. As a result, workers move from worse-paying to better-paying jobs. When a new vacancy is filled by recruiting a worker from a worse-paying job, it creates a new vacancy at the previous (lower-paying) business. This "vacancy chain" helps put additional pressure to raise wages, especially for those employers at the bottom of the job ladder.

Research by John Haltiwanger and his coauthors, published in 2019, provides further insight into the dynamics of reallocation. Analyzing matched employer-employee data from twenty-eight states between 1998 and 2011, they found that high-wage firms tend to poach workers from low-wage firms, effectively moving workers up the job ladder. On net, high-wage firms grow by nearly 1 percent per quarter through poaching, while low-wage firms lose a little over 1 percent of their workforce to higher-paying competitors. Notably, this pattern of poaching is far more pronounced during periods of economic expansion when the labor market is tight. In contrast, when the labor market is slack, job-to-job transitions decrease, largely because workers are less likely to move from worse to better employers.[6]

In essence, running the economy hot creates a "workers' market," where job seekers have more leverage and wage growth is stronger. It's much easier to take Johnny Paycheck's advice and tell your boss to "take this job and shove it" when jobs are plentiful! Put differently, tight labor markets make the economy function more efficiently and reduce the market power of employers.

Tight Labor Markets Before the Pandemic

So, in theory, a tight labor market sounds like a win for workers, promising to raise living standards. But how does it play out in practice? Between 1979 and 2019, there were two notable periods when the United States approached full employment: the late 1990s (1997–2000) and the late 2010s (2017–2019). During these seven years (1997–2000 and 2017–2019), unemployment rates averaged around 4.2 percent, compared to 6.6 percent in the remaining thirty-four years between 1979 and 2019.[7]

What happened during these periods? When we compare wage trends in those seven years of tight labor markets with the other thirty-four years of slack conditions, a striking picture emerges. Figure 3.3 illustrates the differences: During the slack years, real wages fell for the bottom half of the workforce, while rising at the top. But during the tight labor market years, the script flipped—wages grew faster for everyone, with particularly strong gains at the bottom. This shows that tight labor markets deliver broad-based prosperity and help reduce inequality.

This is particularly consequential for those in the bottom half of the pay scale. If an evil genius supervillain snapped their fingers and erased those seven good years of wage growth, everyone would be worse off, but the impact would vary based on income level. Workers at the 90th percentile might hardly notice, as their annualized wage growth would fall only slightly from around 1.1 percent to 1 percent. But for those at the 10th percentile, the loss would be more substantial—their average wage growth would drop from 0.3 percent to 0 percent. In other words, without those seven good years, real wages for the bottom half of workers would have been completely stagnant over the last forty-one years instead of rising slightly. Here is another way to think about this: If instead of seven good years, we'd had twenty years of tight labor markets between 1979 and 2019, America would be a far less unequal society with bigger paychecks for the typical worker. The well-being of low- and middle-wage workers is closely tied to how tight labor markets are.

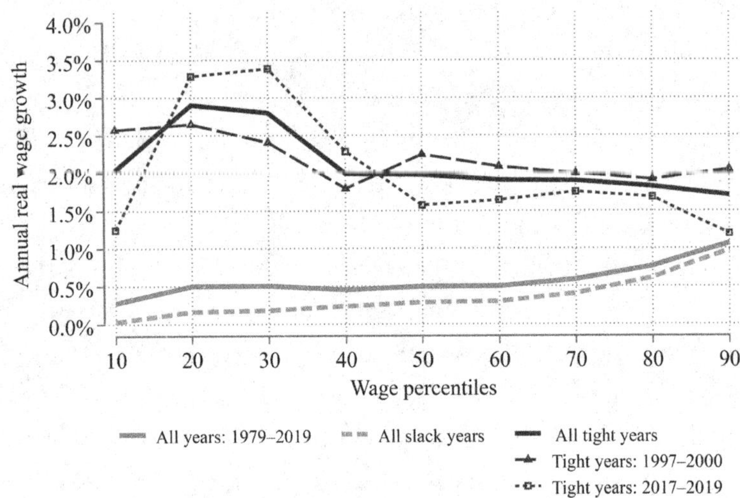

FIGURE 3.3 ANNUAL REAL WAGE GROWTH DURING 1979–2019: SLACK VERSUS TIGHT LABOR MARKETS[8]

To get a better handle on how these episodes of tight labor market came about, and how they helped push back against rising inequality, we will need to dig deeper into the past.

Party like it's 1999

It's hard to remember a time before we had the internet, but before the early 1990s, there were no web browsers, home pages, or e-commerce. The internet is an amazing, emergent phenomenon that came out of a confluence of public investment and private initiative. In the 1960s, the U.S. Department of Defense created ARPANET, a network of computers that could communicate with one another. This was mainly a way for researchers and military personnel to share information and communicate, regardless of their physical location. Over the 1980s, there was additional public investment from the National Science Foundation, followed by private-sector funding in this arena. The original web browser—which was called "WorldWide-Web" at that time—was up and running by 1990, and then Mosaic, the first widely used graphical browser, came online in 1993.[9]

What followed was a period of rapid investment in internet-based companies in the late 1990s. It was a time of great excitement and optimism, as people believed that the internet was going to revolutionize the way we live and work. As a result, many internet-based companies, or "dot-coms," sprang up, offering everything from online retail stores to streaming music services. These companies were able to raise significant amounts of money through initial public offerings (IPOs), as investors were eager to get in on the action. While the internet was initially primarily used for communication and information sharing, as more and more people began to use it, businesses started to see the potential for using it as a platform for commerce.

However, as with other periods of rapid adoption of new technologies, booms sometimes create bubbles and lead to companies with more hype than value. Some of the dot-coms had little or no profits, yet they were still able to go public and raise millions of dollars. Perhaps the most infamous example was Pets.com, which sold pet supplies online and whose marketing campaign was led by its sock puppet mascot that was even interviewed by *People* magazine. But, eventually, the dot-com bubble burst, as it became clear that many of these dot-coms were not as successful as investors had hoped. And the bursting bubble took companies like Pets.com down with it: It turned out that Pets.com didn't really have a viable business plan beyond its catchy (and expensive) advertising campaign.[10] But it was not all for naught. The dot-com era left behind something that has transformed nearly every aspect of our lives, from the way we work and shop to the way we socialize and access information.

The early days of the internet also demonstrated the potential of a private investment-led boom to improve labor market conditions for millions of workers. In the late 1990s, we saw a surge in hiring—not just for tech workers in Silicon Valley but across a wide range of sectors. The boom in investment fueled demand for goods and services both upstream and downstream from the tech sector, affecting industries from manufacturing to janitorial services. This created what many economists have referred to as the "high-pressure" economy of the 1990s, where robust job growth benefited workers across the board.[11]

The unemployment rate dropped from 5.5 percent to 4 percent between 1995 and 1999. While this might seem unremarkable, it's important to remember that a 4 percent unemployment rate is well below what the Federal Reserve at the time believed was consistent with price stability. In 1999, for example, the Fed's estimate of U★ was 5.1 percent. Writing that same year, economists Lawrence Katz and Alan Krueger pointed out what seemed like a puzzle to many contemporary observers: "Though estimates of [U★] . . . are imprecise, the actual unemployment rate has been below 5 percent—the lower bound of the confidence interval for [U★]—for more than twenty consecutive months. Moreover, the rate of price inflation declined in 1997 and 1998."[12]

During the February 1999 Federal Open Market Committee (FOMC) meeting, the vice chair of the Federal Reserve, Alice Rivlin, humorously described the surprising state of affairs: "Most amazing of all, [the cheerful little elves who run the U.S. economy] seem to have figured out how to keep unemployment rates lower than what the [U★] enthusiasts have said for a long time is the drop-dead rate, while wage increases actually have decelerated and inflation does not seem to be a danger at present." At the same meeting, one of the staff economists at the Fed declared, "I would not be as resistant to the notion that [U★] might be below 5 percent or maybe significantly below 5 percent. It is hard to be strongly opposed to that notion based on recent experience."[13]

For the first time since the 1970s, the Fed allowed the economy to experience a tight labor market, letting unemployment drop below its own estimates of U★ and remain there for several years until the boom ended naturally. What followed wasn't out-of-control inflation, as many had feared. In fact, as Katz and Krueger noted, the inflation rate fell during this period. The notion that an unemployment rate below 5 percent was irresponsible had been decisively disproven. This policy "experiment" gave the Fed—and economists more broadly—an opportunity to learn that perhaps the labor market could be allowed to run hotter than we had dared since the 1970s. The broader lesson here reflects a concept from probability theory and machine learning that has a funny name: the *multi-armed bandit problem*. Simply put, without a certain degree of experimentation and risk-taking, we can't generate the evidence necessary for truly informed, evidence-based decision-making. (Want more? Head to appendix A.)

What did we learn from this experimentation? Running the labor market hot led to strong, broad-based, real wage growth and a temporary halt to the rise in wage inequality. A tight labor market is particularly good for workers at the bottom because the unemployment rate among low-wage workers is also much more cyclical than higher-wage workers (say with a college degree). Between 1996 and 2000, for those who were twenty-five years of age or older, the unemployment rate fell from 2.3 to 1.7 percent among college graduates, while it fell from 5.0 to 3.6 percent among those without a college degree—a larger decline. In addition, as we saw, greater tightness fires up the job ladder, allowing particularly low-paid workers within any skill or education group to find better-paid positions. Both forces lead tightness to produce better wage outcomes for those at the bottom. As figure 3.3 shows, during the 1997–2000 period, real wages grew annually by 2.6 percent, 2.2 percent, and 2 percent for the 10th, 50th, and 90th percentiles, respectively. That was quite a difference from a total of −0.9 percent, −0.08 percent, and 0.66 percent annual growth in real wages between 1979 and 1996 for the same percentiles. Not only did wage inequality stop rising in the late nineties, but the real wage decline at the bottom between 1979 and 1996 was reversed in the following four years. These four years demonstrated that the increase in wage inequality we had seen since the early 1980s was not inevitable and at least in part depended on choices we had made about how to run our macroeconomic policy.

The dot-com era showed how a tight labor market can transform the lives of millions of workers, raising wages and making it easier to change jobs. Describing this period, Jared Bernstein and Dean Baker wrote in 2003: "The benefits of full employment are far reaching throughout the economy."[14] The source of the dot-com boom was ultimately not sustainable. But that is not the critical lesson here. Expansions in capitalist economies are inevitably cyclical, and sometimes downturns come from imbalances built up during the expansion itself. In the late nineties, such imbalance came in the form of an asset bubble in tech stocks. The next expansion in the aughts would see a housing bubble, whose collapse would usher in the Great Financial Crisis starting in 2007. Of course, economists and politicians can—and should—take actions such as macro-prudential policies and thoughtful regulation to reduce the risks associated with expansions: Without such regulations, an expansion is more likely to run into a crisis from a sector that veers out of balance. Regulations can also mitigate the harm if a crisis does happen. But the most important policy lesson from that era was this: Letting the economy grow was not only acceptable but beneficial, even when the labor market ran hotter than the Fed's estimate of the sustainable unemployment rate (U*).

Unfortunately, the lesson was learned only partially. The FOMC is the body that meets every month to set the federal funds rate. A reading of the FOMC meeting transcripts and minutes from mid-1999 and 2000 suggests growing concerns that the tight labor market was going to lead to inflation soon, even though there was no actual evidence of such impending inflation. On that basis, the Fed preemptively began tightening monetary policy by raising the interest rate in mid-1999. While policymakers at the Fed recognized that wages were not growing at rates that indicated any inflationary pressures, they thought that such pressures must eventually occur with an unemployment rate this low, despite lack of empirical evidence. Did this tightening shorten the duration of the expansion or make the downturn of 2001 worse than it could have been? It is hard to say for sure. However, having tighter monetary policy than necessary for price stability clearly does not aid the goal of full employment.

Perhaps more importantly, the Fed at the time did not show awareness of how a tight labor market affects the functioning of a labor market—either in terms of reducing employer-side power or affecting wage compression. Going through the FOMC transcripts from 1998 to 2000, it is easy to find discussions about "pricing power" in the product market and how that was being kept in check from various economic forces at the time including globalization. But there was no equivalent discussion of "wage-setting power" or "monopsony power." There was plenty of discussion of "labor shortages," but there was no discussion of how such shortages are often a signature of a market where employers with monopsony power try to avoid raising wages even as it gets harder for them to recruit workers. While there were many remarks on modest overall nominal wage growth, there was little mention of how a decade-and-a-half-long spell of rising wage inequality had been halted from rising wage growth at the bottom of the pay scale. Most critically, there was no discussion of how this high-pressure economy was allowing the labor market to work more effectively and allowing workers to leave low-wage, low-productivity jobs and climb the job ladder to better positions. Without such an understanding of the labor market, any pivot toward a tight labor market policy was bound to remain incomplete.[15]

The long road to recovery after the Great Financial Crisis

The aftermath of the Great Financial Crisis (GFC) of 2007–2009 offers another lens to understand both the incredible costs of labor market slack and the gains that await us when we push for a tighter labor market. The GFC was a period of economic turmoil caused by a combination of factors including a housing market bubble, widespread mortgage fraud, and a lack of regulation in the financial sector. These factors led to a significant increase in foreclosures and a decline in housing prices, causing a wave of mortgage defaults and putting pressure on financial institutions that held large amounts of mortgage-backed securities. The crisis quickly spread beyond the housing market and had far-reaching impacts on the global economy. As financial institutions failed or were forced to seek government bailouts, confidence in the financial system was eroded and credit markets froze. This caused a sharp decline in economic activity and led to high levels of unemployment—the deepest downturn in America since the Great Depression.

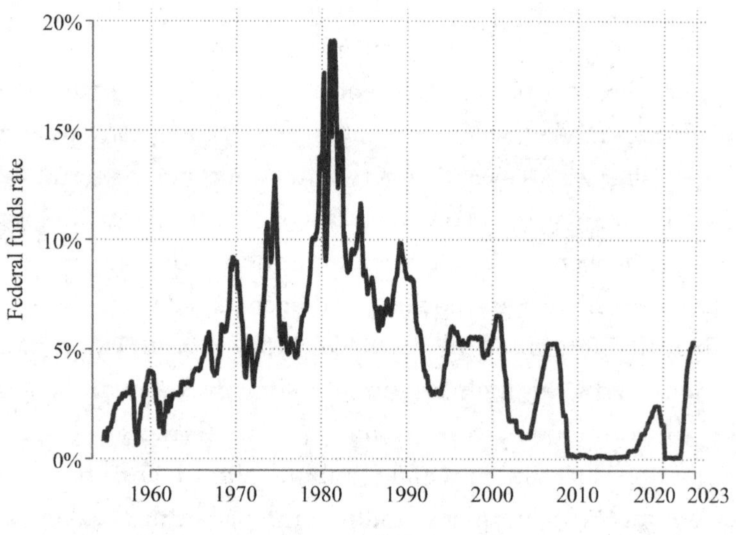

FIGURE 3.4 **FEDERAL FUNDS RATE**[16]

Governments around the world responded to the crisis with a range of macroeconomic policies. The Federal Reserve brought the federal funds rate down close to zero by the end of 2008 and kept it there for seven years. Unfortunately, however, there are limits to what the Fed can do once the interest rate it sets hits zero, a situation known as the "zero lower bound" (ZLB). Yes, it can engage in unconventional monetary policymaking to ease financing, a strategy known as quantitative easing. But the truth is that once we hit the ZLB, we quickly reached the limits of monetary policy to juice the economy.

During these moments when monetary policy becomes ineffective, fiscal policy takes center stage. How can countercyclical fiscal policy help with fighting recessions? And what exactly is it anyway? Fiscal policy refers to debt-financed federal government spending that can include everything from tax credits to households, increased infrastructure spending, more federal aid to state governments, or increased assistance to the jobless. Such spending stimulates demand for more goods and services, which in turn means more hiring and more jobs. This was the idea behind the 2009 American Recovery and Reinvestment Act (ARRA), which was the Obama administration's key weapon to prevent the financial crisis from causing a second Great Depression. The $787 billion bill (in 2009 dollars) did help prevent a calamity. But while the price tag sounds big, the size of the solution was just not big enough given the size of the problem. Even at the time, some economists guessed as much. Writing in 2009, the Nobel Prize–winning economist Paul Krugman observed that "the stimulus was too small given the scale of our economic problems. Unless something changes drastically, we're looking at many years of high unemployment."[17]

How do we really know that it was not enough? First, it was not enough because, as Krugman worried, it took a long time—over a decade!—for key labor market gauges to return to normal. The share of prime-age (twenty-five- to fifty-four-year-old) individuals who were employed peaked at 80.3 percent in early 2007, prior to the crisis. This prime-age employment rate did not reach this level again until late 2019, just prior to the Covid-19 pandemic. It took over *twelve years* for the employment rate to recover following the Great Recession.

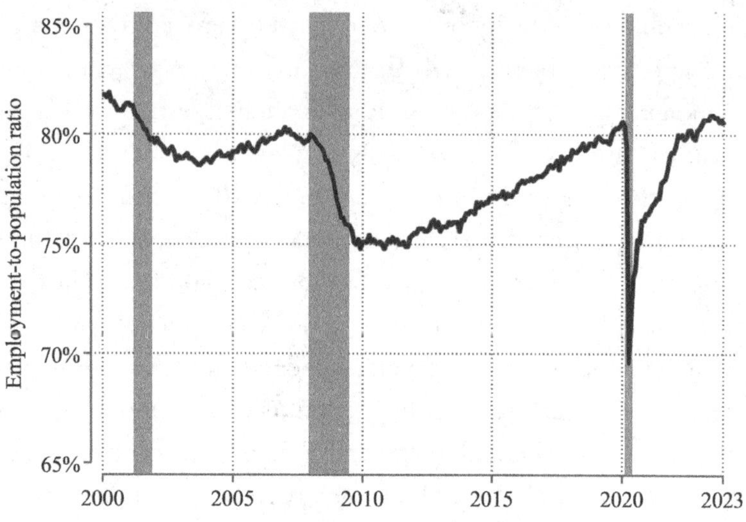

FIGURE 3.5 **EMPLOYMENT-TO-POPULATION RATIO, TWENTY-FIVE- TO FIFTY-FOUR-YEAR-OLDS**[18]

The human cost of the long-drawn-out recovery was particularly steep for the millennials entering the labor force during this time. You may recall that cohorts entering the labor force during downturns are typically scarred by this experience, and it takes many years for them to recover. This is in part because the quality of jobs available during downturns is skewed toward those with worse quality, as high-wage firms are less likely to engage in hiring during downturns; this pushes entrants toward lower-wage (often lower-productivity) employers, who can hire more easily in this environment.[19] In their aptly titled paper "Unlucky Cohorts," Hannes Schwandt and Till von Wachter show that non-college-educated workers entering the labor force following the Great Recession likely lost around 11 percent of their aggregate (or more technically, the present discounted value of) earnings from the first ten years of working. For college grads, the loss was smaller, though still sizable (around 5 percent).[20]

The costs are not just financial. A growing body of research finds that adverse labor market conditions at time of entry is associated with excessive drinking, more smoking, and obesity in middle age. Entering labor markets with high unemployment leads these unlucky cohorts to experience higher rates of heart disease, liver disease, and lung cancer starting in their thirties.[21] Since much of the costs are driven by the fact that these workers have lower-paid jobs than luckier cohorts, they highlight more broadly the human costs of an economy filled with bad jobs as compared to good jobs. When we allow an economy to be driven by low-road employment, we are relegating many workers to a life of economic hardship as well as poor health and higher mortality.

OK, so we know it took a long time for the economy to recover after the financial crisis. But would more government spending have made a difference? Or would it have simply thrown money at the problem without producing real results? Economists have taken a close look at what the American Recovery and Reinvestment Act achieved in terms of job creation. The most compelling evidence comes from studies comparing local areas that received more ARRA assistance (the "treatment groups")—due to somewhat arbitrary factors—to other, similar areas that received less (the "control groups").

This type of analysis is called a *natural experiment*, where random or arbitrary factors help create real-life conditions that mimic the structure of a laboratory experiment. By tracking how outcomes change in treatment versus control groups over time, economists attempt to identify the true causal impact of a policy. It's the same idea behind randomized control trials in medical research, where the effect of a new drug is studied by comparing groups that receive the drug to those that don't.

What does the evidence show about the impact of the ARRA? In a 2019 study, the economist Gabriel Chodorow-Reich reviewed these studies and provided some new estimates of his own. Overall, the analysis found that there was a "local multiplier" of around 1.7.

This means that for every $1 spent on the ARRA, local areas saw an increase in output worth $1.70.

At first glance, that might sound like magic—how can $1 of government spending generate $1.70 in output? But it simply reflects the fact that the economy had unused capacity and idle workers. When government spending increased demand, businesses responded by hiring more workers, who then spent their new earnings, creating a ripple effect. The multiplier being greater than 1 indicates that the economy wasn't operating at full potential, and there just wasn't enough spending to support the available labor and resources.

Chodorow-Reich points out that this local multiplier is likely to be an *understatement* of how much the American economy benefited from each dollar in ARRA spending. Even areas that didn't receive much ARRA assistance probably benefited indirectly, since the places that did receive funds bought goods and services from elsewhere. Overall, these findings suggest that without the ARRA, America would have had *at least* 2.6 million fewer jobs during 2009 and 2010.[22]

In case you're wondering—yes, these added jobs were a big deal. Based on official establishment survey data, total nonfarm employment in 2009 and 2010 was, on average, about 7.2 million below its 2007 level before the recession. According to Chodorow-Reich's estimates, without the ARRA there would have been at least 2.6 million more jobs lost—bringing the total to 9.8 million, or about 36 percent more than what actually occurred. That makes the ARRA a clear success story.

But it also shows how much more could have been done. The high return on investment from the ARRA—combined with the fact that it took more than a decade for the labor market to fully recover—suggests that a larger fiscal package would have delivered even greater benefits. Chodorow-Reich estimates it cost about $50,000 per year to create a job through the ARRA. That cost is small compared to the broader gains from a stronger and faster recovery—not just in terms of reduced unemployment and the health improvements that come with it, but also in helping workers who remained employed avoid being stuck in worse jobs than they could have had in a tighter, more competitive labor market.

So, the economy did not get the help it needed for a faster recovery. Instead, the recovery was slow and prolonged—but it did happen eventually. By 2018, the labor market had largely rebounded, with the unemployment rate falling below 4 percent and the prime-age employment rate reaching around 79 percent and continuing to rise. Here, the choice of policy came back into focus, but this time it was monetary policy that was in the driver's seat once again. Was the Fed going to allow the labor market to find its groove, or was it going to raise interest rates to ward off future inflation, real or imagined?

While the initial policy response to the recession following the financial crisis had been inadequate, and disappointing, we had a better stroke of luck on this front later in the recovery. The Fed did raise its interest rate between 2016 and 2018, but by historical standards, these were modest and stayed below 2.5 percent.

However, as late as September 2018, the Federal Open Market Committee minutes announced the Fed's intention to "continue its gradual approach . . . by raising the target range for the federal funds rate 25 basis points [as in 0.25 percentage points] at this meeting." They cited the "risk of moving too slowly, which could engender inflation persistently above the objective and possibly contribute to a buildup of financial imbalances."[23] This was followed by a further 25 basis point increase in the federal funds rate in December 2018. Core inflation (excluding the volatile energy and food prices) sat at an annual 2.3 percent in December 2018, showing no sign of picking up. And yet the Fed was nervous as the unemployment rate kept falling and the employment rate kept rising. It was starting to look like a replay of the debates in the late 1990s all over again.

Thankfully, in 2019, there was a change in perspective, and some

Fed officials, including James Bullard (president of the St. Louis Fed) and Neel Kashkari (president of the Minneapolis Fed), said the Fed should stop raising rates or it could risk unnecessary trouble. Importantly, the Fed appeared to show an awareness that raising rates when inflation was *below* its 2 percent target was not a prudential course of action. This dovish pivot led the Fed to stop hiking the interest rate and in fact cut the rate from around 2.4 to 1.6 percent during the second half of 2019, even as the unemployment rate had stabilized at around 3.6 percent during that period—a low level by recent standards. This pivot was even more remarkable given the fiscal *stimulus* in 2018 and 2019 resulting from the 2017 Tax Cuts and Jobs Act (TCJA) passed under the Trump administration.[24] This combination of accommodative monetary policy and stimulative fiscal policy contributed to maintaining the full employment economy.

The Fed's pivot signaled a newfound priority to the full employment part of the Fed's dual mandate. Reflecting on the previous cycle, Kashkari had this to say in 2020: "In recent years, we have repeatedly believed we were at or beyond maximum employment only to be surprised when many more Americans reentered the labor market or chose not to leave, increasing the productive capacity of the economy without causing high inflation. To me, maximum employment is the point at which the labor market is just tight enough to deliver 2 percent inflation in equilibrium. . . . By this definition, even in January 2020, we had not yet reached maximum employment."[25]

The tight labor market of the late 2010s brought about another round of wage compression, reminiscent of the late 1990s. Between 2017 and 2019, wage growth was again as strong or stronger in the bottom half of the pay scale than in the top half. After adjusting for inflation, wages grew by an average of 1.2, 1.6, and 1.2 percent at the 10th, 50th, and 90th percentiles, respectively. Growth was especially pronounced at the 20th and 30th percentiles, where wages rose by an impressive 3.3 percent annually. As figure 3.3 shows, the wage patterns during these two periods of tight labor markets, the late 1990s and late 2010s, were strikingly similar. In both cases, wage growth was broad-based and helped partially reverse some of the long-term trends in rising inequality.

We also see how a tight labor market boosts pay, especially at the middle and bottom, when we compare different regions of the country. The American labor market is not a monolithic entity: Sometimes unemployment rates drop more in the South than in the Northeast, or vice versa. We can use these variations across states to further examine how tighter labor markets influence wage growth.

That's exactly what the economists Josh Bivens and Ben Zipperer do in their 2018 study. They investigate how state-level wage growth at the bottom, the middle, and the top of the pay scale correlates with the state's unemployment rate, a statistical relationship often termed a wage Phillips curve. Examining the period from 1980 to 2016, they found that 1 percentage point reduction in a state's unemployment rate was associated with a 0.5 percentage point increase in real wages at the 10th percentile, a 0.4 percentage point rise for the median wage, and a 0.3 percentage point increase for the 90th percentile.[26] A lower unemployment raised wages more at the bottom than at the top.

So, even before the most recent period, we had clear evidence that a tight labor market was a powerful remedy for the dis-equalizing forces that had plagued the American labor market since 1980.

Why do wages grow faster at the bottom—or show signs of compression—during tight labor markets? A major reason is that the job market tends to be more cyclical for lower-wage workers than for higher-wage ones. For instance, unemployment rates spike more sharply during recessions for workers without a college degree than for those with one. We can also observe this pattern in job-hopping behavior. The job-to-job separation rate for workers with a bachelor's degree or higher was around 3.2 percent in slack labor markets (2001–2016), rising to 3.7 percent in the tight labor market of 2017–2019. The difference is more pronounced for workers without a college degree: For high school graduates, the job-hopping rate climbed from 4.3 percent during slack years to 5 percent during 2017–2019.[27]

In other words, when the labor market tightens, it tightens more for middle- and lower-wage workers than for those at the higher end. This underscores the importance of the job ladder in explaining how tight labor markets help reduce inequality. A tighter labor market not only narrows the wage gap between college and non-college-educated workers but also pushes wages up the most for those at the very bottom, helping them escape the lowest-paying jobs. Drawing on survey and ethnographic evidence, Katherine Newman and Elisabeth Jacobs show that, historically, tight labor markets make upward movement along the job ladder more common and more durable: raising pay at the bottom, bringing marginalized workers into the labor force, and reducing deep poverty.[28]

But the clearest evidence on how tight labor markets impact competition and inequality was yet to come, emerging from the unexpected aftermath of a global pandemic.

A Great Reshuffle and an Unexpected Compression

The 2020 Covid-19 pandemic led to the sharpest drop in employment in America since the Great Depression. The share of sixteen- to sixty-four-year-olds with a job fell sharply at the onset of the pandemic, plunging by an unprecedented 9 percentage points from 72 percent in February to 63 percent in May 2020. The employment drop was particularly pronounced for less-educated workers, since the business shutdowns disproportionately affected lower-wage service work such as in hospitality. While the employment rate fell by around 7 percentage points for those with college degrees, it fell by around 10 points for those with no more than a high school degree.

At the same time, although the drop in employment was much sharper for workers with no more than a high school degree, their employment recovery was equally sharp. By early 2022, the employment rate of high school–only adults was 100 percent of its early 2020 level and by mid-2022 it had surpassed its early 2020 levels.[29]

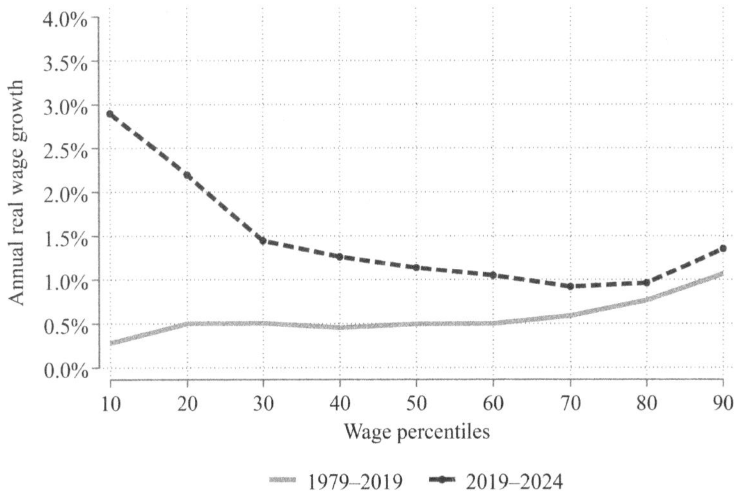

FIGURE 3.6 **ANNUAL REAL WAGE GROWTH DURING 2019–2024: THE "UNEXPECTED COMPRESSION"**[30]

Given where pandemic-related job losses were concentrated, one might have expected *weaker* wage growth for workers at the bottom of the pay distribution. But what happened next was just the opposite. As David Autor, Annie McGrew, and I show in our 2024 study, the post-pandemic wage growth was strongest at the bottom and weaker at the top.[31]

Figure 3.6 illustrates these patterns using the same Current Population Survey data used to track changes in wage inequality in the earlier periods. Despite high inflation during this period, real annual wage growth from 2019 to 2024 was robust for lower-paid workers—nearly 3 percent at the 10th percentile and about 1.5 percent at the 30th percentile. These gains far exceeded the historical averages from

1980 to 2019, aligning with what we've seen during other episodes of tight labor markets.

In contrast, real wage growth for workers in the top half of the distribution was considerably more modest—just 1 to 1.5 percent annually, in line with pre-pandemic norms. The result was an "unexpected compression" in the wage distribution: Wages at the bottom grew faster than those at the top. This pattern marked a sharp reversal from the prior four decades, when inequality had widened. Even during earlier periods of tight labor markets, like the late 1990s and late 2010s, wage compression was not this pronounced, especially when it came to raising pay at the bottom. After accounting for the surge in inflation during this period, real wages at the 10th percentile still rose by a total of 15 percent between 2019 and 2024.

FIGURE 3.7 **WAGE INEQUALITY OVER TIME—THE 90–10 RATIO**[32]

This shift in pay inequality shows up clearly in the 90–10 wage ratio—the wage of a worker near the top of the distribution (90th percentile) divided by that of a worker near the bottom (10th percentile). In 1979, the ratio was 3.5; by 2013, it had climbed to 4.9, meaning top earners were making nearly five times as much as low-wage workers. Since that 2013 peak, the gap has narrowed: It dipped slightly to 4.7 by 2019, then fell more noticeably to 4.4 by 2024. In other words, about one-third of the rise in wage inequality since 1980—as measured by the 90–10 gap—has now been undone, with most of that progress happening after the pandemic, when wages at the bottom rose the fastest.[33]

Tracking the 90–10 ratio over time also makes clear that this recent compression wasn't just a continuation of pre-pandemic trends. While there was some narrowing of the gap between 2016 and 2019, the story changed decisively after the pandemic.

So, what drove the unexpected compression in the wage distribution? While many factors may have played a role, the dominant force was surprisingly straightforward: It was one of the tightest labor markets in American history. And the main way that tightness translated into higher wages at the bottom was through job switching. For workers who stayed in the same job, wage growth was modest across the board—whether at the bottom, middle, or top of the distribution. In contrast, workers who changed jobs saw much larger gains. And during this period, many did exactly that.

We can see the surge in job switching by looking at employer survey data on worker quits from the Census Bureau's Job Openings and Labor Turnover Survey (JOLTS), shown in figure 3.8. In 2021, the overall monthly quit rate hit its highest level since JOLTS began tracking in 2000. The biggest increases were in low-wage sectors—especially leisure and hospitality, including restaurants—where quit rates rose from about 4.6 percent in 2019 to 5.5 percent in 2021. (This spike in quits closely mirrors the rise in job hopping and poaching shown in figure 3.2, based on a different data source.)

The shift was also especially concentrated among younger workers without a college degree. These patterns suggest that the tight labor market gave lower-wage workers more chances to leave bad jobs for better ones, boosting their bargaining position.

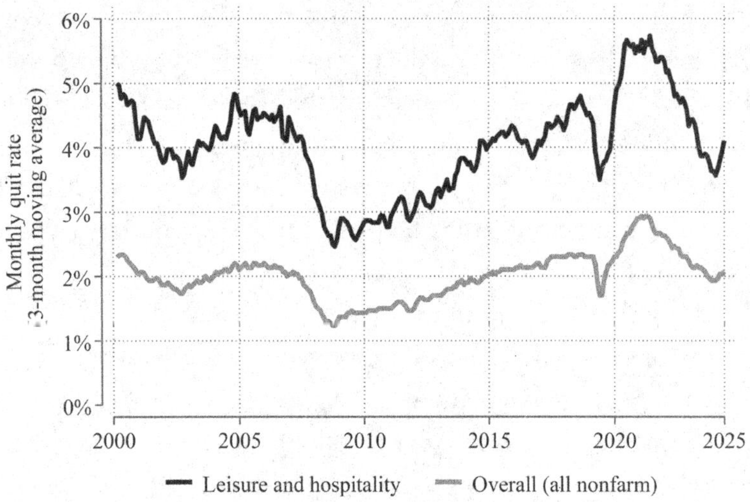

FIGURE 3.8 **MONTHLY QUIT RATE**[34]

Just as the job ladder theory would predict, quits didn't rise evenly across all jobs: They increased most in the ones workers were most eager to leave. In my research with David Autor and Annie McGrew, we show this by looking at job-to-job separation rates across industries, using a detailed (three-digit) industry classification to capture job quality. These categories include everything from fast-food restaurants and retail bakeries to department stores, appliance manufacturers, warehousing and storage, motor vehicle dealers, and internet publishing, among others.

For each of these 280 industries, we construct a measure of job quality based on wages, controlling for education, demographics, and location (for more on this method, see the "Mincer earnings function" entry in appendix B). This gives us the industry wage premium: essentially, the wage advantage (or disadvantage) by industry that remains after accounting for who holds the job. As expected, jobs with higher wage premia tend to have lower quit rates, producing a clear downward-sloping curve. The slope of that curve tells us the "quit elasticity," or how sensitive workers are to wage differences—a key indicator of employer power we encountered in chapter 2.

So how did this change during the post-pandemic period? The story is most pronounced for younger workers under forty without a college degree—the group that experienced the biggest surge in quits. As shown in figure 3.9, the quit elasticity for this group rose noticeably, from −0.8 in the 2015–2019 period to −1.1 in 2021–2023.[35] In particular, we see a sharp jump in job hopping among workers in industries with especially low wage premia (like hospitality).[36]

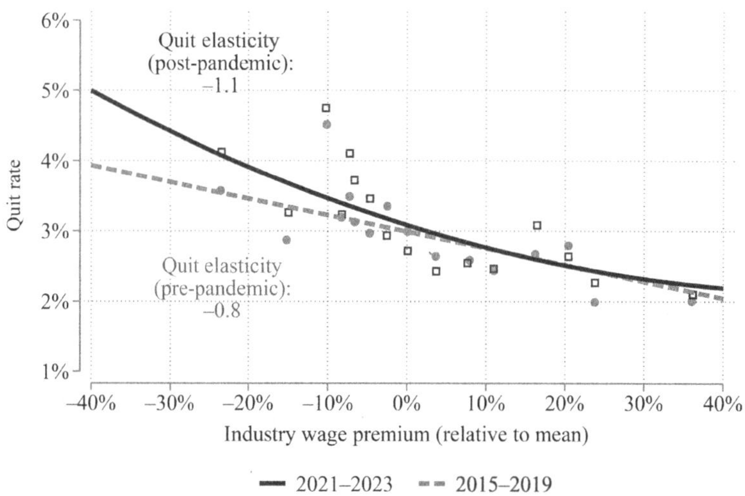

FIGURE 3.9 **A RISING QUIT ELASTICITY FOR WORKERS UNDER FORTY WITHOUT A COLLEGE DEGREE**[37]

All of this meant that the labor market for lower-wage workers became sharply more competitive as workers left poorly paying jobs in droves during the "Great Reshuffling."[38] I use that term instead of "Great Resignation" to describe this period because workers didn't resign and stop working; quite the opposite! Employment rates rose fast during 2021 and 2022. Rather, workers reshuffled or reallocated to better-paying jobs.

And when workers left bad jobs, they increasingly moved to better ones. We can compare the quality of origin and destination jobs, again using industry groups as before. In our research, we found a clear pattern: Between 2021 and 2023, workers left jobs with low premia and entered jobs with higher premia.[39] The share of all workers who in each month moved up from the bottom quarter of industries to better-paying ones clearly rose in the 2021–2023 period. Again, the pattern was particularly striking for younger workers without a college degree: For this group, the chance that any worker made such an upward change in each month rose from around 0.8 percent to 1 percent. If you feel that's a small change, remember this is just a single month; added up over a two- or three-year period, this represents a very sizable shift. In contrast, the chance of moving down from a better-paying industry to one in the bottom quarter did not change noticeably. Added together, this means low-wage workers *in net* reallocated toward better-paying (and likely higher-productivity) employers.

What fueled this Great Reshuffle? For one, we put in place policies like the Coronavirus Aid, Relief, and Economic Security (CARES) Act and the American Rescue Plan (ARP) Act, which put money in people's bank accounts. The U.S. government also provided generous unemployment benefits to those who lost jobs during the pandemic recession—much more so than it had during past downturns. The $600/week supplement in 2020 and the $300/week supplement in 2021 represented a more than doubling of the unemployment benefits workers usually get. As a result, spending was boosted, and average consumption did not fall among those experiencing job loss in 2020 or 2021 when the supplements were available, which was a historic achievement.[40] At the same time, the cost of borrowing was kept low by the Federal Reserve, which further allowed greater consumption and investment by businesses. Together, the additional demand stemming from consumer behavior, fiscal policy, and monetary policy contributed to a tight labor market and a historically fast recovery following a downturn. Our approach to the Pandemic Recession was in striking contrast to the Great Recession following the financial crisis, where a small fiscal response likely drew out the downturn for many more years than necessary.

Besides the tightness-based factors that come out of the job ladder model, there may also be other factors that contributed to an increase in the sensitivity of quits to job quality. Most obviously, the sudden detachment of workers from their workplaces at the onset of the pandemic could have disrupted search behavior. While most other advanced industrialized countries used public payments to employers to retain workers during lockdowns (e.g., the furlough policy in the UK), the United States used its unemployment benefits program to provide relief, leading to temporary (and sometimes permanent) layoffs.

The use of unemployment benefits led to a *disruption* in the work relationship. Because there was less certainty about when workers would be called back to work, if at all, some workers looked for and found jobs elsewhere. The disruption may also have altered perceptions of the availability of better-paying jobs, as workers started looking around for alternatives due to the uncertainty. It is also possible that once some workers started leaving low-paid jobs for better-paid ones, their co-workers updated their beliefs about outside opportunities. In an interesting study, Simon Jäger and coauthors found that workers in particularly low-paid jobs often underestimate their outside opportunities.[41] Simply put, workers in bad jobs think their jobs are better than they are. In contrast, workers at good jobs know that they have a good deal. In such a world, if (for whatever reason) some workers quit and move to better-paid jobs, this provides information to other people, who may start looking around for greener pastures themselves. Especially during the height of the Great Reshuffle in late 2021 and early 2022, the act of quitting a job became a performance art. TikTok videos of quitting went viral. Social media posts like this one showing screenshots of texts with bosses leading to an "I quit!" moment became commonplace:

When people quit bad jobs in such a public manner, it can create a snowball effect, where each departure prompts others to consider quitting as well.[42] It's hard to know exactly how important this type of social learning was in moving job-change behavior. But the fact that job quality differed so much here in America, combined with evidence on systematic bias in beliefs among those holding particularly bad jobs, suggests it is a serious contender in explaining some of the dynamics behind the Great Reshuffle.

I brought up some of these ideas in 2021 at the onset of the Great Reshuffle. Picking up on this, Paul Krugman wrote the following in his November 2021 column in *The New York Times*:

> As [Dube] says, there's considerable evidence that "workers at low-wage jobs [have] historically underestimated how bad their jobs are." When something—like, say, a deadly

> pandemic—forces them out of their rut, they realize what they've been putting up with. And because they can learn from the experience of other workers, there may be a "quits multiplier" in which the decision of some workers to quit ends up inducing other workers to follow suit.

As with many periods of rapid change, social multipliers or contagion effects can play an important supporting role. While direct evidence is limited, this explanation fits with how social media curated and spread stories about quitting bad jobs during the post-pandemic recovery.

The Promise and Limits of Tightness

If tight labor markets offer significant benefits, why don't we aim to sustain them more often? Are they just fortunate occurrences, or do they stem from deliberate policy choices? And if they are choices, are they really a "free lunch" or are there some trade-offs that we must consider?

First things first. As we have seen, we used to spend more times with unemployment close to or below the U* than we have in the past forty-five years. The 1990s boom offered a glimpse into a world of broad-based wage growth reminiscent of the pre-1980 period. The key ingredient was a tight labor market. So, the real question becomes: What policy tools can we use to re-create and sustain such a high-pressure economy?

In the years leading up to the pandemic, we saw how accommodating monetary policy could produce low unemployment and strong wage growth without sparking inflation. Had the pandemic not disrupted the momentum, we might have experienced an extended period of high-performing labor markets, with broad-based prosperity not seen in recent times.

Fiscal policy also plays a crucial role, especially when pulling the economy out of deep downturns. A key lesson from the Great

Recession was that we didn't do enough. The fiscal stimulus was too small, which resulted in a prolonged period of high unemployment and weak wage growth. It wasn't until the final years before the pandemic that we finally saw strong, inclusive wage growth, low unemployment, productive reallocation of workers through job-to-job separations, and a competitive labor market. If we had implemented a more aggressive fiscal policy in the aftermath of the 2008–2010 period, we could have achieved a tight labor market much sooner, allowing for a more equitable recovery.

We can see this clearly by comparing the recovery from the financial crisis to the one after the pandemic. The labor market took twelve years to recover after the financial crisis, but just two years after the pandemic. This swift recovery was partly due to unprecedented fiscal relief, first with the CARES Act of 2020 and then with the American Rescue Plan Act of 2021. This included direct Economic Impact Payments ("stimulus checks") and an expanded child tax credit, but just as crucial was the generous support for the unemployed. The Federal Pandemic Unemployment Compensation (FPUC) temporarily boosted unemployment insurance (UI) by $600 per week in 2020 and $300 per week in 2021, providing much-needed relief. Typically, UI only replaces about 45 percent of a worker's previous weekly earnings, varying significantly across states. In 2019, this replacement rate ranged from just 31 percent in Alaska to 53 percent in New Mexico.

Providing more generous unemployment benefits during downturns makes both social and economic sense. It helps individuals and families get by when jobs are hard to find, but it also stimulates the broader economy because unemployed workers tend to spend most of their benefits. This boosts demand and helps accelerate the recovery. Unemployment benefits are one of the most effective "automatic stabilizers" in our economy. The pandemic made this clear, and it's a lesson we should carry forward into future downturns. The current patchwork of state-level unemployment benefits is inadequate. We need a more uniform, generous system that can provide stronger support, especially during times of crisis. Economists who have studied the issue are strongly in favor of such reforms, recognizing the power of unemployment insurance not only to help individuals but to jump-start the economy when it's most needed.[43]

But did more generous jobless benefits hold workers back from reentering the labor market? This concern was frequently raised during the pandemic, with critics warning that the extra support would deter job seekers. However, the evidence tells a different story. Peter Ganong and his coauthors analyzed millions of financial transactions from families receiving unemployment insurance benefits, using data from JPMorganChase bank accounts. Their findings were clear: The more generous benefits significantly boosted consumption among unemployed households during a tough time. Yet, these benefits had only a minimal impact on how quickly jobless individuals exited unemployment.[44] In related work, my coauthors and I analyzed financial transactions of low-wage unemployed workers in states that ended the more generous benefits in June 2021 and compared them to their counterparts in states that kept these until September 2021. Like Ganong and his team, we found that generous benefits lifted spending but had a surprisingly small effect on job-finding rates.[45]

These findings suggest that bolstering automatic stabilizers like UI can soften the blow of economic downturns without creating substantial disincentives for job seekers. Additional fiscal relief, such as tax credits or public investments in infrastructure, can further boost demand and support recovery efforts. At the same time, an accommodating monetary policy that doesn't prematurely choke off growth is crucial to sustaining recoveries. Together, these fiscal and monetary tools can foster the kind of tight labor markets that drive broad-based, shared prosperity—the type of economic dynamism we've seen all too little of over the past four decades. Ultimately, a tight labor market allows the economy to work as it should, creating both a bigger economic pie and a larger share for those in the middle and at the bottom.

At the same time, there are limits to relying solely on macroeconomic policy to solve labor market problems. Monetary policy can be a blunt instrument, and it's often difficult to predict how interest rate hikes will impact the real economy. Fiscal policy, too, tends to get bogged down in partisan gridlock, as we saw in both 2009 and 2021. These tools are powerful but imprecise, making it easy to either undershoot or overshoot. One natural concern when overshooting is the risk of inflation.

As you likely know, inflation spiked sharply beginning in mid-2021, posing a serious challenge for policymakers. The causes of this surge were varied, including the global reopening after the pandemic, supply chain disruptions, and geopolitical shocks like the war in Ukraine. These factors led to a worldwide inflationary trend that affected countries across the board. But heightened demand also played a role, particularly in the United States, where fiscal policies such as stimulus payments likely fueled demand, especially as it pushed against a (temporarily) constrained supply in the wake of the pandemic.

During 2021–2023, there was a debate about how much fiscal policy contributed to this inflation. Some economists, like Lawrence Summers, argued that it played a major role, while others, such as Joseph Stiglitz, pointed mainly to supply-side issues. Paul Krugman took a view where supply and demand may both play a role and interact, but that fundamentally disinflation would occur as the economy put itself back together after the pandemic, a process he dubbed the "recombobulation."[46] In contrast, Summers predicted a high cost of bringing inflation down, which he argued would require five years of unemployment above 5 percent.[47]

How much fiscal and monetary policy contributed to the inflation burst remains a matter of disagreement, and economists will likely study this question for a long time. However, the fact that inflation surged substantially in both the United States and other advanced economies suggests that global factors—like supply chain disruptions, pandemic-related upheavals, and geopolitical shocks—played a central role. By mid-2024, inflation had eased without a significant rise in unemployment. It turns out inflation was transitory, and the disinflation process was relatively "immaculate," occurring without the predicted spike in joblessness. Although the extended period of high prices was painful for consumers, this suggests that fiscal policy, while a factor, wasn't the main culprit. Instead, much of the inflation in the United States stemmed from the global reopening and rebalancing of economies after the pandemic—Krugman's "recombobulation" at work. Careful analysis supports the idea that while fiscal policy contributed, it wasn't the dominant driver of the inflation spike.[48]

We can also ask a more specific question: Did the tighter labor market raise real wages, or were the higher nominal wages merely passed through as higher prices, making the wage hikes self-defeating? We have some tentative answers from comparing states with varying levels of labor market tightness. My work with David Autor and Annie McGrew shows that while labor market tightness was associated with somewhat higher price growth, it was linked to wage growth that was even larger. For those in the bottom quartile, wage growth was substantially higher than price inflation. In short, higher prices didn't cancel out the wage gains, especially for low-wage workers.

When we look beyond the United States, the benefits of a tight labor market become even clearer. America was the only G7 country to see notable real wage gains after the pandemic. Between late 2019 and early 2024, American workers saw a 2.8 percent increase in real wages (adjusted for inflation), while workers in other major economies saw stagnant or declining wages—with a 9 percent drop in Italy and only a 0.2 percent rise in Canada.[49] This comparison highlights the critical role that strong fiscal policies played in the American recovery. Without such policies, we likely would have dealt with much of the same inflation but without the wage gains fueled by a tight labor market.

So where does this leave us? Macroeconomic management through fiscal and monetary policy is a powerful tool for improving labor market efficiency and equity. Tight labor markets strengthen workers' leverage, making the job market work better for everyone. However, macroeconomics is not an exact science, and changing the course of an economy is like turning an ocean liner: It takes time and carries risks. We should strive for better macroeconomic management, including a focus on fostering tight labor markets, as seen before the pandemic as well as after. Remember that raise we talked about at the beginning of the book? It's much easier to make that happen in a full-employment economy.

But history also shows we should look beyond macro-level tools alone. Relying solely on tight labor markets is a high-risk strategy for durable, broad-based wage growth: By mid-2025, signs suggested that some tightness-driven wage compression was starting to unwind as job growth cooled.[50] The good news is that we have other safeguards at our disposal. At the micro level, we can encourage high-road employment practices through public pressure, antitrust policies, and targeted interventions. At the meso level—the middle ground of policy—we have the minimum wage, collective bargaining, and sectoral standards, which reach large groups of workers and are essential for making sure economic growth translates into bigger paychecks for workers throughout the labor market.

Why combine macro, micro, and meso strategies? Because even effective tools have side effects, and relying on a single approach risks diminishing returns or unintended consequences. A diversified tool kit is more likely to achieve our goals while keeping downsides in check.

In the coming chapters, we'll take a closer look at these tools and how they can help rebuild the wage standard.

CHAPTER 4

The Treaty of Detroit

The Rise and Fall of the Postwar Wage Standard

For many years, the prevailing wisdom held that securing a job at a large, well-known company was a stroke of luck. This belief was grounded in reality. Following World War II, major corporations like General Motors provided well-paying positions spanning from assembly line workers to engineers. Even into the early 1980s, companies with around ten thousand workers paid around 47 percent more than companies with around one hundred workers, largely due to higher wages for otherwise similar workers. But as Nicholas Bloom and his coauthors show, this wage advantage had plummeted to 20 percent by 2013.[1] Strikingly, this decline was far more pronounced in lower-paid sectors like retail and transportation, in contrast to higher-paid sectors such as finance. While larger companies continued to offer favorable employment opportunities for white-collar employees, they were no longer a gateway to high-quality jobs for blue-collar workers.[2]

In fact, a significant portion of the rise in wage inequality in America since the early 1980s can be traced to the declining quality of major companies where blue-collar workers found employment. As a result, many lower-wage workers increasingly joined companies like Walmart, while higher-wage workers gravitated toward higher-paying industries such as banking, pharmaceuticals, and consulting.

Even within these industries, top earners were more likely to work for better-paying firms. As we saw in chapter 2, high- and low-wage workers are increasingly sorted into separate worlds, a shift from the past when large corporations like GM offered middle- and lower-tier workers premium wages.[3]

What drove these changes? Technological advancements and shifts in trade dynamics certainly influenced employer decisions. Whether it was early electrification, later automation, or the recent rise of artificial intelligence, technology has consistently shaped corporate behavior. However, even in the face of these forces, employers have made distinct choices at different times. This challenges the idea that market forces alone, such as technology, dictate corporate behavior. Employers have a certain degree of power in the labor market, allowing them to shape wage policies.

Depending on external pressures, various wage strategies emerge. In certain periods, leading companies took a "high road" approach—offering higher wages to reduce turnover and build loyalty. At other times, companies opted for a "low road" strategy—paying lower wages and accepting higher turnover. Both approaches can be profitable: So what determines the prevalence of these strategies and the overall wage landscape?

As we have seen, the business cycle plays a key role. During periods of tight labor markets, competition compels companies to elevate wages, redirecting work toward higher-wage firms. In contrast, lower-wage companies struggle to attract workers under such conditions.

In this chapter, we broaden our perspective to explore how these wage policies take shape initially. We discover that companies are significantly influenced by the prevailing spirit of the age during their formation and expansion. This zeitgeist becomes ingrained in corporate culture, establishing enduring wage norms. The concept of norms is a squishy one, but important to understand. And as we will see in this chapter, social forces surrounding wage-setting—such as labor unrest and union bargaining—have played a crucial role in shaping such norms and setting a wage standard.

To fully grasp the past landscape of company pay practices at major employers like GM—which once offered a path to the middle class for countless American workers—we have to delve into a tumultuous period in history over a century ago. By digging into the history and the forces that shaped wage norms, we may uncover paths to reversing the negative changes that have hit middle- and low-wage workers in recent decades.

The Great Compression

Labor and the Great Depression

The Roaring Twenties were a time of great promise in America. In the aftermath of World War I and the devastating Spanish flu pandemic, the country's economy experienced a powerful surge. Income per person, when adjusted for inflation, grew by a remarkable 23 percent between 1919 and 1929. This growth was fueled by increased productivity, thanks to the widespread adoption of electric power.[4] As the economic historian Paul David argued, power acted as a game changer much like computers did in the 1990s, revolutionizing various sectors and boosting production. Output per hour of work jumped by an impressive 27 percent during that decade, following a rather lackluster period of growth earlier in the twentieth century.[5]

But the America of the twenties was also a very unequal society. The share of income going to the top 1 percent stood at 22 percent in 1929—an all-time high—while the bottom 50 percent's share stood at 14 percent. Between 1919 and 1929, the bottom 50 percent saw their pre-tax income grow by a total of 14 percent, while those in the top 1 percent saw their income grow by a considerably larger 21 percent. This income growth at the top was in part fueled by a strong stock market: The S&P 500 grew by more than 150 percent during the same ten years.[6]

Despite the inequality, the 1920s also witnessed improved living standards due to high productivity and low unemployment rates. The transition to electrification helped boost hiring and demand for workers. The unemployment rate hit a record low of 2.3 percent in 1919 and reached 2.9 percent in 1929.[7] Although those in the bottom half saw less income growth compared to the top earners, their incomes still rose considerably. Workers had plenty of grievances at the workplace, but the relative ease of finding a job kept most workers away from the other way of pushing for better terms of employment: joining a labor union.

Since the advent of factories in the nineteenth century, workers have often tried to form unions, which are organizations that represent their interests at the workplace. Unions can serve as a collective voice for employees in negotiations with employers, advocating for fair wages, better benefits, and improved working conditions. The most important role of labor unions is to negotiate for better compensation. Especially when employer power is pervasive, unions can help balance the playing field between workers and employers. As the economist Lloyd Ulman—a leading voice of the "California school" of industrial relations—wrote in the mid-twentieth century, "[F]irst and foremost, collective bargaining was championed as an instrument to provide equal justice . . . in a marketplace where . . . competition frequently afforded inadequate protection against oppression."[8] Besides wages, unions can also play a vital role in providing workers with a voice, empowering them to raise concerns, address grievances, and participate in decision-making processes that affect their working lives.

During the industrial era, when workers faced poor working conditions or inadequate wages, it often led to strike waves and labor unrest. The year 1919 saw a peak in such unrest, with major strikes occurring among dockworkers in Seattle, steelworkers in Gary, Indiana, and police officers in Boston. Unfortunately, these strikes were met with repression from both the government and employers, sometimes resulting in violence.[9]

Due to a combination of repression, a relatively low unemployment rate, and real wage growth, the 1920s saw a decline in workers' interest in joining labor unions.[10] This made unions less influential at the workplace and in determining wages during that decade. Union membership dropped from 4.6 million in 1920 to around 3.3 million in 1929.[11] And after reaching a high of around 18 percent in 1920, union density—or the share of the workforce belonging to a union—fell back down to around 10 percent by the end of the decade (see figure 4.1). Furthermore, most union members at that time were part of skilled craft-based unions associated with the American Federation of Labor (AFL). The labor movement faced challenges in organizing workers in the ascendant mass-production industries like steel, automobile manufacturing, and textiles, which predominantly employed semiskilled workers rather than skilled craftsmen.

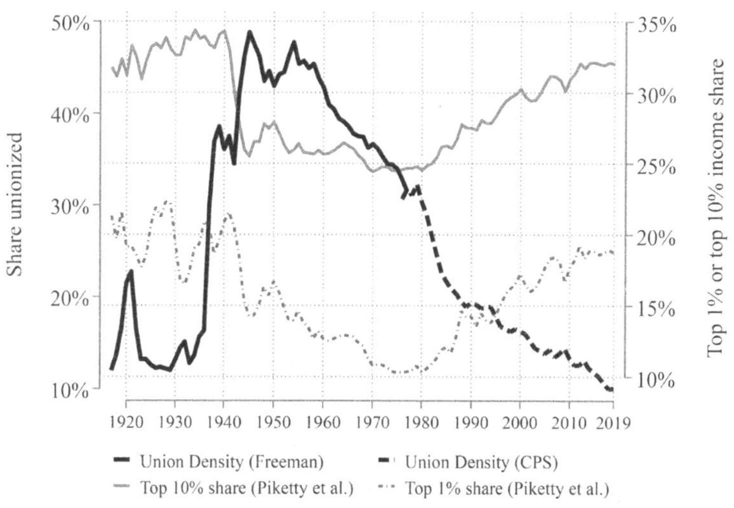

FIGURE 4.1 **UNION MEMBERSHIP AND THE GREAT COMPRESSION**[12]

All of that changed with the onset of the Great Depression. As the investment boom and the associated stock market bubble collapsed after 1929, it left behind failed banks, tightened credit, and falling product demand in its wake. Production fell precipitously as companies cut hours and employment, along with wages and prices. The concurrent wage and price deflation meant real wages did not fall as much. However, from the workers' perspective, nominal wage cuts were a major source of consternation that—along with general economic insecurity and resentment from the high levels of inequality—helped fuel labor organizing at a scale that had not been seen before or since in America.

A key to the scope and durability of the union spurt of the thirties was a supportive policy environment. During the nineteenth and early twentieth centuries, local, state, and federal governments, as well as the courts, often sided with business owners and repressed strike activity and union organizing. For example, in the 1919 steelworkers' strike in Gary, Indiana, the mayor called in the state militia to bar picketing or rallies by the striking steelworkers. Subsequently, the U.S. Army was brought in to enforce martial law, eventually leading to the defeat of the strikers.[13] The courts also often sided with employers, leading to injunctions against labor actions like boycotts and strikes, based on a narrow reading of antitrust laws.

In contrast, the thirties saw a movement in the opposite direction in the legal arena. First, the Norris–La Guardia Act was signed into law by President Hoover in 1932, which tilted the playing field partly in favor of unions. The act expressly exempted labor from court-issued injunctions that had often stymied collective action by workers. It also barred "yellow dog" contracts—where workers had to agree not to join a union to get the job.

But the biggest changes would come after President Roosevelt took office in 1933. First, as part of the National Industrial Recovery Act (NIRA), Roosevelt granted industrial workers the right to organize. The act read: "Employees shall have the right to organize and bargain collectively through representative of their own choosing, and shall be free from the interference, restraint, or coercion of employers." This was a watershed moment in American labor history.

And yet, the NIRA labor boards ran into many problems, including difficulty in the enforcement of the rules, and were eventually found unconstitutional by the U.S. Supreme Court.

The National Labor Relations Act of 1935 (also known as the Wagner Act) rose from the ashes of the NIRA labor law. It was designed to better withstand a legal challenge at the Supreme Court—which it did successfully in 1937. The Wagner Act enshrined workers' right to organize and endorsed the principle of exclusive representation by a union based on majority rule. It also compelled an employer to bargain in good faith with the union representing the workers after the employer recognized the union, either voluntarily or following a successful union recognition election. Importantly, the Wagner Act created the National Labor Relations Board (NLRB) to help enforce the new law.

The combination of economic and social upheavals and the change in legal environment led to a massive wave of organizing. The most iconic of these organizing efforts was the unionization of General Motors—the largest and most important employer at the time. The United Auto Workers union was not a member of the old AFL. Rather, they were a part of the newly formed Congress of Industrial Organizations (CIO), a breakaway faction in labor that had a different model of organizing. While the AFL-affiliated craft unions usually focused on organizing the skilled trades in a guild-like structure, the CIO took a wall-to-wall approach of organizing the entire workforce at a company, regardless of their occupation or skill status.

Organizing the whole of GM was exactly the plan when an initial seven hundred autoworkers took over the Fisher Body Plant No. 1 owned by GM in Flint, Michigan, on December 30, 1936. Unlike other work stoppages, at these "sit-down strikes," workers took control of the plant itself, which was in the legal gray area at the time (they would be found illegal today). Other plants followed suit over the course of the next few months, leading to a virtual shutdown of

America's biggest employer. After forty-four days of striking, GM relented and signed a deal. The agreement that ended the strike was only four pages long. But in it, GM recognized UAW as the sole representative of the workers with whom it pledged to bargain in good faith.[14] This was a new dawn in American labor relations.

The strike at GM was both a catalyst and an example of broader changes at play. Between 1933 and 1939, union membership rolls rose by nearly 6 million, resulting in a surge in union density from 11 to 28 percent over the same period.[15] Interestingly, even after 1935, not all of the new organizing came through elections: For example, a majority of newly organized workers joined a union through a strike for union recognition in 1936 and 1937, much like at GM. However, by 1940, nearly all new organizing was occurring through NLRB elections. And even when the employer recognition of the union happened through a strike, the threat of the NLRB election loomed large and helped push many employers to cease fighting the union.

The role of the government had changed in other ways as well. For example, during the Flint strike, Governor Frank Murphy of Michigan mediated between the two sides, meeting with the UAW when GM management was refusing to do so. The governor also sent in the Michigan National Guard. But unlike times past, they were not sent in to evict the strikers but rather to protect them from the police and strikebreakers.

How did this union spurt in the United States compare to what was happening in other countries? In his analysis of union organizing spurts, Richard Freeman compared unionization trends across ten high-income countries during the 1930s.[16] His data shows that the 17 percentage point rise in union density in America between 1933 and 1939 was greater than the average increase of 13 points across all high-income countries, placing the United States behind only Norway and France. At the same time, Freeman's analysis confirms that the rapid increase in unionization during the 1930s was more the rule than the exception across much of the Western world.

The union wave continued through the Second World War, aided in large part by the creation of the National War Labor Board (NWLB), a wartime institution designed to avoid further labor unrest and ensure uninterrupted production. While the NWLB imposed restrictions on unions' ability to strike, it simultaneously curtailed employers' resistance to organizing drives. As a result, union density surged again during the war years, rising from 26 percent in 1940 to 34 percent by 1945. The NWLB not only mediated labor disputes but also played a significant role in wage-setting. Much like the Office of Price Administration—charged under the Emergency Price Control Act of 1942 with imposing price ceilings and administering civilian rationing—the NWLB stabilized wages and capped top-end wage growth between 1942 and 1945. As we'll see, this wage stabilization policy also directly contributed to the reduction in pay inequality during the 1940s.

In sum, the combination of rising union membership and proactive state intervention set the stage for a new and very different process of wage-setting in America—one that would shape labor relations for decades to come.

The Treaty of Detroit and a new wage standard

By 1945, the Second World War had ended, even as a new Cold War was in the making. Trouble was brewing at home, too. The pivot to the peacetime economy brought shortages and price hikes from pent-up consumer demand. The economic conditions of the time were tumultuous, with inflation being a primary concern. During the war, price controls were put in place to control inflation, but they were lifted in 1946, leading to rapid price increases for goods and services and an annual rate of inflation of around 18 percent that year. As a result, workers' purchasing power was weakened.

At the same time, an increasingly vocal labor movement began to demand better wages. The War Labor Board was disbanded, and the National Labor Relations Board was back to mediating labor disputes. With an unemployment rate of only around 4 percent and a labor movement that had grown over the past decade, workers had confidence in making strong wage demands. This set the stage for a showdown between labor and capital that would shape the postwar accord.

Once again, at the center of the action was America's largest employer, General Motors, where workers were fed up with lackluster wages. In November 1945—nearly a decade after the Flint sit-down strike—the United Auto Workers called for another strike against GM, demanding a 30 percent wage increase and better working conditions. As in the thirties, what was happening at GM reflected broader realities across the American labor market and economy. The number of American workers on strike rose from 2.1 million in 1944 to 4.6 million in 1946, the highest in history. As noted by the Bureau of Labor Statistics, wages were the most important single issue, fueled by lost purchasing power from the postwar inflation: "[A]s living costs rose . . . real earnings declined. Wages . . . became the key issue in about 45 percent of all work stoppages which ended in 1946."[17]

The strike at GM—which involved more than three hundred thousand workers and was to last 113 days—would turn out to be yet another watershed moment in American labor history and the story of the postwar wage standard. In the end, the UAW did not get the 30 percent raise it had sought. GM agreed to a 17.5 percent wage increase, similar to deals the UAW had recently struck with Chrysler and Ford. But this was just the beginning. In 1947, the auto employers agreed to additional cost-of-living adjustments (COLA) and other improvements in working conditions. Finally, in 1950, following a strike at Chrysler, the Big Three auto manufacturers signed five-year contracts with not only substantial wage increases but also expanded paid vacation time, employer-sponsored health insurance, and pension benefits. This was the first time that major American employers took responsibility for broad-based retirement security.[18]

Fortune magazine dubbed this contract the "Treaty of Detroit"—an agreement that set the standard for labor-management relations for the postwar era and established a framework for collective bargaining that was used throughout the industry. This process came to be known as "pattern bargaining," whereby the deal or pattern set by the leading companies was adopted partly or fully by other employers. In a 1960 study of nearly one hundred companies, the economist Harold Levinson found that around two-thirds of the automobile industry's collective bargaining contracts in the 1946–1949 period adopted either the exact or an equivalent pattern set by the Big Three manufacturers.[19] The Treaty of Detroit would play a critical role in setting the stage for the postwar wage standard.

The Evidence on the Great Compression and Inequality

What was the overall impact of this turbulent period on wage and income inequality? In their influential 1992 study, economists Claudia Goldin and Robert Margo examined this question and coined the term the "Great Compression" to describe the dramatic narrowing of the wage distribution between 1940 and 1950.[20] Their findings revealed a substantial reduction in wage inequality, driven by notable wage growth at the lower and middle segments of the distribution.

To illustrate this shift, I replicated Goldin and Margo's analysis using the same Census data on working-age men, but focused specifically on hourly (rather than weekly) wages. As shown in figure 4.2, real (inflation-adjusted) wages rose much more sharply at the bottom and middle of the distribution than at the top. Between 1940 and 1950, workers in the bottom half saw real wages grow by over 35 percent, while wages at the 90th percentile rose by around 15 percent. These patterns reflect a major reduction in wage inequality between the top and middle of the pay scale during the 1940s. The term the "Great Compression" couldn't be more apt.

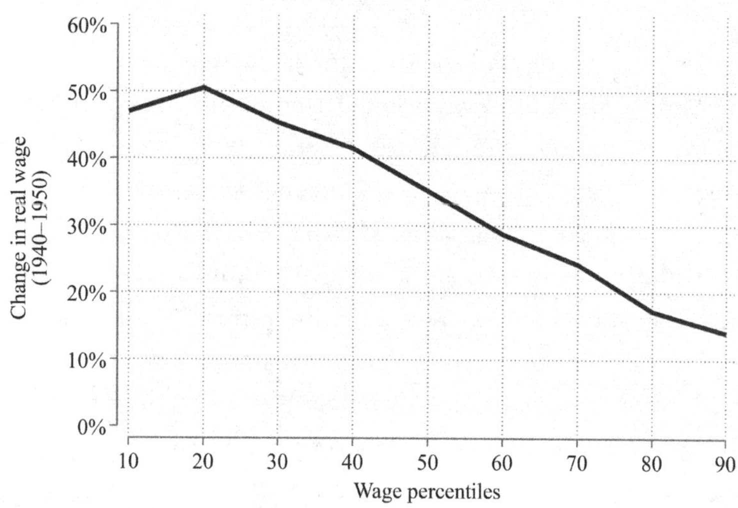

FIGURE 4.2 **THE GREAT COMPRESSION IN WAGES: CHANGE IN REAL HOURLY WAGES BETWEEN 1940 AND 1950 BY WAGE PERCENTILE (EIGHTEEN- TO SIXTY-FOUR-YEAR-OLD MEN)**[21]

Shifting focus from wage to income inequality, as figure 4.1 shows, the share of pre-tax national income going to the top 1 percent dropped from around 21 percent in 1940 to 17 percent in 1950 and continued to decline to 14 percent by 1953. These figures demonstrate a significant decrease in income inequality during this transformative period.

To be clear, the Great Compression was shaped by a variety of factors. A robust economy, increased production during wartime, and technological advancements—particularly electrification—all contributed to a higher demand for blue-collar workers. However, what sets the Compression apart is the rapidity of its occurrence and its geographic pattern. These two aspects suggest that institutional changes, extending beyond market forces alone, were at play. Among these changes, the surge in union membership and the establishment of the National War Labor Board stand out. Determining the precise causal factors amid a multitude of contenders is a challenging task, but there are intriguing pieces of evidence that shed light on the matter.

In a landmark study published in 2021, a team of economists—Henry Farber, Daniel Herbst, Ilyana Kuziemko, and Suresh Naidu—provided compelling evidence regarding the causal impact of labor unions on the Great Compression. A key innovation in their work was the discovery of a new source of data on both union membership and the incomes of union members. Unlike today's government-collected household surveys that routinely ask about union membership and income, such inquiries weren't standard practice in the 1940s and 1950s. However, the research team unearthed a series of annual surveys conducted by Gallup during that era, which did ask about union membership within households alongside household-level income. This overlooked dataset proved to be a treasure trove for investigating the impact of the wave of unionization that characterized this transformative period.[22]

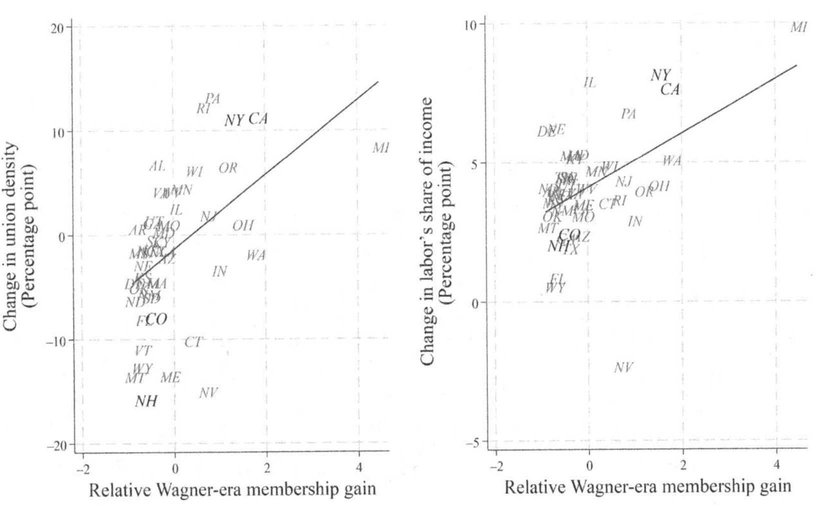

FIGURE 4.3 LONG-TERM IMPACT OF 1930S ORGANIZING ON UNION DENSITY AND LABOR'S SHARE OF INCOME[23]

To discern the causal effect of unions on the Great Compression, the researchers employed two ingenious *natural experiments* that resulted in divergent increases in union membership across different states during the 1930s and 1940s. The first natural experiment focused on the passage of the Wagner Act in 1935, while the second centered on pro-union defense contracting between 1940 and 1945. By examining these sharp institutional shifts and by comparing across geographic areas, the study avoided conflating union growth with other factors that could affect inequality—like strong demand for a local export good or a local downturn. In economic parlance, this type of analysis is called an *instrumental variables* technique, which leverages an exogenous shift in the key explanatory variable to get at causal effects. (If you want to nerd out on this, check out the glossary in appendix A.)

Figure 4.3 illustrates the contrast between California and New York—both of which experienced significant union growth during the "Wagner shock" of 1935–1938—and states like Colorado and New Hampshire, which saw much smaller increases in union membership. The surge in organizing in California and New York not only contributed to a durable increase in union membership for decades but also resulted in a larger share of income going to labor (and to the bottom 90 percent of families), as compared to Colorado and New Hampshire. Importantly, I selected these states based on the general statistical patterns identified by the authors rather than cherry-picking specific cases. The broader statistical fit (represented by the dashed line) reveals that those states with the most significant organizing efforts during the Wagner era experienced lasting reductions in inequality.

The researchers also leveraged the peculiarities of how certain local areas relied more heavily on wartime purchases during the 1940–1945 period. For example, the federal government purchased a greater volume of war-related goods from New Jersey than Iowa, which coincided with a more pronounced increase in union density in New Jersey than in Iowa. This wasn't an anomaly—the pattern held across states, indicating that higher defense procurement during wartime significantly boosted union membership, even after accounting for differences in industrial structure. Why? Federal war purchases came with pressure on employers to avoid obstructing union efforts, particularly under the union-friendly Roosevelt administration. These wartime procurement policies left a lasting imprint on union density in those states.

So what impact did the surge in union density have on income inequality? As union density rose, inequality fell. On average, a 5 percentage point increase in union density from Wagner-era organizing raised labor's share of income by 1.4 percentage points between 1937 and 1948.[24] It also increased the share of income going to the bottom 90 percent by 2.6 percentage points over the same period (not shown in the figure). Similarly, wartime spending–driven gains in union membership boosted both labor's share and the bottom 90 percent share. In sum, the unionization waves of the Great Depression and World War II clearly lifted workers' earnings and reduced inequality. This happened in two ways: first, by increasing wages at unionized jobs, which were concentrated in the bottom and middle of the income distribution; and second, by raising wages at nonunion jobs—a spillover effect that we will return to later in this chapter.

Unionization also reduced inequality by limiting income growth at the top. Historically, determining the impact of unionization on top earners has been a challenging task due to limited data linking high-income individuals to company-level information. However, a 2011 study by Carola Frydman and Raven Molloy helped shed light on this topic by constructing a comprehensive database that included compensation data for executives from nearly 250 of the largest companies during the 1940s.[25]

Their findings reveal a sharp decline in inequality between executives and other workers from 1940 to 1949. Although executive pay rose in nominal terms during this period, it did not keep pace with the earnings of most workers. For instance, in 1940, the median executive in their sample earned twenty-four times the average annual earnings in the broader economy. By 1949, this ratio had dropped to seventeen times. Crucially, the role of unions in this trend cannot be overstated. Frydman and Molloy found that the sharpest reductions in executive pay occurred in unionized sectors. Furthermore, they observed that as union membership and power grew throughout the 1940s, unions increasingly curbed executive pay.

In addition to the surge in union membership during the 1930s and 1940s, another institutional force behind the Great Compression was the wage-setting mechanism implemented during wartime through the War Labor Board. As the federal government ramped up wartime production, it also imposed wage and price controls. From 1942 to 1945, raising wages required approval from the National War Labor Board, which oversaw a significant number of wage increase applications and handled potential violations. The NWLB established rules that tended to favor wage increases for lower-paid workers more than those at the top of the scale. For example, employers were allowed to raise wages by up to 40 cents per hour (about $7.50 in 2023 dollars) without needing the board's explicit approval.

Additionally, the NWLB created "brackets"—expected wage ranges—by industry and occupation in each region. Wages that fell below the designated bracket could be increased to meet it without special permission, while raises for wages already above the bracket were generally prohibited. The explicit goal of the NWLB was to reduce wage disparities across businesses for the same job by encouraging wage increases at the lower end. In line with this goal, the work of Goldin and Margo found that the greatest reduction in wage inequality during the war occurred in low-wage industries like textiles, where wages were allowed to rise even as wage growth was restricted at the top.

But did wartime wage regulations leave a lasting mark? To investigate the persistent effects of the NWLB on inequality, economists

Chris Vickers and Nicolas Ziebarth combined newly digitized archival data on NWLB-mandated maximum allowable raises with microdata from the decennial Census.[26] The NWLB's bracket policy represented a unique experiment, exerting control over wages for the majority of private-sector workers.

To track its impact on earnings inequality over time, the researchers used regional variation in bracket levels. They found that higher brackets—i.e., rules allowing larger raises—were linked to significantly smaller wage gaps between the top (90th percentile) and the middle (50th percentile). Strikingly, the effects of these wartime wage caps persisted for decades: The compression of wage differences between the middle and the top remained visible through about 1980. This pattern supports the idea that union wage standards, shaped in part by the NWLB era, helped lift middle wages—at least while union density remained strong. In short, the NWLB's wage regulations had a durable impact on narrowing wage disparities and helped shape the trajectory of postwar income inequality.

Tax policy also appears to have played a role in facilitating the Great Compression, as argued by Thomas Piketty, Emmanuel Saez, and Stefanie Stantcheva in their 2014 work.[27] Starting in the 1930s, the top *marginal tax rate* (the tax you pay on an additional dollar of income) on ordinary income in America underwent a dramatic increase, reaching over 90 percent by the early 1940s. (The glossary in appendix A goes into marginal tax rate in more detail.) This elevated top tax rate remained in place until 1964, when it was lowered to 70 percent under Johnson, and it has gradually declined to the current rate of 35 percent.

A high personal income tax rate at the top inherently reduces post-tax incomes of top earners. But how might it impact their *pre-tax* income? Piketty, Saez, and Stantcheva argue that a high tax rate at the top limited the incentives of upper management and business owners to cut workers' pay. For example, imagine a situation where management decides against giving a raise to workers, saving the business $1 million, which is then funneled into a bonus for the CEO. Under a 90 percent top income tax rate, the government would take a substantial portion of that sum, leaving the CEO with only $100,000 after taxes. In this scenario, diverting pay from workers to management becomes far less appealing. By contrast, with today's lower top tax rate of 35 percent, the CEO would retain around $650,000 of that $1 million, making cost-cutting measures that benefit management far more attractive. In this way, high top-income tax rates can limit *rent-seeking behavior,* where top earners redistribute income to themselves rather than creating additional value.

This theoretical explanation has merit, but does it square with the evidence? At a broad level, the rise and fall of the top tax rate in America over the twentieth century certainly does look like the mirror image of the share of pre-tax income going to the top 1 percent. But such historical correlation can be driven by any number of other factors that were at play during this period—like unionization. So, the question remains: Did taxation genuinely have a causal impact on top earners' earnings?

To answer this question, Piketty, Saez, and Stantcheva conducted a cross-country analysis, comparing countries like the United States and Great Britain—which saw substantial reductions in top tax rates between 1960 and 2009—with countries like Germany and Switzerland, where such reductions were less pronounced. The researchers found a strong negative relationship: The share of the top 1 percent income grew more in the United States and Great Britain than in Germany and Switzerland. Similarly, countries like Australia and Canada, which experienced moderate reductions in the top tax rate, saw moderate increases in the top 1 percent income share.

While this cross-country evidence is not definitive, it suggests that the high top tax rates of the postwar period likely played a role in limiting excessive income growth at the top. Individual companies could still thrive and expand, but this did not translate into disproportionately large compensation packages for C-suite executives.

In such an environment, the benefits of resisting broader wage growth were muted, as any saved labor costs were more likely to be paid as taxes than channeled into post-tax profits or outsize executive bonuses.

Piketty, Saez, and Stantcheva find some tantalizing evidence on how the top tax rate might affect rent-seeking behavior by executives. It's well known that sometimes CEO pay rises from pure luck—like an executive at a petrochemical company getting a raise following a global oil price shock.[28] Tellingly, CEO pay doesn't usually diminish when the oil price falls, which is a signature of rent-seeking behavior. As it turns out, this relationship between executive compensation and lucky events is much weaker when the top tax rate is high. In other words, higher taxes at the top seem to curb the extent to which top earners engage in rent-seeking practices.

In sum, a combination of forces during and in the aftermath of World War II created a set of rules for the economy that fundamentally altered pay setting in America—at least for a time. The rapid rise in union membership led to a rise in wages, especially for those in the middle and the lower end of the pay scale. Wartime wage regulations further compressed pay differences, and these more equal wage structures persisted even after the war ended, pointing to the lasting influence of wage norms. We saw how wage-setting practices evolved within individual companies, like GM, and how other companies followed suit—whether through collective bargaining, market competition, or likely by emulation. Collectively, these changes established a set of unwritten rules that most major employers adhered to when determining blue-collar pay. At the same time, unions and tax policy likely played a role in restraining top pay. In this economic framework, wages across the board rose in tandem with overall productivity, representing a rising tide that genuinely lifted all boats.

Of course, this period was far from perfect. Some workers were left behind, particularly those who were not white men. Employment opportunities for women were limited, and those who did work faced considerable barriers. Racial discrimination was rampant, with a stark wage gap between white and Black workers. Yet, despite these significant shortcomings, for the typical worker in the economy, the postwar era was a time when prosperity was more broadly shared.

The Demise of the Treaty of Detroit and Private-Sector Unionism

But as we know by now, this shared prosperity of the postwar era was not to last forever, and by the 1970s, ominous signs were appearing on the horizon. While technological advancements and trade policies undoubtedly played a role in reshaping the labor market, the significance of institutions cannot be overstated. And the key institutional change that influenced the trajectory of the labor market was the decline of unions.

Union density reached its peak in the early 1950s, only to undergo a steady decline thereafter. Various factors contributed to this decline, including the 1947 passage of the Taft-Hartley Act, which allowed states to enact right-to-work laws. The so-called right-to-work laws are designed to weaken unions by making it hard to collect union dues, needed to fund the organizations. These laws, in turn, incentivized unionized industries such as steel and automobile manufacturing to relocate to states with more favorable labor conditions.

However, the shortcomings did not solely lie with the Taft-Hartley Act and right-to-work laws. The Wagner Act itself, although instrumental in protecting workers' rights, had flaws in its focus on workplace-level bargaining. In contrast, in many other industrialized countries, wage bargaining happens at the national level between unions and employers. The bargained standards apply to most workers either because their employer is a party to the negotiations, or because the resulting contract is extended to cover most positions in the sector, whether they are held by union members or not. As a result, countries like Denmark, Austria, and France faced similar globalization and technological changes as America but managed to sustain high levels of collective bargaining *coverage* (share of jobs where wages are determined by collective bargaining), even when the share of workers who are members of a union fell. Unfortunately, the same cannot be said for America, where the declining union membership and coverage went hand in hand. We will return to sectoral versus enterprise bargaining and the difference it can make later in the book. For now, the key takeaway is that given the enterprise-level bargaining system in America, the labor market was much more exposed to a fall in union membership than it was in other countries.

This impact of de-unionization on inequality within the American labor market was substantial. The possibility of such a catastrophic turn of events was conjectured as early as 1984 by the economists Richard Freeman and James Medoff in their influential book, *What Do Unions Do?* Freeman and Medoff provided an array of evidence on how unions raise wages of union members and how wages at unionized jobs are less varied.[29] The first channel means the gap between union members and nonmembers rises, which tends to raise overall inequality somewhat. However, the bigger impact comes from the second channel: By compressing pay differences among members, unions lower overall pay inequality. So, when unionization falls, we can expect overall wage inequality to rise. The book's concluding paragraph contained a prescient warning: "All told, if our research findings are correct, the ongoing decline in private-sector unionism—a development unique to the United States among developed countries—deserves serious public attention as being socially undesirable." While the decline in unionism did not end up being unique to America, the impact of the decline ended up being just as concerning as Freeman and Medoff had warned us.

A large body of evidence in economics and sociology has confirmed that the decline in unionization contributed significantly to increased inequality in America after 1980. In their 2021 study, the economists Nicole Fortin, Thomas Lemieux, and Neil Lloyd provide a comprehensive account of how de-unionization affected pay inequality in America by examining varied unionization trajectories across different states.[30] Importantly, their study takes into account how unions not only affect wages at unionized positions but can also influence pay at nonunion jobs—through the spillover effect. Accounting for these spillovers is crucial for a more accurate evaluation of the union effect.

So, how do Fortin and her coauthors quantify these effects? Their approach turns on leveraging diverse experiences with de-unionization across industries and geographical regions. Between 1979 and 2017, national-level unionization rates fell substantially in industries that were historically characterized by high levels of organizing—like manufacturing. But crucially, this fall was not uniform across the country. Union density in these sectors fell much more in the Midwest (from around 42 to 25 percent) than in other parts of the country. In essence, Fortin and her coauthors look to see what happened to wages in these traditionally high-unionization sectors like manufacturing, comparing states like Michigan that saw big union declines with states like South Carolina where union rates were low to begin with. Since some industries never had much unionization in either Michigan or South Carolina, those allow the researchers to control for other types of economic shocks that may have affected Michigan or South Carolina in different ways.

Comparing across states, Fortin and coauthors find that a 10 percentage point reduction in the union membership in an industry was associated with a 2 to 3 percent lower union wage (the "direct effect") and a 1 percent lower nonunion wage (the "spillover effect") in that industry in the 1979–2017 period. In a labor market with monopsony power, strengthening the wage standard in unionized jobs can therefore have a positive spillover on nonunion jobs, as nonunion employers have to compete with unionized employers to recruit and retain workers. There are other channels for spillover as well. When confronted with the possibility that their employees may join a union, employers often raise pay to lower the threat of unionization. When unions are in decline, such threat effects are less likely to boost wages at nonunion jobs.

Interestingly, the biggest declines in wages from de-unionization occurred toward the middle of the pay distribution. For example, nonunion wages toward the middle of the pay scale (or the median) declined by around three times as much from de-unionization as did wages lower down or higher up the pay scale (the 25th and 75th percentiles, to be more precise). This reflects the fact that unionization tends to be most prevalent among jobs paying around the median wage.

Overall, accounting for spillovers roughly doubles the contribution of de-unionization on the growth of wage inequality since the early eighties. In the case of men, the direct role of de-unionization can explain around 20 percent of the growth in the pay gap between the top (90th percentile) and the middle (the median) between 1979 and 2017. When we add in the fall in wages in the nonunion sector as well, de-unionization explains around 37 percent of the growth in the pay gap between the top and the middle for men over this period. Women were historically less likely to be in unionized jobs. For this reason, de-unionization explains a smaller share (13 percent) of the growth in pay gap between the top and the middle for women. For the workforce as a whole, de-unionization played an important role in weakening the wage standard in the post-1980 period.

The consequences of de-unionization present a stark parallel to the historic Treaty of Detroit era. In the mid-twentieth century, the deals struck at major employers not only shaped wage bargains within their own ranks but also had positive spillover effects on wages across the labor market. This contributed to the Great Compression, where wages rose more broadly for nonunion workers in the middle and lower pay scales. However, as union membership waned and their influence diminished in the latter part of the twentieth century, a similar process played out—but in reverse.

With reduced union density, the availability of well-paying union jobs for those without a college degree declined, and competitive pressures on nonunion companies to raise wages were alleviated. The outcome was a steady breakdown in the availability of good jobs for working Americans and a gradual erosion of acceptable pay levels for blue-collar jobs. When the countervailing power of unions eroded, it left behind a market marred by mostly unchecked power of employers and a diminished wage standard.

The erosion of wages wasn't primarily due to past leading unionized companies like GM or Ford lowering their pay standards, although that did occur to some extent. Instead, the labor market underwent a transformation into a service-oriented economy during the 1970s and 1980s. This shift brought forth new companies with different business models and managerial strategies. Crucially, these emerging companies were largely nonunion and unburdened by the wage norms established during the era of the Treaty of Detroit. As we will see in the next chapter, these newcomers played a pivotal role in reshaping the wage-setting landscape for the twenty-first century.

CHAPTER 5

Corporate Pay Strategies

From Walmartization to Voluntary Minimum Wages

Throughout history, leading companies have played a crucial role in shaping wage norms that ripple across the broader labor market. These norms include both internal wage-setting practices within iconic firms like General Motors and the overarching principles guiding pay structures market-wide. When a dominant company sets a wage standard, others frequently follow—either driven by competitive pressures to attract talent or by simply emulating industry leaders. For instance, nearly all employers benchmark new hire compensation against their competitors, creating strong imitative and inertia-driven forces within the labor market.[1]

As American union power waned and the postwar wage standard—famously embodied in the Treaty of Detroit—began to unravel, new wage-setting norms emerged. In this evolving landscape, the concept of monopsony power proves particularly insightful for understanding wage changes since the 1980s. Unlike the competitive supply-and-demand model, monopsony offers a compelling lens to explain modern labor markets, especially as firms gained substantial discretion in wage-setting, unrestrained by union rules or historical norms.

Monopsony power allows firms considerable latitude in determining wages, enabling internal culture, corporate history, and broader social influences to significantly shape pay structures. Why does this happen? Somewhat counterintuitively, when employers wield market power, their profits become less sensitive to the exact wages they pay. Under monopsonistic conditions, higher wages can yield offsetting benefits, such as reduced recruitment costs and easier workforce growth. The more market power a firm holds, the more pronounced these profit-offsetting advantages become. Additional gains from higher wages—like increased worker productivity—can also materialize. This does not imply that wage hikes fully "pay for themselves," but rather that an additional dollar in wage costs does not necessarily translate into an equivalent dollar-for-dollar reduction in profits.[2] The actual profit reduction might be substantially lower, allowing a broad range of possible wage levels with similar profit outcomes—but with very different implications for workers. In our research, Alan Manning, Suresh Naidu, and I show how monopsony power can explain seemingly puzzling pay practices, such as the frequent use of whole-numbered wages or uniform pay scales across multiple worksites, because firms are less sensitive to small wage variations under these conditions.[3]

In markets characterized by monopsony, wage policies from dominant employers can profoundly impact competitors. A major company's decision to raise wages can spill over to other firms in the market, not only through competitive pressures but also via emulation. As we come to realize that the labor market doesn't mirror the "perfect competition" ideal where workers are solely rewarded for their contributions to the employer, the concept of wage norms gains more coherence. Norms can emerge from a combination of market dynamics, social pressures, and historical exigencies. And these norms can transmit across workplaces, becoming an integral part of a new equilibrium in wage determination. As economist Samuel Bowles argues in the moral-economy tradition, social preferences—such as fairness, reciprocity, and identity—help set the very terms of market exchange.[4]

But while norms are resilient, they are not set in stone. In this chapter, we will see how established companies sometimes alter wage standards in response to social pressures, with significant consequences for the broader market. When influential firms adjust their pay policies—whether raising or lowering them—they can help redefine what constitutes a "going rate" for millions of workers.

The retail sector offers a particularly clear window into this dynamic. Since the 1980s, it has been a central arena for both the erosion and the partial rebuilding of wage standards. Companies like Walmart and Amazon have played an outsize role—first in pioneering a low-wage labor model and more recently in responding to public pressure to raise wages. Examining what shapes these corporate decisions sheds light on the forces that undermine wage norms and the levers that can rebuild them.

The Beast of Bentonville

Few companies embody this transformation more vividly than Walmart, the retail giant that redefined the industry. Unlike the Big Three automakers—whose wage policies were forged through the tumultuous labor struggles of the Great Depression and enforced wartime labor peace—Walmart emerged from a very different setting: a nonunion, right-to-work region centered in Bentonville, Arkansas. From its first store in Rogers, Arkansas, in 1962, Walmart expanded rapidly through the 1980s and 1990s, ultimately becoming the largest private employer in the United States. This explosive growth not only elevated Walmart to national prominence but also helped establish a new template for workplace practices and wage-setting norms across the economy.

Spread of Walmart

Walmart's exceptional expansion during the 1980s and 1990s can be attributed to a number of strategic initiatives, including technological advancements, efficient supply chain management, and an unwavering commitment to cutting costs.[5] Walmart's growth was underpinned by the vision and leadership of its founder, Sam Walton. Walton's core philosophy centered around providing "everyday low prices" to customers instead of offering periodic deals or bargains, which set Walmart apart from its competitors. This vision emphasized the importance of cost control, operational efficiency, and passing on savings to customers—a significant value proposition.

During this period, Walmart harnessed technology to gain a competitive edge. The company was an early adopter of computerized inventory management systems, allowing for accurate tracking of sales, inventory levels, and customer preferences. These systems enabled Walmart to streamline its supply chain, reduce costs, and optimize its product assortment, leading to increased market share.

Walmart's expansion into new markets was a key driver of its growth during this period. As Walmart spread out geographically from its home base in Bentonville, the company strategically opened stores in rural and suburban areas, targeting relatively underserved areas. This expansion into previously untapped markets allowed Walmart to reach a broader customer base and establish a dominant presence across the United States. Walmart's market share grew rapidly between 1980 and 2000, and in 2002 it topped the Fortune 500 list as America's largest corporation. By then, Walmart had also become the largest private-sector employer in America, employing over a million workers.

The Walmart Effect

The dazzling rise of Walmart was undoubtedly impressive, and the company transformed the retail industry and redefined consumer expectations. However, that success came with some darker undersides: the significant impact of Walmart's expansion on the erosion of wage standards. Walmart's model of low wages stood in stark contrast to the postwar labor relations exemplified by the Treaty of Detroit.

What was the source of Walmart's power to shape the wage standard? Walmart's rapid expansion and its subsequent establishment as a dominant retail player granted the company substantial leverage over labor markets. Walmart's immense size and market power also allowed it to dictate terms to suppliers, pressuring them to cut costs and trim their own labor expenses. In turn, this translated into a race to the bottom, with suppliers compelled to reduce wages and benefits, exacerbating the broader issue of wage stagnation across the industry and the local labor market.

It may seem misleading to compare Walmart to General Motors given that they occupy different sectors of the economy. But Walmart's low-wage model was not just a consequence of it being in retail as opposed to being in manufacturing. Walmart's wages have historically ranked lower than most other major retailers. In a 2005 report with Steve Wertheim, we looked at wage data that had been recently released by Walmart and compared it with public data on retail pay.[6] We found that Walmart's wages lagged by 15 percent compared to large retailers at the time and around 26 percent if we compared it to other large retailers in the general merchandising category, even after adjusting for the fact that Walmart tended to locate in somewhat lower-cost areas.

However, the impact of Walmart's growth on wages is a more complicated matter. While it's true that Walmart Supercenters may have displaced unionized, higher-wage grocery chains like Safeway and Albertsons—companies that typically paid their workers more—it also displaced smaller mom-and-pop retailers and dollar stores, which were far from being examples of high-wage employers. The story doesn't end there. If Walmart's entry into a local market ended up being a net job creator, it could have boosted demand for workers and pushed wages higher across the board. Conversely, if Walmart's growth enabled it to exercise market power—both in hiring and in setting terms with local suppliers—this could have exerted downward pressure on wages, especially for workers in low- to middle-wage jobs.

As it turns out, the earlier research that tried to disentangle these effects found mixed results. My own work with William Lester and

Barry Eidlin in 2007,[7] as well as independent work by David Neumark and coauthors published in 2008,[8] devised a new way of estimating the impact of Walmart on the local economy. We observed that Walmart's expansion followed a highly radial pattern, spreading outward from its "ground zero" in Benton County, Arkansas, over time. This growth pattern was driven by Walmart's ability to exploit economies of scale in distribution. For us, this provided a way to address a persistent problem: Walmart often opened stores in locations that were systematically different in terms of underlying pay trends or job growth. To solve this, we used a distance-based approach—comparing places closer to Benton County with those farther away—as a predictor of when Walmart would enter. This *instrumental variables* strategy aimed to mitigate the complications that might arise from analyzing the impact of individual store openings in isolation.

Our findings showed that Walmart's entry was associated with a reduction in retail earnings in the counties it entered.[9] However, this approach wasn't without its critics. Emek Basker, for instance, raised concerns about the distance-based method, arguing that places farther from "ground zero" differed from closer ones in their underlying economic trends, which could confound our findings.[10]

This disagreement lay dormant for many years until recently, when economist Justin Wiltshire took a new look at the old data, using both new statistical tools and a broader perspective.[11] Wiltshire's focus lay less on exactly what happened to retail-sector jobs or earnings—the focus of the earlier literature—and more on the overall impact of Walmart's entry. Namely, he aimed to quantify how a new Walmart Supercenter affected overall jobs and wages after factoring in those spillover effects on competitors and suppliers, and how Walmart may be able to exercise more labor market power from being a big employer.

To address concerns that Walmart Supercenters open in highly selective locations, Wiltshire built a "control group" to answer the question: What would have happened if Walmart hadn't entered, but all other conditions remained the same? He did so in two steps. First, for each county where a Supercenter opened (the "treatment" group), he identified counties where Walmart tried to enter but was blocked by local opposition. These counties were more economically similar to successful entry sites than places Walmart never targeted. Second, he applied a statistical model that put more weight on control counties that more closely matched the treatment counties in terms of employment and earnings trends prior to the store opening.[12]

So, what would have happened if Walmart had not opened a Supercenter in these areas? Wiltshire found that, on average, counties without a Walmart would have had higher overall earnings. Specifically, his estimates suggest that the presence of a Supercenter reduced annual earnings per worker by about 3 percent, or around $1,200 (in 2023 dollars). He also observed a decrease in employment, leading to an estimated 5 percent loss in aggregate earnings across all workers in the county.

The earnings losses occurred not only in directly affected service sector jobs (like in retail), but also in the manufacturing sector. Walmart often sourced its products from national or international suppliers, reducing demand for local goods, which in turn disrupted the usual economic benefits associated with new business entries. According to Wiltshire and other researchers, this shift in sourcing not only changed where goods were produced but also put downward pressure on wages.[13] Walmart's immense leverage allowed it to force suppliers to cut costs, which often meant lower pay for workers at those companies. Historian Nelson Lichtenstein documented one such case with Ferris Fashions, a small Arkansas clothing manufacturer that began supplying Walmart exclusively in 1985. Under relentless pressure to reduce costs, the company ended up paying its workers low wages.[14]

Overall, the entry of Walmart Supercenters seems to have lowered both wages and employment—contrary to what might have been expected. One potential explanation is that Walmart's presence increased monopsony power in the labor market, allowing the company to set wages lower than in more competitive markets. But was this really the case? To test this hypothesis, Wiltshire examined how areas with and without Walmart stores responded to the federal minimum wage increase in 1996–1997. This policy change is interesting because the response to a higher minimum wage can reveal monopsony power in a labor market. In a perfectly competitive market, as described in Econ 101, raising the minimum wage would lead to job losses, as some employers find it unprofitable to pay the higher wage, resulting in more workers chasing fewer jobs.

However, in a market with monopsony power, the story is different. We'll dig into the details in the next chapter, but here's the gist: When employers have some power over setting wages, they often keep pay low, even if it makes it harder to hire and keep workers. Why? Because raising wages to attract new hires would mean paying more to everyone already on the payroll. The result is that both wages and employment end up lower than they would be in a competitive market. When the government steps in with a minimum wage increase, it can actually improve hiring by forcing wages up, even if it cuts into profits. That's why a minimum wage increase that produces no job losses, or even job gains, is often a telltale sign of monopsony power at work.

What does Wiltshire's data show? In counties where Walmart opened a Supercenter, subsequent minimum wage increases tended to have a more positive effect on employment compared to counties that blocked Walmart's entry. This finding supports the idea that Walmart's expansion in the 1980s and 1990s increased monopsony power in the low-wage labor market, contributing to lower wages.

It's important to note that these findings don't suggest that Walmart was a net negative for the American economy. There is evidence that Walmart significantly improved productivity in the retail and logistics sectors during the 1980s and 1990s. Additionally, Walmart's ability to provide low-cost goods has helped ease the financial burden on many American consumers.[15]

However, even if Walmart's expansion was inevitable due to its productivity advantages, its impact on wages was not. In the past, high productivity "superstar" firms also gained market share, which increased market concentration. While this could have enhanced their monopsony power, countervailing forces limited its negative effects. For instance, the unionization wave of the 1930s and 1940s was more pronounced in these superstar firms. More generally, during the postwar Treaty of Detroit era, large firms often set wage standards in an upward direction. Newly digitized administrative wage data reveals that even as late as the late 1970s, large, unionized establishments exhibited not only lower levels of wage inequality within the workplace but also reduced inequality across workplaces.[16] Historically, then, large employers sometimes played an equalizing role, despite the added power that came with their size.

That role changed after 1980. New entrants like Walmart charted a different course, unencumbered by the wage standards of the past or by the strength of worker organizing, as unions were in a state of decline. At the same time, the broader economic climate shifted: Persistently high unemployment in the post-1980 period gave employers more leverage to set the terms of employment, further weakening workers' bargaining power.

Another key factor was the retreat of the federal minimum wage, which had long served as a foundation for wage standards. For the first time since its creation in 1938, the federal minimum wage was frozen for nearly a decade, remaining unchanged from 1981 to 1990. This stagnation allowed inflation to erode its real value, especially for workers in the bottom third of the wage distribution. As we'll see, this contributed directly to rising inequality. Combined with slack labor markets, the weakened wage floor made it easier for employers to adopt "low-road" pay strategies—especially for workers without a college degree.

In short, the 1980s marked a turning point, as market conditions, institutional dynamics, and policy safeguards all shifted in favor of employers—ushering in a new era of wage-setting practices. Walmart became a prominent example of this shift, as it grew to be the largest employer in the country. But it was not alone—Walmart's rise reflected broader, more pervasive changes in wage norms across the American labor market.

The Erosion and Evasion of Wage Norms

A core proposition of this book is that historical changes in pay patterns are more than just shifts in supply and demand. They reflect broader wage-setting behavior. A market with monopsony power gives employers leeway in setting wages, but the pay levels are influenced by a myriad of other forces including institutional pressures, organizational history, and notions of fairness. These forces can reinforce each other through both market processes of recruiting and retaining workers, as well as institutional processes like salary benchmarking. So, while there are many constitutive microeconomic components, it can be helpful to use the broader conceptual category of wage norms to understand how interrelated pressures and ideologies may affect pay setting.

But norms are also difficult to pin down. Unlike simple statistics like union density or the unemployment rate, or even compared to more complicated ones like market power, norms are more a state of mind than a hard number. They are like catalysts or inhibitors that can nudge wage-setting processes in one direction or another. To get a handle on norms, ideally we would peer into the minds of those who are setting pay—the managers—to glean insight into their approach to pay determination, and then link it to what they actually did in real life. Of course, that's easier said than done.

Fortunately, new research by economist Daron Acemoglu and coauthors provides intriguing evidence on the shift in managerial attitudes and practices starting in the 1980s, and how that contributed to wage suppression and a reduction in workers' share of the pie.[17] What makes their evidence compelling is that they can document *who* were setting wages. Before the 1980s, top managers were often promoted from within the company, with their training rooted in hands-on experience and tacit knowledge accumulated over time. But by the late 1970s, this started to change. Increasingly, managers were not homegrown; instead, they came from business schools. A business degree became almost a prerequisite for those aspiring to become top managers at major companies. In 1980, around 26 percent of workers were employed at companies led by a CEO with a business degree. By 2020, that number had risen to 43 percent.

There are good reasons to believe that this shift in managerial training altered how companies approached wage-setting and sharing the benefits of their success—what economists call *rent-sharing*. Starting in the 1970s, the idea of maximizing "shareholder value" gained dominance. This shift was best captured by the influential free-market economist Milton Friedman's 1970 declaration that "the social responsibility of business is to increase profits."[18] Business scholars like Michael Jensen argued that corporate managers were too focused on other stakeholders and not enough on maximizing shareholder value.[19] These ideas quickly made their way into business school curricula, as well as the popular corporate finance textbooks of the time.[20] One way in which managers could increase shareholder value was to cut costs. For example, by the early 1990s, the management literature increasingly emphasized "reengineering" of the work processes to streamline the workflow. Another body of work drew from the concept of the "lean corporation," which centered on reducing waste. These and other approaches often shared a common emphasis of driving cost efficiencies that—in practice—*could* lead to cutting labor costs and reexamining pay practices.

Acemoglu and his coauthors set out to test this hypothesis rigorously. They compiled data on all publicly traded companies in the United States, linking the educational backgrounds of top managers with administrative wage data covering nearly all workers at those companies from the 1980s to the 2000s. With this rich dataset, they could examine what happened when a company hired a CEO with a business degree for the first time. They compared the wages and profits of companies that brought in a "business manager" to those that continued to be led by nonbusiness managers.

It turns out that the appointments of CEOs with business degrees led to fundamental changes in pay setting. When a company shifted to a CEO with a business degree, wages declined by about 6 percent on average. This wage suppression was even more pronounced for low-wage workers, who saw a 9 percent reduction, compared to a 5 percent drop for higher-wage workers.

Importantly, these shifts in pay didn't correspond with improved company performance. The arrival of a business manager didn't affect employment, output, investment, or productivity, but it did reduce workers' share of the company's output. The labor share of company output fell by about 5 percentage points. Meanwhile, stock prices and return on assets improved, reflecting the increased profits from lower wages. But this wage suppression came with costs: Quit rates increased, and the resulting turnover likely moderated the company's profit gains. At the same time, business managers themselves enjoyed pay raises, earning 5 to 8 percent more than their non-business-school peers. In sum, these companies redirected economic rents toward owners and top management, largely at the expense of workers—particularly those at the bottom.

Acemoglu and his team took various steps to ensure that their findings were truly capturing the causal impact of business managers on wages. One clever strategy involved looking at CEO appointments brought about due to managerial retirements and deaths, events that are less likely to be influenced by other confounding factors. Even when focusing solely on these unplanned transitions, they found the same pattern: Wages dropped when the new CEO held a business degree. This bolstered their argument that it was the business managers themselves driving the observed reductions in wages and labor's share of company output. These findings show that the cost-cutting strategies pursued by GE executive "Neutron Jack" Welch and his protégés, discussed earlier in the book, were not isolated cases. Instead, they reflected the broader managerial philosophy of the era—one shaped by the teachings of leading business schools.

The implications of this research are profound. The findings suggest that rising wage inequality and the decline in labor's share of income can be attributed, at least in part, to the practices and values instilled in managers through business education. Business schools, with their emphasis on shareholder value and cost cutting, have led managers to prioritize profits over equitable sharing of economic gains with employees. This echoes arguments made by scholars like William Lazonick and Mary O'Sullivan, who have described how the rise of the shareholder value model has exacerbated income inequality in America.[21] The managerial focus on maximizing returns for investors has often come at the expense of workers, reinforcing a system where profits are prioritized over wages, contributing to the widening income gap.

The shift toward business managers reflects a broader erosion of pay norms in the post-1980 period. Employers adopted various strategies to alter pay-setting practices, including giving managers more discretion in determining wages. Throughout much of the twentieth century, blue-collar wages were frequently determined based on job title and seniority. However, beginning in the 1970s, companies increasingly turned to managerial discretion, relying on supervisors' evaluations of worker performance. Pay rates ceased to be "standardized" and became more personalized, based on the judgments of managers.

How did this departure from standardized pay practices impact the wages of blue-collar workers? As it so happens, the Department of Defense, tasked with setting pay rates for federal employees, gathered data from roughly fifty thousand private-sector workplaces between 1974 and 1991. This data offered a unique window into wage levels and pay-setting methods across detailed occupations. Maxim Massenkoff and Nathan Wilmers analyzed this data and found that the adoption of discretionary pay-setting almost doubled—from about a quarter of workplaces in the mid-1970s to around half by the early 1990s.[22]

The impact of this shift was significant. When a company used non-standardized pay setting, workers in the same job, in the same region and sector, earned roughly 8 percent less than their counterparts in companies with more standardized systems. Tellingly, when companies abandoned standardized pay practices in favor of managerial discretion, wages dropped almost immediately. This transition helps explain much of the decline in real wages among service workers—such as janitors and food service employees—during this period, accounting for around 20 percent of the wage decline for these workers. Similarly, it accounts for about 16 percent of the wage decline for trades workers, including electricians and mechanics, between the late 1970s and the early 1990s.

Employers have not only contributed to the *erosion* of wage norms, but they have also increasingly resorted to methods to *evade* them. In addition to adopting practices that lowered wages for employees within their organizations, employers found cost-cutting opportunities through outsourcing parts of their workflow to lower-cost contractors. This outsourcing allowed companies to sidestep one of the constraints on wage-setting: concerns about fairness.

Historically, when a company established a reputation as a good employer, it tended to pay a salary premium to most of its employees. For a manufacturing plant to pay its machine operators very well while underpaying the cleaning staff could lead to morale problems among the latter, who may feel they were being treated unfairly.[23] The concept of fairness usually involves a comparison to a reference group. When everyone works for the same employer, it's natural to compare wages within the company. However, when the cleaning staff works for an outside contractor, their reference group may shift to other workers under the same contractor. This change in the formal employer's identity can alter workers' reference groups, enabling employers to lower wages for "peripheral" workers while maintaining a wage premium for their "core" employees.

Ironically, outsourcing became especially prevalent in historically higher-paying sectors and companies, which stood to save the most on labor costs by transferring service roles to lower-wage contractors. This shift created a "social distance" between lower-wage and higher-wage workers, even though the nature of the work itself remained the same. As a result, modern companies have become more occupationally homogenous compared to their twentieth-century counterparts, with service workers like janitors or security guards increasingly concentrated in low-paying, specialized employers—as we saw in chapter 2. The economist (and former administrator of the Wage and Hour Division of the Labor Department) David Weil famously described this restructuring as the creation of a "fissured" workplace.[24]

These changes were not inevitable. Had there been different institutional safeguards in place to shield janitors' or security guards' wages from decline, employers would have had fewer incentives to reduce pay by circumventing fairness norms and altering the boundaries of formal employment.

Even more importantly, these changes are not irreversible. While much of the discussion in the book so far has centered on the unraveling of wage standards, if there is one thing I want to emphasize, it is the potential for positive change. Pay norms did erode, but they can also emerge to elevate and safeguard workers' wages. Remarkably, some of these positive changes began to emerge during the drawn-out recovery process following one of the most severe economic downturns in American history—the 2008 financial crisis.

Corporate Minimum Wages and the Rebuilding of the Wage Standard

In February 2014, the retailer Gap Inc. made a groundbreaking announcement that reverberated across the corporate landscape. It wasn't about a new fashion line or a flashy advertising campaign. Instead, Gap took the lead as the first major American company in recent memory to set a corporate minimum wage. The company raised its minimum pay to $9 per hour, with plans for a further increase to $10 per hour the following year. Considering the prevailing federal minimum wage of $7.25 per hour at that time, Gap's initiative represented a small but significant step toward higher standards in the wage-setting arena.[25]

Importantly, the clothing retailer declared its intention to raise the minimum wage for its workers voluntarily—not because it was compelled to do so by law or a collective bargaining agreement. Gap's announcement evoked comparisons to Henry Ford's celebrated $5-a-day wage in 1914, marking a rare moment when a large nonunion employer publicly framed a wage increase as a standard-setting move.

But while the corporate minimum wage was voluntary, it did not occur in isolation. At the heart of Gap's decision was the broader context of the Fight for $15 movement. Originating in 2012, the Fight for $15 movement was a grassroots campaign advocating for a $15-per-hour minimum wage for fast-food workers and other low-wage employees. It quickly gained momentum, spreading to cities across the nation, and mobilized thousands of workers, activists, and supporters demanding higher wages and better working conditions. The movement spearheaded a series of small-scale strikes and protests across the country, demanding higher wages and improved working conditions for low-wage workers. Fast-food employees, retail workers, and other service industry personnel united under the banner of the movement, staging walkouts and setting up picket lines in front of prominent businesses.[26]

By amplifying the voices of low-wage workers and using direct action strategies like strikes and protests, the Fight for $15 movement successfully brought the issue of low wages to the forefront of national conversations about economic inequality. In November 2013, the movement won its first legislative victory when the small city of SeaTac in Washington State passed a referendum authorizing a $15 minimum wage policy.[27] But Gap's announcement was the first sign that the arguments for reforming corporate wage policies was being heard in corporate boardrooms.

Gap's decision was also influenced by a tightening labor market during the recovery from the Great Recession. After years of a weak job market following the financial crisis, employers felt little pressure to compete on wages. But by 2014, there was finally some kindling in the competition for workers providing employers with an impetus to raise pay. Still, it was clear that Gap's decision wasn't just a response to market conditions. The establishment of a new wage *floor* also reflected mounting pressure from social movements, underscoring how external forces can drive meaningful change in corporate wage practices.

In the wake of Gap's announcement, Walmart, the largest private employer in the United States, initially downplayed the idea of a nationwide voluntary minimum wage (VMW) increase, asserting that wage decisions should be made at the local store level. However, just a year later, in February 2015, facing mounting public pressure, Walmart unveiled a $9 VMW, with a pledge to raise it to $10 in 2016. Walmart's move sparked a chain reaction throughout the retail sector, as major competitors felt the pressure to respond. In April 2015, Target, the second-largest retailer in the United States, followed suit, announcing an increase in its VMW to $9 and promising to raise it even higher in subsequent years.[28]

Then in 2018, Amazon, the e-commerce giant, drew national attention with its decision to establish a minimum wage of $15 per hour by 2019 for all its U.S. employees. Amazon's decision was

	2014	2015	2016	2017	2018	2019 //	2023
Walmart	$9.00	$9.00	$10.00	$10.00	$11.00	$11.00	$14.00
Amazon	.	.	.	$11.00	$11.50	$15.00	$15.00
Kroger	$7.95	$7.95	$7.95	$9.00	$9.00	$9.00	
Costco	$11.50	$11.50	$13.00	$13.00	$14.00	$14.00	$17.00
Home Depot	$8.00	$9.00	$10.00	$11.00	$11.50	$11.50	$15.00
CVS	$9.00	$9.00	$9.00	$9.00	$9.00	$9.00	$15.00
Target	.	$9.00	$10.00	$11.00	$12.00	$13.00	$15.00
Lowe's	$8.00	$9.00	$10.00	$11.00	$12.00	$13.00	
Albertsons	.	$7.25	$7.25	$9.00	$9.00	$9.00	
Walgreens	.	$9.00	$9.00	$9.00	$9.00	$9.00	$15.00

TABLE 5.1 **VOLUNTARY MINIMUM WAGES AT MAJOR U.S. RETAILERS**[29]

viewed as a significant step toward addressing income inequality and received widespread attention. “We listened to our critics, thought hard about what we wanted to do, and decided we want to lead,” said company CEO Jeff Bezos, who topped Forbes’ list of the world’s billionaires that year. And the critics took notice as well. After spending years skewering Amazon for paying poverty wages, the progressive stalwart senator Bernie Sanders sounded much more upbeat. “Today I want to give credit where credit is due. . . . I want to congratulate Mr. Bezos for doing exactly the right thing.”[30]

By 2019, the biggest American retailers had implemented VMWs ranging from $11/hour at Walmart to $15 at Amazon. Within a brief span of just five years, a key segment of the American labor market had undergone a remarkable transformation. Gone were the days when top retailers like Walmart were leading the way in putting downward pressure on wages. Instead, it seemed like major retailers were embracing a new approach. A combination of public and market pressure—facilitated by effective macroeconomic management—seemed to be shifting the attitudes of American corporations when it came to setting pay. The swift adoption of these wage floors across many leading companies illustrated how norms can emerge and evolve.

Impact of voluntary minimums

Despite these positive developments, questions lingered about the true impact of these corporate minimum wages. Were these announcements primarily aimed at winning public relations battles? Or did they genuinely make a difference for workers in the bottom half of the pay scale?

One early piece of evidence came from research I conducted with Suresh Naidu and Adam Reich, where we examined wage distribution within one company in particular—Walmart.[31] As discussed in chapter 2, we conducted a survey of Walmart workers in 2019 using Facebook ads to recruit participants nationwide. This allowed us to reach roughly ten thousand employees and gather detailed information on their wages, job satisfaction, and other characteristics.

In the absence of a binding wage floor, it's unusual to see a large share of a company's workforce earning exactly the same wage. When this happens, it's known as "bunching" in the pay distribution—a pattern that typically signals the presence of an external force, such as a wage policy or legal requirement, pushing wages up to that level. In our data, about one in six Walmart workers reported earning exactly $11 per hour—the company's stated minimum wage in 2019—indicating clear bunching at that wage point (figure 5.1, panel A). This indicates that Walmart's policy was indeed binding for a substantial part of its workforce. It wasn't a blanket raise for all workers, but instead likely boosted the pay of those at the bottom.

The story doesn't end there. Curiously, a common feature of corporate minimum wages is their uniformity across the country, despite wide regional differences in wage levels. For instance, retail wages tend to be higher in the Northeast than in the South, even though Walmart's voluntary minimum wage policy was applied uniformly nationwide. If Walmart's $11 minimum wage in 2019 was more than just a PR move, we would expect to see more workers in the South bunched at exactly $11 than in the Northeast. And that's precisely what we found.

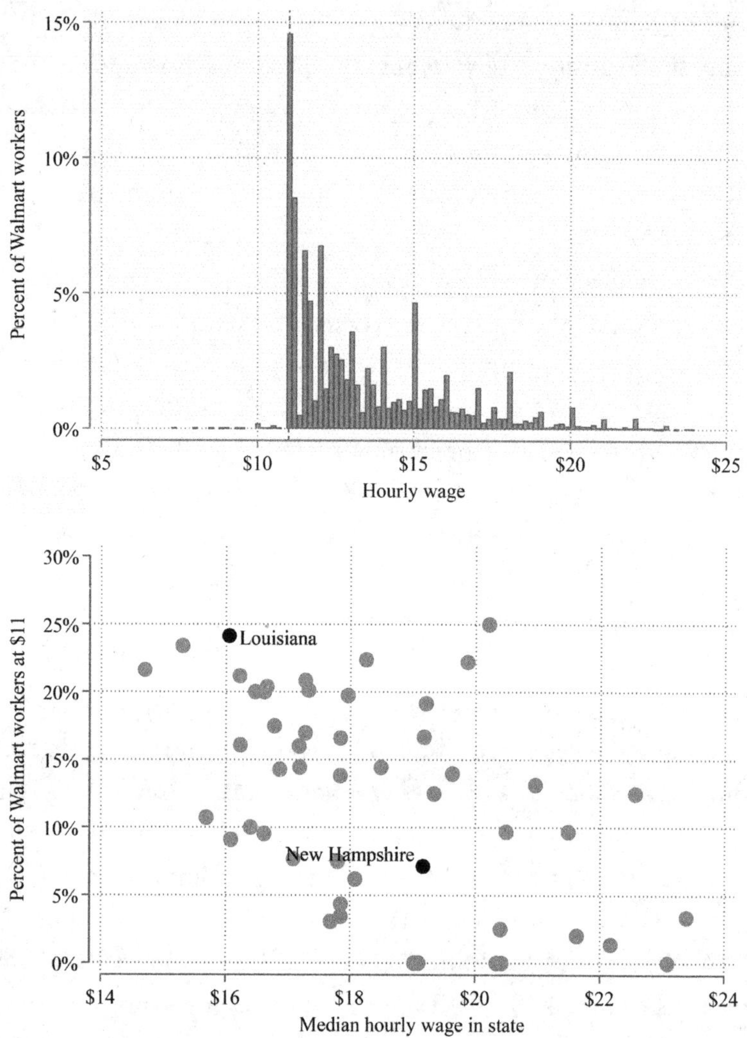

FIGURE 5.1 **HOW BINDING IS THE WALMART MINIMUM WAGE?**[32]
A. Walmart Wage Distribution (2019)
B. Share of Walmart Workers Earning Exactly $11/hour by State Median Wage

The bunching at $11 was more pronounced in low-wage states like Louisiana than in higher-wage states like New Hampshire (figure 5.1, panel B). New Hampshire is especially interesting because, unlike most New England states, it doesn't have a state minimum wage. Yet only about 7 percent of Walmart workers there reported earning exactly $11 per hour, compared to nearly 24 percent in Louisiana. This difference wasn't driven by legal wage requirements but by local labor market conditions. Many workers in New Hampshire would have earned more than $11 even without Walmart's policy. In contrast, in Louisiana, Walmart's policy ensured that a significant portion of workers earned more than local managers might have otherwise chosen to pay.

This explains the greater bunching at $11 in Louisiana—and also sheds light on why Walmart workers there reported higher job satisfaction than those in New Hampshire. The corporate wage policy had a more tangible impact on raising job quality in lower-paying regions. Taken together, this pattern of wage distribution and worker satisfaction across states provides strong evidence that Walmart's voluntary minimum wage genuinely raised pay for a significant share of its workers.

While our findings were informative, the most comprehensive evidence on the impact of voluntary minimum wages comes from a major recent study by Ellora Derenoncourt and David Weil.[33] They assessed the effects of corporate wage policies at five major retailers by analyzing payroll data from over 18 million hourly positions—at these retailers as well as other employers. The results were striking. When three major retailers adopted a $15 minimum wage, the share of workers earning exactly $15 jumped from around 10 percent to over 60 percent (see figure 5.2). This dramatic increase in wage bunching mirrored what we saw at Walmart, but on an even larger scale.

The data revealed that wages at these retailers rose by about 10 percent on average after the introduction of the $15 minimum wage, as compared to other similar companies. This wage increase wasn't limited to those earning close to $15; it had ripple effects, raising wages for workers earning above the new floor as well. The immediate impact was a significant pay boost for the lowest-paid workers, many of whom were previously earning near the legal minimum wage. The effect was most pronounced in regions where local minimum wages were much lower than $15, amplifying the importance of the corporate policy.

The wage increases also had a profound effect on employee retention. By making these jobs more attractive, higher pay substantially reduced turnover—especially among the lowest-paid workers, who had previously been the most likely to leave for better-paying opportunities. This decline in churn highlights the important role that wages play in retaining workers, particularly in high-turnover sectors like retail. The estimated quit elasticity—measuring the sensitivity of worker quits to wage changes—was around –1. This provides another high-quality natural experimental data point on monopsony power, consistent with the evidence we discussed in chapter 2. Taken together, these findings point to substantial employer power in these labor markets.

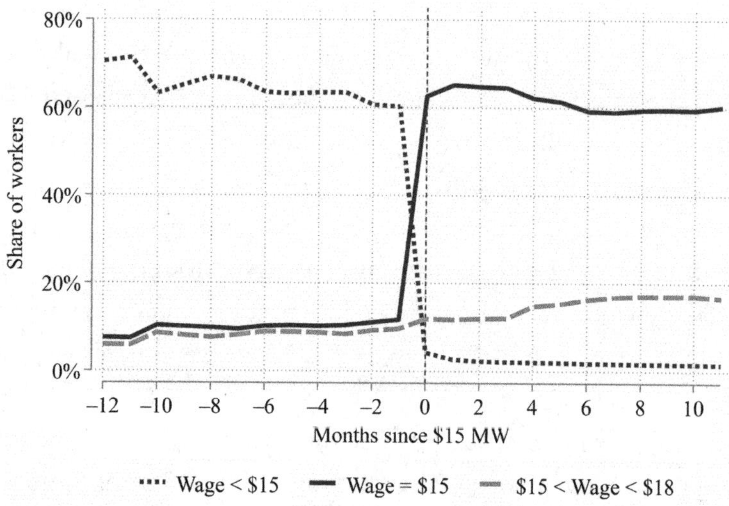

FIGURE 5.2 **SHARE OF WORKERS IN DIFFERENT WAGE RANGES AT THREE MAJOR RETAILERS ADOPTING A $15 VOLUNTARY MINIMUM WAGE**[34]

How many American workers have seen their wages rise due to these corporate policies over the past decade? Derenoncourt and Weil estimate that approximately 3 million workers were directly affected by voluntary minimum wages (VMWs) at the major retailers they studied. However, this is an undercount of the full impact of all VMWs, as it only reflects the impact of these policies at five large retailers. While the retail giants are the most visible adopters of VMWs, other employers have joined the trend. Numerous restaurant chains, including McDonald's (for centrally hired workers only, not franchises), and more recently, Starbucks, have implemented similar policies. What's particularly interesting is that companies traditionally associated with higher wages, such as banks, have also followed suit.

Bank of America made headlines in 2017 by setting a minimum wage of $15 per hour, making it one of the first financial institutions to do so. The bank further raised this to $20 in 2019, $22 in 2022, and plans to reach $25 by 2025. In a notable extension of the policy, Bank of America requires its vendors to maintain a minimum wage of $15, meaning the ripple effects of this policy likely spread beyond the bank's direct employees.

Other major banks have followed Bank of America's lead, including Citi, JPMorganChase, Wells Fargo, PNC Bank, U.S. Automobile Association Bank, and Truist Financial. Many of these wage standards have been revised upward in recent years. For instance, Truist raised its minimum wage to $22, up from $15 to $18, and JPMorganChase now pays between $20 and $25 per hour, depending on location, well above its previous range of $15 to $18.[35]

The banking sector examples are significant for several reasons. First, they show that the recent wave of corporate minimum wage policies isn't confined to industries like retail and hospitality. These wage hikes have extended to sectors that typically pay better, like finance. Second, the minimum wage levels in the banking sector, often between $20 and $25 per hour, are quite high—roughly in line with the median wage in the United States, which was $22 in 2022. This means that these policies are raising wages not just for those at the bottom but for workers across a wider range of the pay scale.

Finally, while there isn't an exact estimate of how many workers in the banking sector have benefited from these policies (since surveys like the Shift Project didn't include bank workers), given the large size of these institutions, it's reasonable to estimate that several hundred thousand workers have been affected. When combined with the estimates from the retail sector, it suggests that around 3.5 million workers, and possibly more, have directly benefited from corporate VMW policies in the past decade.

These pay standards have had a tangible impact on workers. Recent research by Nathan Wilmers and coauthors shows that corporate minimum wage policies not only raised wages but also significantly reduced working poverty among affected families—and helped narrow racial and gender disparities in the workplace.[36]

Return of the Large Employer Wage Premium?

The recent embrace of voluntary wage standards by prominent companies is intriguing, especially considering the history of the firm size pay premium presented at the start of this chapter. In the postwar decades, large firms like GM consistently paid better than smaller companies. But that pattern unraveled after 1980, particularly for low-wage workers. As we've seen, individual wage policies at companies like Amazon, Target, Walmart, and Bank of America likely raised pay for their lowest-paid employees. Still, while these firms rank among the nation's largest employers, a broader question looms: Are we witnessing a return of the large employer wage premium? And more specifically, has this shift benefited workers at the lower end of the pay scale?

To answer these questions, I leverage the matched employer-employee data from Oregon, first introduced in chapter 2, to evaluate changes in pay structures at big firms. Here I classify companies as either "small companies" (those with fewer than one hundred employees) or "large companies" (those with twenty-five hundred or

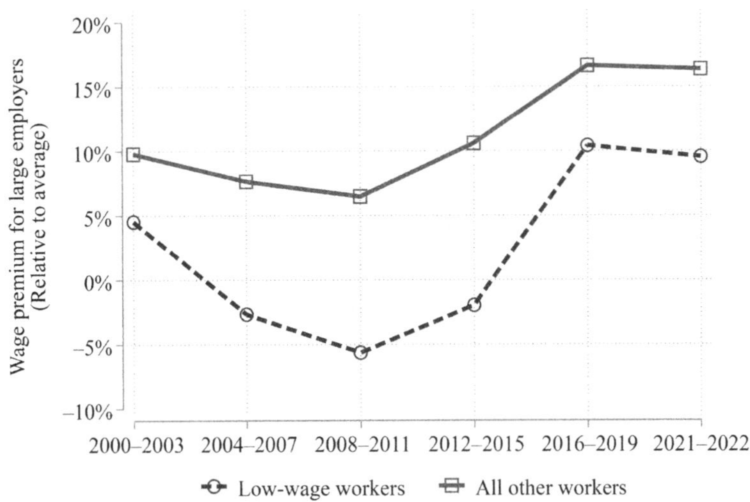

FIGURE 5.3 **LARGE EMPLOYER WAGE PREMIUM**[37]
Percentage Differential in Wages Paid by Large Versus Small Companies to the Same Worker

more workers). As in chapter 2, by focusing on how workers' pay changes when they move between firms, we can control for differences in worker quality and isolate a "pure" company pay premium. We can then compare the average of these premia between large and small companies over time. The analysis spans the period from 2000 to 2022, broken into four-year intervals, with the final section covering the two years from 2021 to 2022.

The results, shown in figure 5.3, are telling. During the early 2000s, the large firm pay premium fell from around 9.8 percent to 6.5 percent. However, this trend reversed dramatically between 2016 and 2019, with the premium jumping to 16.6 percent. The story is even more pronounced for low-wage workers—those expected to be in the bottom quartile of the wage distribution. For this group, large firms stopped offering a pay premium altogether in the mid-2000s. But by 2016–2019, the premium made a notable comeback, rising to over 10 percent for the first time in this century. Importantly, the pay premium for large firms appears to have remained steady after the pandemic, signaling that the changes might be more durable than cyclical.

The timing of this shift, and its greater impact on low-wage workers, coincides with the introduction of corporate VMW policies. While it would be an oversimplification to attribute these gains entirely to VMWs, they likely played a significant role. Other forces, such as a tightening labor market, also contributed. Hiring dynamics at large firms tend to be more cyclical, making their pay structures more responsive to economic conditions than those of smaller firms. But it's noteworthy that, even when labor markets were similarly tight at the start of the twenty-first century, the large employer pay premium for low-wage workers was significantly lower than it was by the end of the 2010s. This suggests that worker activism, public advocacy, and state-level policies during this period likely nudged many big employers to partly reorient their wage policies for blue-collar workers.

Are Voluntary Standards Enough?

The combination of public pressure and macroeconomic policies that fostered a tight labor market played a significant role in pushing employers to rethink wage-setting practices, particularly for workers at the bottom and middle of the pay scale in the years following 2015. As we'll explore further in the next chapter, the rise of state minimum wages, driven by the Fight for $15 movement, also contributed, especially in large states in over half the country. There's growing evidence that companies tend to set wage policies uniformly across locations, despite the diversity of local labor market conditions.[38] When an employer operating nationally has to raise wages in California, New York, and Florida, it may be simpler—both logistically and reputationally—to raise wages across the board.

These shifts have contributed to a partial rebuilding of wage norms—the unwritten rules that govern how wages are set in the labor market. Such standard-setting doesn't happen organically through impersonal market forces; it requires external pressure and evolving societal views on what constitutes a fair wage. In recent years, the question of what a large, successful company like Amazon or Bank of America ought to pay its workers has gained renewed prominence, resulting in meaningful wage increases for millions.

Of course, institutions and markets are not merely additive factors. A tight labor market has not only given employees more leverage through exiting a bad job; it can make it less costly for workers to exercise their voice at work by organizing into unions. Atulya Dora-Laskey, a Chipotle worker who helped organize a store in Lansing, Michigan, in 2022 recounts asking his co-workers what would happen if Chipotle closed the store as retaliation. Dora-Laskey said that they would respond, "Oh I'd just get a job at Qdoba, they're hiring for $14 an hour."[39] In his words, "it's a tight labor market that is giving people a lot of power right now." Similarly, workers fired by Starbucks for alleged retaliation against union-organizing efforts have often been able to find comparable jobs with ease.[40] Full employment is thus crucial not only for giving workers more power to exit undesirable jobs but also for lowering the risks and costs associated with staying and exercising their voices through unionization.[41]

Moreover, tight labor markets make companies more responsive to "nudges" toward adopting high-road strategies—such as raising wages or improving working conditions—because these strategies make more sense in a full-employment economy. When competition for workers is fierce, it becomes more attractive for businesses to pursue policies that retain talent and build goodwill among employees. Grassroots organizing and political pressure can be powerful forces when deployed at the right time and under the right macroeconomic conditions. The Fight for $15 campaign and broader labor activism successfully pressured many companies to adopt voluntary wage standards, resulting in real gains for workers. In her 2014 book, *The Good Jobs Strategy*, Zeynep Ton argues how companies could benefit from investing in employees.[42] As it turns out, given the right impetus, a good number of businesses adjusted their wage policies in line with this approach. And according to research by Natalia Emanuel and Emma Harrington, at least for one Fortune 500 company, the move to a higher wage even paid for itself through lower turnover and higher productivity.[43] This echoes the conclusion reached by Daniel Raff and Lawrence Summers that Henry Ford's $5-a-day largely paid for itself.[44]

There is certainly room for progress through pushing leading employers to adopt stronger wage standards, especially when paired with better systems for enforcement and periodic evaluation to ensure that promises of higher pay are actually fulfilled. But there are real limits to building standards one workplace at a time. Strategies like public pressure and workplace organizing under current labor laws may move the needle at some major companies, yet are likely to leave many other employers untouched. Voluntary minimum wage policies have directly raised pay for an estimated 3.5 million workers—roughly 2.5 percent of the overall workforce, or about 4 percent of U.S. workers without a college degree. While that represents meaningful progress, it remains limited in scope. Importantly, Derenoncourt and Weil found that while the companies adopting these voluntary minimum wages saw strong wage increases, other employers in the same local labor markets did not follow suit. Although the adoption of national VMWs seemed to exhibit considerable spillovers, they were less effective in prompting regional competitors to raise their pay. Finally, voluntary floors may not last: Notably, Gap's path-breaking $10 per hour VMW from 2014 has not been followed with any new announcement.

The limitations of voluntary minimum wages call for broader approaches to setting standards than solely relying on piecemeal efforts at the micro level or on macroeconomic policies alone. There are tools that operate in the middle ground—what I describe as the meso level. This is where reforming or retooling some of our labor market institutions can play a powerful role in helping build and protect a wage standard. In the next chapters, we will see how some of this work is already underway, and what more we can do.

CHAPTER 6

The Minimal Cost of Higher Minimums

The Science of Setting the Minimum Wage

In the sun-drenched cities of Tucson, Arizona, and San Antonio, Texas, where the straight roads stretch on endlessly, you might expect the stories of fast-food workers to be quite similar. In 2023, both cities had living costs about 6 percent below the national average and their median wages were roughly $21 (in 2023 dollars)—about 12 percent lower than the national median.[1] In many ways, these urban centers seemed to follow parallel paths. Yet, when it comes to the low-wage workforce, their realities sharply diverged.

Consider someone working the counter or drive-thru around 2023 in Tucson, where the median fast-food wage was $14.01 per hour. In San Antonio, her counterpart earned only $12.14—a 15 percent difference. This gap wasn't due to a lower cost of living in San Antonio, where rent and childcare costs were just as high. Instead, it came down to the state minimum wage policies.

Arizona voters had passed a 2016 ballot initiative to raise the state minimum wage from $8.05 to $12 per hour by 2020, with annual cost-of-living adjustments. By 2023, the minimum wage had risen to $13.85 per hour, and most fast-food workers earned close to that amount. Meanwhile, Texas adhered to the federal minimum wage of

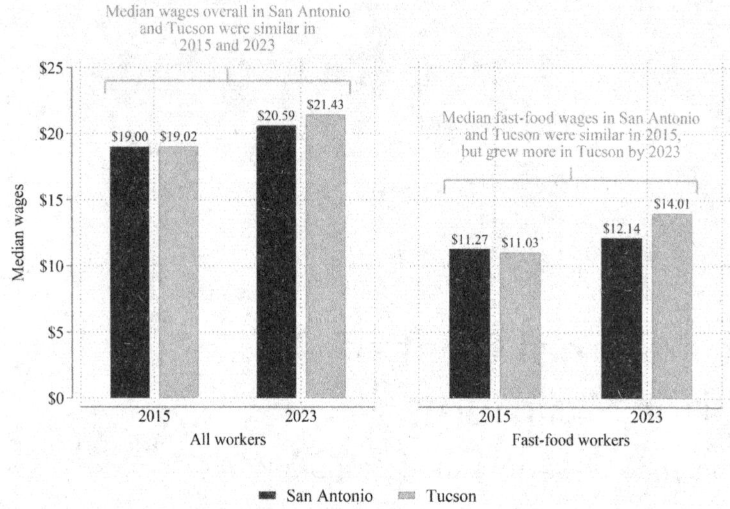

FIGURE 6.1 **A TALE OF TWO CITIES: MEDIAN WAGES IN SAN ANTONIO AND TUCSON**[2]

$7.25, unchanged since 2009 and mostly irrelevant for local workers because it is so low. Arizona's higher minimum wage directly lifted pay for many hospitality workers, explaining the wage gap between these two cities.

As figure 6.1 shows, while the overall median wage in both Tucson and San Antonio moved roughly in tandem between 2015 and 2023, the story for fast-food workers was different. In 2015, the typical fast-food worker in Tucson earned 2 percent less than their peer in San Antonio. But by 2022, their paycheck had grown to be 15 percent larger than that of their Texan counterparts. Clearly, minimum wage policies had a tangible impact on this group.

These numbers may seem like dry statistics, but they tell a powerful story about the real-world effects of minimum wage policies. In 2023, a full-time fast-food worker in Tucson earned about $3,700 more annually than one in San Antonio.[3] To put that into perspective, $3,700 could cover more than a year's worth of basic food expenses for a single adult in San Antonio, according to the MIT Living

Wage Calculator.[4] That kind of wage difference can significantly affect the lives of low-income workers and their families.

This highlights the practical stakes in the debate over regulating the low-wage labor market. Texas, like nineteen other states, has not raised its minimum wage above the federal level. As a result, nearly 40 percent of Americans—including residents of Texas—live in places where the minimum wage is too low to meaningfully impact their earnings.[5]

Meanwhile, many states and cities have passed their own minimum wage laws. Nearly every time it's put to voters—whether in blue, purple, or red states—minimum wage increases win approval. Yet, the issue remains contentious in state legislatures and Congress. Many businesses, along with some politicians and voters, argue that raising minimum wages represents dangerous government overreach into the private sector's wage-setting process. So, what drives the push for a higher minimum wage, and why is it controversial?

These are questions I have engaged with for more than two decades—by analyzing data, evaluating policies, and advising policymakers. In this chapter, I lean on what that work has taught me, including a recent deep dive on the minimum wage I did with Attila Lindner for the *Handbook of Labor Economics*, the go-to guide most economists reach for on this topic.[6]

The roots of the federal minimum wage trace back to 1938 when President Franklin D. Roosevelt signed it into law as part of the Fair Labor Standards Act. President Roosevelt's vision was clear: American workers should earn "a fair day's pay for a fair day's work." He tapped into a sentiment that had taken root years earlier when he declared, "No business which depends for existence on paying less than living wages to its workers has any right to continue in this country. . . . By living wages, I mean more than a bare subsistence level—I mean the wages of a decent living."

This vision behind the federal minimum wage was to ensure that working families could achieve a basic standard of living, reflecting the belief that public policy should step in when market wages fall below what society deems a "living wage." This is a wage that, as economist Robert Pollin put it: "enables workers . . . and [their] family members to lead lives that are at least minimally secure in a material sense."[7]

The push for a minimum wage also reflects a deeper concern for what is considered fair compensation for labor. As psychologists and behavioral economists have shown, fairness is a powerful motivator in human psychology, with many individuals willing to sacrifice their own benefits to penalize those who act unfairly.[8] People support the banning of transactions they perceive as exploitative, even when it involves economic costs. This sense of injustice becomes more acute when wage inequality rises and wages at the bottom fail to keep up with the rest of the economy—precisely the situation that has characterized America since the 1980s.

While a social preference against very low market wages is evident, it is not enough for setting policy. Such preference must be weighed against the potential costs of imposing a minimum wage standard. Even staunch advocates for low-wage workers have to carefully consider the trade-offs, as high costs might nudge us toward alternative strategies for supporting these workers. These costs could include higher prices for goods and services produced by minimum wage labor or reduced profits for businesses hiring low-wage workers. But the central concern in minimum wage debates is about potential unintended consequences for low-wage workers themselves—specifically, whether employers might cut back on hiring, leading to fewer job opportunities for those at the bottom of the wage scale.

This concern is rooted in the fundamentals of supply and demand: When labor becomes more expensive, employers may reduce their workforce. In the standard model of a competitive labor market, wages reflect a worker's *marginal productivity*—what they contribute to the economy. Higher-wage workers earn more because their contributions are greater, often due to superior skills, while lower-wage workers earn less for the opposite reason. The model also assumes that a worker's contribution declines as more workers are hired, leading to the downward-sloping demand curve for labor: The higher the wage, the lower the demand for labor. Market wages, in this framework, are set where the supply of workers meets employer demand, barring intervention from the government or unions. If a government-mandated wage exceeds this equilibrium, the competitive model tells us that it must lead to job losses, as some positions may no longer be profitable for businesses at the higher wage.

Of course, the presence of *some* job loss doesn't automatically make a policy undesirable. What matters is the magnitude of potential job losses. The basic supply-and-demand framework suggests that job losses might be larger when low-wage workers can be easily replaced by machines or by more skilled employees. It also predicts more significant job cuts in sectors where consumer demand is highly sensitive to prices. In these cases, employers may struggle to pass higher costs on to consumers, leading them to cut back on production and hiring. Conversely, even in a competitive labor market, job losses may be minimal if low-wage workers are not easily substitutable or if businesses can readily absorb or transfer those added costs.

Yet, as we've seen, the labor market is rarely perfectly competitive, and wages aren't set solely by market forces and skills. In a labor market with monopsony power, the effects of a higher minimum wage can look very different. Under monopsony, employment isn't limited just by employer demand for labor but also by the supply of labor available to the firm. For example, if McDonald's is required to pay a higher wage, fewer of its workers might leave for other opportunities, reducing vacancies at McDonald's. Unable to poach from McDonald's, other employers may now hire workers who were previously unemployed. And even if some lower-wage employers reduce hiring or shut down, their workers may find jobs at higher-paying companies. This reallocation is a key feature of labor markets where employers have power over wages.

These dynamics can help prevent unemployment from rising in response to minimum wage hikes. While some employers might cut back on creating new positions, others may find it easier to recruit and retain workers. As a result, moderate minimum wage increases can reduce vacancies and turnover without significantly reducing employment. Lower turnover also cuts recruitment and training costs, raising productivity, while higher wages can motivate workers, further offsetting higher labor costs.

Of course, these offsets have their limits. As the minimum wage rises, it eventually reaches a point where labor demand becomes the limiting factor. At that point, employers may be unwilling to fill vacancies, even when they can, which could reduce overall employment. In other words, there's a "Goldilocks zone" for setting minimum wages, where we balance job quantity with job quality.

This discussion underscores that when employers have monopsony power, the effect of a minimum wage increase on employment is an empirical question. As we'll see, while the debate on minimum wage and employment remains contentious, we've made significant progress in gathering better data and clearer natural experiments. Economists' views on the topic have shifted over time, with more convincing evidence shaping our understanding.

In this chapter, we'll trace the historical evolution of minimum wage policies in America. This will shed light on how this trajectory may have contributed to the erosion of the wage standard, particularly starting in the 1980s. We'll assess the wide-ranging effects of the minimum wage, focusing on its role in wage inequality, employment, and other economic consequences. Drawing on both domestic experiences and international evidence, we close with the big question: How ambitious can minimum wage policies be in our efforts to rebuild the wage standard?

The Arc of the Federal Minimum Wage

The story of minimum wage legislation in America begins in the early twentieth century. In 1912, Massachusetts took the pioneering step of passing the first state-level minimum wage law, setting the stage for other states to follow suit over the next two decades. However, this momentum was abruptly halted by the Supreme Court's decision in *Adkins v. Children's Hospital of D.C.*, which ruled that minimum wages violated employers' and workers' rights to contract freely under the Fifth Amendment, effectively nullifying state-level minimum wage protections.

It wasn't until 1938, during the closing years of the Great Depression, that the federal government succeeded in establishing a national minimum wage. Three years after Congress passed the National Labor Relations Act, and one year after the Supreme Court overruled *Adkins*, President Roosevelt signed the Fair Labor Standards Act (FLSA) into law. This landmark legislation introduced a minimum wage, a forty-four-hour workweek, and protections against child labor, aiming to improve living standards. The initial minimum wage was set at 25 cents per hour, which is equivalent to about $4.52 per hour in 2023 dollars.[9]

At its inception, the 1938 FLSA covered roughly half of the American workforce, including sectors like manufacturing, transportation, wholesale trade, and finance. Roosevelt's original vision was more ambitious—he wanted the minimum wage to cover the entire economy. However, strong opposition in Congress, particularly from Southern Democrats, resulted in a compromise. The law's coverage was limited to employees involved in interstate commerce or in producing goods for interstate commerce.

From 1938 onward, the federal minimum wage saw gradual increases every few years, outpacing inflation and rising alongside labor productivity over the first three decades. During this period, wages across the board generally increased together, allowing the minimum wage to keep pace with the earnings of most workers.

Figure 6.2 illustrates how, during this era, the real federal minimum wage consistently tracked the average wage of non-managerial workers, who made up most of the private-sector workforce.

Over time, a series of amendments aimed to expand the minimum wage's reach. The most significant expansion came with the 1966 FLSA amendments, which extended coverage to sectors like agriculture, nursing homes, hotels, restaurants, schools, laundries, and hospitals bringing an additional 8 million workers under the law. By 1968, the minimum wage had reached its peak value, equivalent to $11.85 in 2023 dollars. Although the wage floor lost ground during the Great Inflation of the 1970s, it still held between $10 and $11 (in 2023 dollars) by the decade's end. Two nominal increases in 1980 and 1981 pushed its real value to $10.64 at the start of 1981.

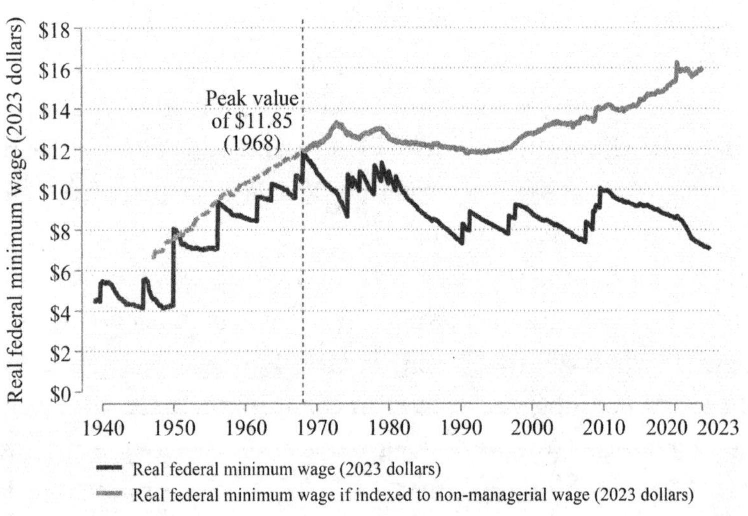

FIGURE 6.2 **VALUE OF THE FEDERAL MINIMUM WAGE: ACTUAL VERSUS INDEXED TO AVERAGE NON-MANAGERIAL WAGES**[10]

However, the pattern of regular minimum wage increases changed dramatically after the 1980 presidential election when Ronald Reagan took office. President Reagan, who viewed the minimum wage as harmful to the economy, left the federal minimum wage unchanged during his two terms, from 1981 to 1990, marking what was then the longest period of inaction in its history. As a result, the real value of the minimum wage steadily declined, dropping from around $10.64 in early 1981 to about $7.32 in March 1990 (in 2023 dollars). This 31 percent decline had major implications for wage-setting and contributed significantly to rising inequality and the erosion of real wages for American workers.

Since 1991, the federal minimum wage has been updated only twice: a two-step increase in 1996 and a three-step increase in 2007. The most recent increase was implemented in 2009, marking over sixteen years—longer than a generation—without any change to the federal wage floor. Between 2009 and 2023, the real value of the minimum wage fell by almost 27 percent, mirroring the decline of the 1980s.[11]

To put this decline in perspective: Had the minimum wage kept pace with overall labor productivity since 1968, it would have stood at just under $25 in 2023.[12] Had it grown at the same rate as the average wage for non-managerial workers (as it did from the 1940s to the 1970s), it would be around $16 in 2023. Economists also measure the strength of the minimum wage by comparing it to the median wage, a measure known as the Kaitz index. During the 1960s, the minimum wage ranged between 50 percent and 60 percent of the median wage, peaking at 61 percent in 1968 (as shown in figure 6.3). If it had stayed at 61 percent, the minimum wage in 2023 would have been slightly under $15 per hour.[13]

Interestingly, a minimum wage of $15 in 2023 would have better aligned us with our peer countries based on the Kaitz index. Most countries around the world have instituted some form of a minimum wage. On average, OECD countries set their minimum wage at 61 percent of the median wage in 2023. As figure 6.3 reveals, over the past twenty years, this index has been steadily rising in these countries, as nations like the United Kingdom and Germany have implemented ambitious national minimum wage policies. However, the

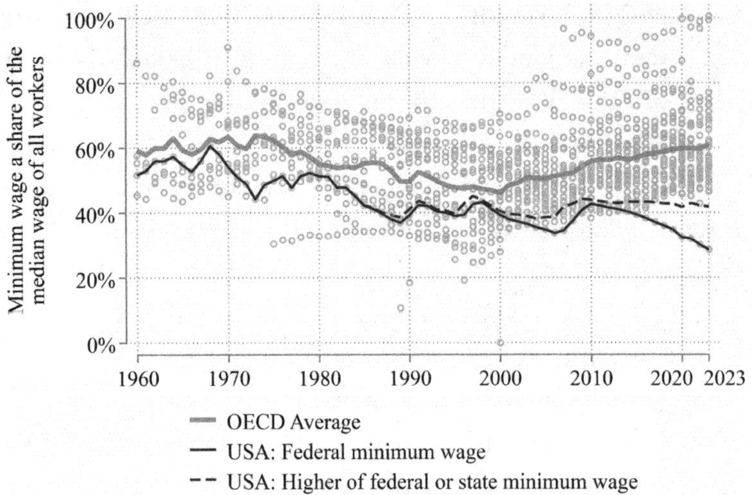

FIGURE 6.3 **MINIMUM WAGE RELATIVE TO THE MEDIAN WAGE: AMERICA AND PEER COUNTRIES**[14]

American experience has been quite the opposite. In 2023, the federal minimum wage was at 30 percent of the median wage, making it the absolute lowest among all OECD nations.

States and Local Areas Step in After Federal Inaction

States have the authority to set their own minimum wage rates, allowing them to account for regional differences in cost of living and wage levels. This feature of American federalism served as a partial solution during periods when the federal minimum wage stagnated, starting in the 1980s. By 1995, nine states had higher statewide standards. By 2007, the number of states with wages above the federal minimum had grown to thirty-one. However, with the incremental federal increases in 2007, 2008, and 2009, this number temporarily declined. But by 2023, thirty states once again had minimum wages above the federal level, with rates ranging from $8.75 per hour in West Virginia to $15.74 in Washington State. Fourteen states had minimum wages exceeding $12.50; seven had rates above $14. Additionally, nineteen states had implemented automatic indexation, ensuring their minimum wages would rise annually, often based on cost-of-living adjustments.

Another significant shift occurred with the emergence of the Fight for $15 movement in the 2010s. Until then, local governments rarely set their own minimum wages, aside from the District of Columbia (starting in 1993) and the cities of San Francisco and Santa Fe (starting in 2004). That all changed in 2014 when Seattle became the first city to take the lead in setting higher wage standards.

Since then, local wage policies have expanded significantly. Today, sixty-seven localities—mostly cities—have their own minimum wage laws, adding further texture to the minimum wage landscape. These cities are largely in Democratic-leaning states like California, Washington State, Colorado, and Illinois. In contrast, twenty-five states, mostly Republican-leaning, have passed laws preventing cities from setting their own minimum wages.[15]

More generally, today we have a stark divide across the country. Twenty states, such as Texas, have yet to implement an effective state minimum wage, largely relying on the federal standard, which is too low to be a relevant factor in determining paychecks at this point. This divergence is illustrated in figure 6.3: While the Kaitz index (minimum to median wage ratio) based on the federal floor has significantly declined over the past fifteen years, the Kaitz index that includes both state and federal minimum wages has remained stable, though still at a relatively low level. This underscores the growing role of state policies in shaping wage floors, while federal policy has remained stagnant.

As the face of minimum wage policy has transformed, so, too, has the profile of the low-wage workforce. To understand the impact of minimum wage policies, it's crucial to have a clear sense of who today's minimum wage workers are. Are they predominantly teenagers earning "pocket money," or are they single mothers struggling to support their families on meager wages? While both opponents and advocates of minimum wages often spotlight specific cases, it's helpful to examine the broader demographic composition of the minimum wage workforce.

Minimum wage workers tend to be somewhat younger than the overall workforce, but it's important to note that those under twenty make up less than 25 percent of minimum wage earners. Moreover, the minimum wage workforce is aging, with an increasing proportion in their twenties and thirties. Approximately 60 percent of minimum wage workers are women, and an expanding segment (around 30 percent) have received some college education.

Another key question in policy debates concerns the role of minimum wage jobs as potential stepping stones to higher-paying positions. If these jobs primarily serve as entry-level positions from which workers quickly move on to better opportunities, concerns about their quality might be alleviated. However, the reality is different: Low-wage workers are increasingly spending longer periods in minimum or near-minimum wage jobs. About half of minimum wage workers under twenty-five and two-thirds of those aged twenty-five or older remain in such positions for three years or longer. This share has significantly risen over the past two decades, highlighting the growing importance of minimum wage jobs in the long-term career paths of low-wage workers.[16]

Stagnant Minimums, Unequal Wages

Between 1981 and 1990, the federal minimum wage remained frozen at $3.35 per hour, causing its purchasing power to decline by 31 percent due to inflation. Around the same time, wages in the lower half of the pay distribution began to stagnate or even fall, contributing to heightened inequality. Was there a connection between the decline in the real minimum wage and this rising inequality?

There are compelling reasons to believe the answer is yes. Here it's crucial to distinguish between two distinct mechanisms at play.

First, by raising the bottom wage, a higher wage floor directly reduces wage disparity between the bottom and the top of the pay scale. Secondly, minimum wage adjustments can trigger "spillover" or "ripple" effects, where workers slightly above the minimum wage range also receive raises, further diminishing wage inequality. There are several reasons why we observe such spillovers. One reason is that workers consider not just their own pay level compared to other jobs but also their pay relative to their co-workers. So, if frontline workers receive a raise due to a minimum wage increase, the company may need to boost the pay of shift supervisors to maintain a certain differential.[17]

Another factor comes into play in markets where employers have some monopsony power, leading to wage disparities among similar workers. A higher minimum wage compels an increase in pay at the lowest-paying jobs, making them more attractive to workers. This, in turn, exerts pressure on jobs higher up the scale to also raise wages to preserve their pay advantage over the lowest-paying competitors. When firms have monopsony power, spillover effects can also arise as unproductive firms shut down when the minimum wage goes up, and their workers transition to higher-paying and more productive firms.[18] Such a reallocation channel is more likely to occur for larger and more permanent changes in the minimum wages, a point we will revisit shortly.

While the theory behind the spillover effects of minimum wages is clear, what does the evidence reveal about the role of the declining real minimum wage in driving wage inequality? There are some initial hints of a connection. As real minimum wage fell by 31 percent between 1981 and 1990, the 10th percentile wage also fell in real terms by around 10 percent.[19]

But while the timing of these trends suggests a link, establishing a causal relationship requires more robust evidence. This is where state-level minimum wage policies entered the scene, transforming states into laboratories. As states introduced different minimum wage policies at various times, these changes provided real-world *natural experiments.* These experiments allow researchers to compare outcomes across areas—such as Texas and Arizona—under varying policy conditions, offering valuable insights into how minimum wage changes affect wages, employment, and other outcomes.

When it comes to the impact of minimum wages on inequality, economists largely concur: The declining real minimum wage played an important role in driving up wage inequality in America. Three key studies have substantially contributed to our understanding of this phenomenon. Economist David Lee's pioneering 1999 research was one of the first to comprehensively examine how minimum wages shape wage inequality. His analysis focused in part on how the erosion of the federal minimum wage played out differently across states, depending on whether their overall wage levels were high or low.[20] He found that increases in the minimum wage led to substantial ripple effects, raising wages not only at the bottom but also higher up the pay scale. Notably, he argued that nearly all the growth in inequality within the bottom half of the wage distribution during the 1980s could be attributed to the erosion of the minimum wage's real value due to inflation.

However, Lee's findings raised some perplexing questions, particularly the apparent suggestion that a higher minimum wage not only elevated wages at the bottom compared to the middle but also led to higher wages at the top relative to the middle, a concern that left some economists unconvinced of Lee's research design.

A subsequent study by David Autor, Alan Manning, and Christopher Smith in 2016 introduced a more refined methodology studying state-level minimum wage changes. Importantly, they addressed some technical issues in Lee's construction of the minimum wage measure.[21] In Lee's analysis, both the explanatory variable (the minimum wage) and the outcome variables (such as the 10th, 20th, or 90th percentile wage) were divided by the median wage. This was done to leverage the substantial variation in how binding the federal minimum wage was across high- and low-wage states. However, this inclusion of the median in both the explanatory and outcome variables created a mechanical and spurious correlation. When Autor and his coauthors corrected for this problem, the results showed a smaller but still significant impact: A 10 percent increase in the minimum wage raised the 10th percentile wage by approximately 1.5 percent. Additionally, their research identified spillovers extending up to the 20th or 25th percentile of the pay distribution, beyond which ripple effects became negligible.[22]

Their results show that the minimum wage was a key driver of the gap between the 50th and 10th wage percentiles (inequality in the lower half of the distribution), but spillovers were smaller than in Lee's analysis, implying a more modest impact on overall inequality. Even so, they estimate that simply maintaining the real minimum wage at its 1979 level would have prevented around half of the increase in bottom-half wage inequality (the gap between the 10th and 50th percentiles) during the eighties. Importantly, the effects were stronger for women, who are more concentrated in lower-wage jobs.

More recently, research by Nicole Fortin, Thomas Lemieux, and Neil Lloyd revisited the minimum wage–inequality link and offered fresh insights. Their approach blended elements from both federal policy analyses (like Lee's) and state-level minimum wage variation (like those studied by Autor and coauthors). To analyze the 1980s, a period with little variation in state minimum wages, they looked at how far up the wage distribution the federal minimum wage was binding in each state before its real value began to decline. This innovative method allowed them to estimate the spillover effects of the federal minimum wage during the 1980s and to study the effects of more varied state policies in the 1990s and 2000s.[23]

They found that spillover effects in the 1980s were large—

comparable in size to Lee's estimates—and extended throughout the bottom third of the wage distribution. In contrast, spillovers in later decades were more modest, typically affecting only the bottom fifth of workers or less. These differences make intuitive sense: In a labor market with employer power, a large and prolonged decline in the real minimum wage could invite lower-wage, lower-productivity employers into the market, displacing better-paying blue-collar jobs. The contrast across time periods helps reconcile Lee's earlier findings with the smaller spillovers identified by Autor, Manning, and Smith in more recent data.

Like Lee, Fortin and her coauthors concluded that the stagnation of the federal minimum wage largely explains the dramatic rise in bottom-half wage inequality during the 1980s, and its relative stability since. However, unlike Lee's analysis, their method avoided overstating the reach of minimum wage effects. They found that spillovers were concentrated among lower-wage workers, with no artificial effects observed at the top of the pay scale.

In summary, while scholars have disagreed on the precise magnitudes (with recent work narrowing those differences), the conclusion is clear: The decline in the real minimum wage significantly contributed to the rise of pay inequality, particularly within the lower half of the wage distribution, with a more substantial impact on female workers. And the ripple effects of the minimum wage were likely greater during the 1980s, when the federal minimum wage held significant sway and the changes in minimum wage were durable—just as a theory of the market with monopsony power would indicate.

This last point is critical. As we return to the question of how high a minimum wage can go, it is useful to recognize that we are likely to boost the inequality-fighting power of the minimum wage when we consider more ambitious targets, not only because a higher minimum wage directly raises pay for more workers but also because it sends more potent ripples up the wage scale.

But What About Jobs?

While the minimum wage clearly raises pay for low-wage workers, a key question remains: Does it hurt their job opportunities? To fully understand its effect on workers' well-being, we have to look at how it impacts employment.

The debate over the minimum wage was fraught from the early days of the policy. During the 1940s, institutionalist economists such as Richard Lester used survey evidence and case studies to argue that within a range, minimum wages' impact on jobs was unlikely to be substantial.[24] To the surprise of many, the survey results painted a different picture than what the standard framework had long predicted. While conventional economics had emphasized the role of wages as a primary determinant of employment levels, Lester's findings offered a contrasting perspective. According to the executive officers he surveyed, the key factor influencing a firm's employment level was the current and prospective market demand for its products. The importance of wages ranked relatively low in their considerations. These findings were also consistent with the institutionalist view that there was a lot of variation in wages across businesses hiring low-wage workers, and there was room to push up wages without harming overall low-wage employment.

A different view was proposed by the increasingly dominant neoclassical school of economists such as George Stigler of the University of Chicago, who argued that employers competed fiercely for talent, and wages in a market settle to an equilibrium reflecting price of skills. Stigler and his followers argued that in such a competitive market, government-imposed wages will surely lead to job losses as some workers are "priced out" of the labor market.[25] Another neoclassical critic, Fritz Machlup, argued that once more sophisticated versions of the neoclassical model were considered, the business surveys of the type Lester conducted no longer had a close correspondence with the theoretical question, and so could not adjudicate between different theories.[26]

A more foundational criticism of the institutionalist perspective came from arguably the most famous University of Chicago economist, Milton Friedman. In his essay "The Methodology of Positive Economics" in 1953, Friedman argued that asking business leaders about how they respond to policies was much less informative than one may think. Much like skilled pool players or proficient drivers intuit the laws of physics without studying mathematical models, business leaders made intuitive decisions "as if" they were the agents described in the neoclassical models. In essence, as long as the neoclassical model of supply and demand predicted outcomes accurately, the unrealistic assumptions behind them were inconsequential, Friedman argued.

As we saw in chapter 2, by the 1960s, the neoclassical perspective on the labor market—focused on skill, supply, and demand—became the dominant paradigm in economics. But what about evidence? In the absence of significant variations in minimum wage policies across states, most studies relied on comparing employment levels of low-wage groups (most commonly teenagers) at the national level before and after minimum wage increases. This kind of "time series" analysis had limitations that economists didn't fully appreciate at the time, because federal minimum wage hikes often coincided with other national shifts, making simple before–after comparisons misleading. Even so, while the evidence was far from uniform, a consensus of a sort emerged, likely aided by a prior faith in competitive markets. Summarizing this view, economist Charles Brown and his coauthors wrote in 1982: "Time series studies typically find that a 10 percent increase in the minimum wage reduces teenage employment by one to three percent."[27]

The consensus, however, was not to last. The proliferation of state-level minimum wages paved the way for what's called the "new minimum wage research" starting in the early 1990s. Unlike the old "time series" evidence, the new approach leveraged differences in minimum wages across states, providing economists with before-and-after data on changes in employment, wages, and other outcomes across states with and without minimum wage increases. This new research approach would soon raise serious concerns about the quality of previous empirical work, as well as the conventional theoretical models.

To better understand how the new minimum wage research challenged the orthodoxy, it is useful to start with the key challenges faced by the researchers when conducting this research. One challenge is to identify groups for which the minimum wage is genuinely binding—that is, where it raises the wages of many workers in the group. If only a few individuals of the group receive a raise, their impact can get lost in the background noise. To interpret any employment effect meaningfully, we need to observe a wage effect for many workers in that group. Therefore, economists often focus on groups in which a large portion of workers earn close to the minimum wage. This frequently involves studying specific low-wage demographic groups like teenagers or low-wage sectors like restaurants or retail. Retail and restaurant industries together have typically employed a majority of minimum wage workers.

The more difficult task is constructing a credible counterfactual—a "what if" scenario that tells us what would have happened in the absence of a minimum wage increase. Would wages have stayed flat? Would employment have followed a different path? Early studies based on national time-series data lacked a clear control group. Instead, they tried to infer the effects of the minimum wage by controlling for broad economic indicators like the national unemployment rate.

The introduction of state-level variation in minimum wage policy enabled a major step forward. With some states raising their minimum wages while others did not, researchers could now compare otherwise similar places to better estimate what would have happened in the absence of a change. These studies brought the analysis closer to the logic of a controlled experiment. While economists still lacked true laboratory conditions, they increasingly relied on natural experiments and carefully chosen comparison groups to approximate the counterfactual and isolate the causal effects of minimum wage policy.

Perhaps the most influential study in the minimum wage literature was conducted by David Card and Alan Krueger in 1994. They examined the impact of New Jersey's 1992 minimum wage increase—from $4.25 to $5.05 (equivalent to roughly $8.50 to $10.10 in 2023 dollars)—on fast-food employment.[28] To estimate what would have happened without the policy change, they compared fast-food employment trends in New Jersey (the "treatment group") to neighboring eastern Pennsylvania (the "control group"), where the minimum wage remained at $4.25. While differences between the two regions certainly existed, the key assumption was that absent the minimum wage increase, employment *changes* in fast food would have followed a similar trajectory in both areas. This study became a foundational example of the *difference-in-differences* approach in economics, using a natural experiment to identify causal effects. Card was later awarded the Nobel Prize in Economics in 2021 for his methodological innovations, including this study.

Card and Krueger surveyed 410 fast-food restaurants to measure the policy's impact. They found that prior to the policy change, starting wages in New Jersey and Pennsylvania were quite similar. Following the increase, starting wages in New Jersey rose by about 10 percent more than in Pennsylvania. Yet when it came to employment, fast-food jobs declined in Pennsylvania in 1992, while they slightly increased in New Jersey. In other words, there was no evidence of job losses resulting from the higher minimum wage.

They also analyzed data within New Jersey, comparing restaurants that had to increase wages significantly with those already paying wages close to or at $5.05. Again, they found no indication of greater job losses (or slower job gains) at restaurants that had to raise wages more. In their 1995 book, *Myth and Measurement*, the duo summarized and expanded on this evidence using various research

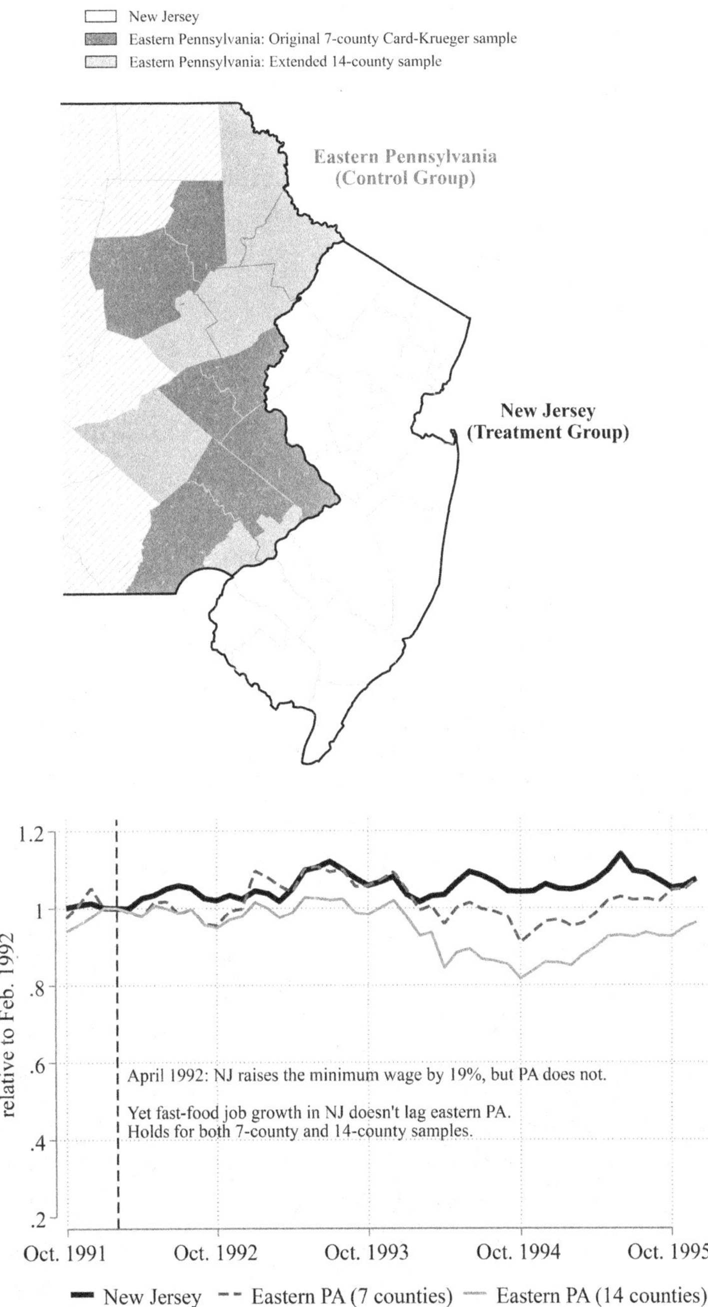

FIGURE 6.4 A NATURAL EXPERIMENT IN NEW JERSEY—FAST-FOOD EMPLOYMENT AND MINIMUM WAGE[29]

methods, all of which failed to suggest that minimum wages led to job losses.[30]

These findings defied conventional economic wisdom, challenging deeply entrenched beliefs about the functioning of the low-wage labor market and about the effect of minimum wages. Some responses to this research were quite extreme, with Nobel laureate economist James Buchanan warning against economics becoming a "bevy of camp-following whores" in a *Wall Street Journal* op-ed.[31] Even among more composed economists, skepticism remained.

Most notably, economists David Neumark and William Wascher challenged the findings, raising concerns about the quality of the underlying data.[32] The initial study had relied on a self-collected survey because no suitable public data existed at the time. In response, Card and Krueger conducted a follow-up in 2000, this time using administrative payroll records from nearly all fast-food restaurants in New Jersey and Pennsylvania.[33] As figure 6.4 shows, they again found no decline in New Jersey restaurant employment after the 1992 minimum wage hike, whether compared with the seven eastern Pennsylvania counties in the original study or an expanded set of fourteen.

Subsequent research has built upon Card and Krueger's methodology, greatly benefiting from more state-level experimentation and better data access. Data derived from the administrative payroll records used in Card and Kreueger's 2000 study is now publicly available through the Quarterly Census of Employment and Wages (QCEW) program. In a 2010 study with William Lester and Michael Reich, we examined 504 contiguous counties along state borders with continuous data from 1990 to 2006. Of these, 337 counties in 288 pairs had differing minimum wage levels. Using QCEW data, based on administrative records from nearly all businesses, we compared wage and employment changes in the restaurant sector across border counties with different minimum wage policies. Like Card and Krueger, we leveraged neighboring areas as control groups, which shared similar market conditions. However, our analysis covered dozens of minimum wage changes across the country and over a longer period.[34]

Our results showed that restaurant earnings rose more on the side of the border with the higher minimum wage, while the difference in employment was negligible, and statistically indistinguishable from zero. This pattern persisted up to four years after the wage hike. These results suggested that significant job losses following minimum wage increases were unlikely. Card and Krueger's core findings held up when using more and better data.

Since 2010, data and methods have advanced further. We've had many more natural experiments, with some involving much larger minimum wage increases, and more sophisticated techniques for aggregating the evidence. In a 2024 follow-up study with Michael Reich, Akash Bhatt, and Denis Sosinskiy, we used 420 border county pairs and analyzed 42 major minimum wage increases between 1990 and 2019 to reassess their impact on employment in the restaurant sector.[35] This was equivalent to conducting 42 different New Jersey–Pennsylvania case studies and averaging the results. Across these events, the minimum wage rose by 25 percent—a bigger increase than in the New Jersey case study. As figure 6.5 shows, restaurant earnings grew by about 6 percent more on the side of the border that raised the minimum wage, while restaurant employment, which had been growing similarly on both sides of the border before the hike, continued to grow at similar rates afterward. There was no loss in restaurant jobs, even five years following the increase. Restaurant employment actually grew slightly more (1.6 percent) on the side of the border raising the minimum, though this was not statistically different from zero.

We also used various other approaches to creating control groups—such as analyzing areas within the same commuting zone (an alternative way of defining local labor markets) or simply comparing outcomes between states that raised their minimum wage or did not around the same time. In each case, our results confirmed the same finding: The overall impact of minimum wage increases on restaurant employment remained minimal. These newer techniques and data further reinforced our earlier conclusions, providing straightforward and transparent evidence for the case for modest employment effects from raising minimum wages in this low-wage sector.[36]

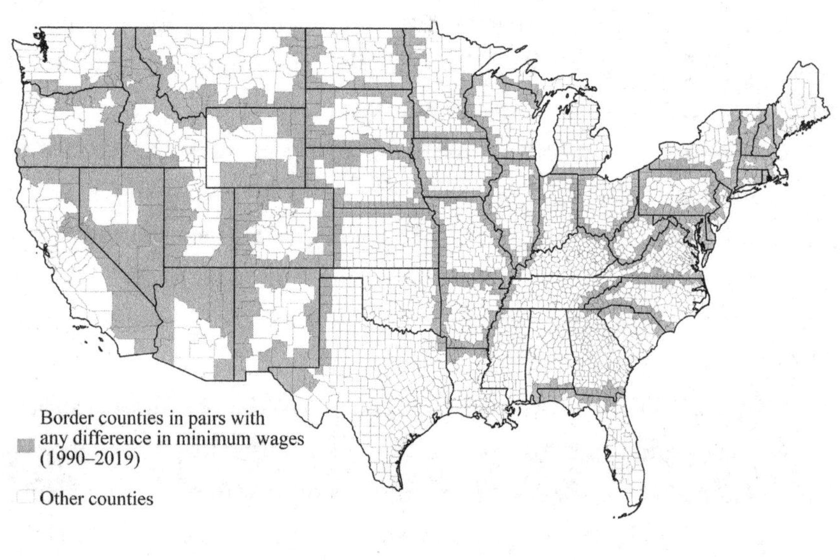

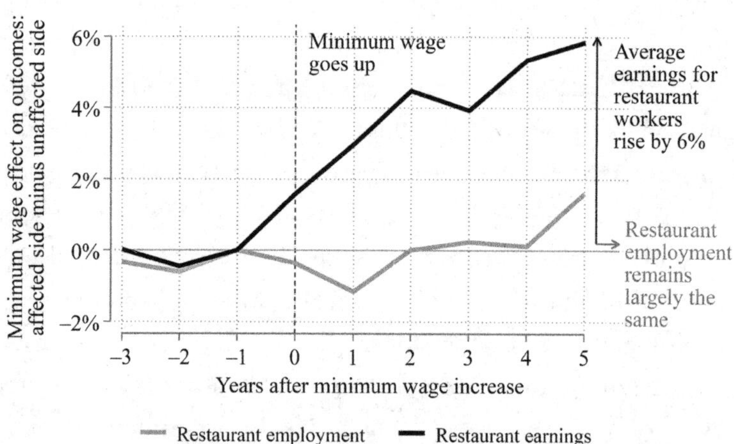

FIGURE 6.5 **COMPARING ACROSS THE BORDER: EARNINGS AND EMPLOYMENT IN RESTAURANTS FOLLOWING FORTY-TWO MAJOR MINIMUM WAGE INCREASES**[37]

The Bigger Picture on Jobs

Although these prominent studies suggested minimal employment effects of minimum wage increases, the broader literature includes many more studies focusing on various groups and employing diverse methods, sometimes yielding different conclusions. Rather than delving into each study individually, which would be a laborious task, it's more informative to gain an overall perspective of the literature's findings. To do so, we first need a way of quantifying any job losses, which will help us determine whether they are economically "big" or "small."

Historically, researchers have used a measure called the "minimum wage elasticity" (MWE) to assess the impact of minimum wage increases. The MWE is calculated by dividing the percentage change in employment for a particular group by the percentage change in the minimum wage. For example, an MWE of −0.1 means that a 10 percent increase in the minimum wage results in a 1 percent drop in employment for a group like restaurant workers. However, this metric has limitations. It's not particularly useful when comparing the effects of minimum wages across different groups or experiments with varying wage increases. For instance, an MWE of −0.1 among restaurant workers could reflect very different scenarios depending on how much the 10 percent minimum wage increase actually raises average restaurant wages. If it raises wages by 5 percent in one case but only by 1 percent in another, the trade-offs between wage gains and job losses are quite different.

A more revealing way to assess a minimum wage hike's impact on employment and earnings is to use "own-wage elasticity" (OWE). This measures how a group's employment responds to the resulting increase in that group's average wage. Mathematically, OWE is calculated by dividing the percentage change in employment (%ΔE) by the percentage change in wages (%ΔW) brought about due to the minimum wage hike.

For a longer explanation, take a look at appendix B, "Five Equations

That Explain How Wages Are Set in the Labor Market." But here is the basic point: An OWE of −1 means that job losses fully cancel out wage gains, leaving total earnings unchanged. More generally, an OWE of −0.1 implies job losses are small, and erase only 10 percent of the potential gains: so total earnings rise to about 90 percent of the no-job-loss benchmark. In contrast, an OWE of −0.8 means 80 percent of the potential gain is lost, indicating much larger job losses. Although any threshold is somewhat arbitrary, OWE values less negative than −0.4 can be considered small, indicating that the policy is quite effective at helping low-wage workers. In contrast, values between −0.4 and −0.8 are medium, and anything more negative than −0.8 is large, suggesting a relatively ineffective policy.

In practice, not all minimum wage studies report the effect on the average wage of the group, making it challenging to compare employment estimates. Nonetheless, focusing on studies that do report both wage and employment changes allows for a more informative evaluation of the evidence. Fortunately, reporting this statistic has become almost standard in contemporary research, permitting economically meaningful comparisons.

In 2024, Ben Zipperer and I created an online repository with all available OWE estimates, updated regularly to incorporate new studies.[38] At the time of writing, there were a total of seventy-two estimates from as many published studies; we used the broadest estimate representing the authors' preferred approach from each study. Fifty-eight of these estimates were based on data from the United States, from studies conducted since 1992. In figure 6.6, I present a snapshot of this database to provide an overview of the academic literature on American minimum wages.

These fifty-eight estimates come from studies using a variety of methods and covering a wide range of worker groups. Among these, twenty-four estimates are positive and thirty-four are negative, but most suggest economically small impacts. Approximately 74 percent fall into the "small negative" or "positive" categories (less negative

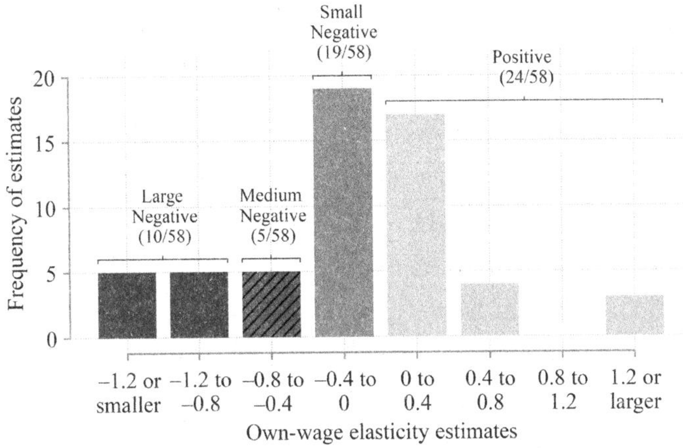

FIGURE 6.6 **FREQUENCY DISTRIBUTION OF EMPLOYMENT ELASTICITY (OWE) FROM THE U.S. MINIMUM WAGE LITERATURE**[39]

than –0.4). The median own-wage elasticity is around –0.11, indicating a minor job effect: For every percentage increase in wages, employment falls by only about one-ninth as much. In short, the data shows that minimum wage increases tend to raise overall earnings for low-wage workers by about 89 percent of what would be expected if there were no job losses. These studies collectively suggest that minimum wage policies generally raise pay more than they reduce employment, if at all, ultimately increasing total earnings for low-wage workers. The broader literature reaches a conclusion similar to our 2010 border county-study (with an OWE of 0.07) and our 2024 follow-up.

One limitation of these estimates is that most (forty-five out of fifty-eight) are based on narrow subgroups. For instance, fifteen estimates focus on teens, a frequently studied group. The median OWE from these fifteen U.S.-based teen studies is –0.17, which is still quite small, though the range spans from +1.3 to –1.9.

Indeed, teens have played an outsize role in the minimum wage literature. The modern debate on teens and minimum wages began in 1992, with opposing papers by David Card on one side and David Neumark and William Wascher on the other. Neumark and Wascher found more negative employment effects for teens than Card did in his 1992 study or in his 1995 book with Alan Krueger, where they revisited the topic. Fast-forward twenty years, and the debate was still ongoing.[40] Between 2011 to 2017, there were multiple exchanges between David Neumark, William Wascher, Ian Salas, Sylvia Allegretto, Michael Reich, Ben Zipperer, myself, and others, with much of the focus on teen employment. Reviewing these debates in 2021, economist Alan Manning wrote that "no clear evidence of a negative effect on [teen] employment has been found." Yet, he also expressed frustration, describing the debate as resembling trench warfare, with both sides battling over a small patch of ground that may not hold much strategic importance.[41] After all, teens now make up a small and shrinking share of the minimum wage workforce in America.

This underscores the importance of looking beyond narrow groups to grasp the broader impact. Recent advancements in research techniques now allow us to assess the effects of minimum wages on most low-wage workers or jobs. In a 2019 publication coauthored by Doruk Cengiz, Attila Lindner, Ben Zipperer, and me, we provided what is arguably the most comprehensive view to date of how minimum wages affect low-wage jobs.[42] Our methodology was novel yet conceptually straightforward.

Imagine a scenario where the minimum wage rises from $8 to $12 per hour in Arizona. Following this policy change, there should be fewer jobs paying below $12 in Arizona. Some of these jobs that previously paid below $12 now pay $12 or perhaps slightly more. Others may be eliminated if the costs of these jobs to employers now exceed the benefits. To gauge the impact, then, we can compare the increase in jobs in Arizona paying $12 per hour or slightly above to the reduction in jobs paying below $12. This difference would tell us about the change in the total number of low-wage jobs in Arizona. However, some of this change might have occurred independently of

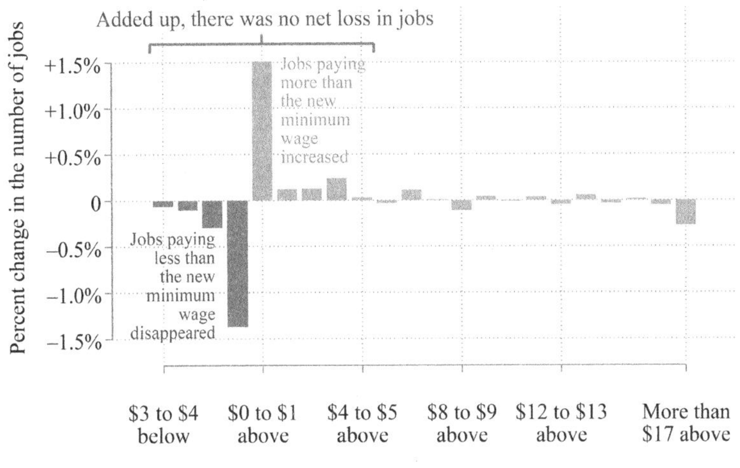

FIGURE 6.7 **WHAT MINIMUM WAGE HIKES DO TO JOBS AT DIFFERENT WAGE LEVELS**[43]

the minimum wage policy. To account for this "counterfactual," we can compare the total change in low-wage jobs in Arizona to analogous changes in other states—like Texas—that did not raise the minimum wage, after accounting for differences in population growth. This *difference-in-differences* estimate reveals the total number of jobs lost (or gained!) due to the minimum wage increase. Our study aggregated findings from all major minimum wage changes across states between 1979 and 2014.

As depicted in figure 6.7, minimum wage increases led to a clear reduction in the number of jobs that previously paid below the new minimum wage, confirming that the minimum wages under examination were binding. So, what happened to these "missing jobs"? We found that the decrease in jobs paying below the minimum wage was counterbalanced by a similarly sized increase in jobs paying the new minimum wage or up to $4 above the new minimum (picking up some of the ripple effects we saw earlier). In summary, we estimated that low-wage workers experienced an average wage gain of approximately 7 percent following a minimum wage increase, with minimal changes in employment over the five years following the policy change. The own-wage elasticity for employment from our study was +0.41, and the margins of error were tight enough to statistically rule out all but small job losses resulting from the policies.

Our methodology also incorporated additional checks, such as examining employment changes at higher wage levels. We found essentially no changes in employment for jobs that already paid well above the minimum wage, which was reassuring. It's unlikely that a minimum wage increase would significantly impact these positions. This mirrors the earlier discussion on how a similar diagnostic helped assess the policy's impact on wage inequality.

Another approach to measuring the overall impact of minimum wages on jobs comes from our 2022 study coauthored with Cengiz, Lindner, and David Zentler-Munro.[44] Like much of the previous literature, in this analysis we employed demographic information to identify probable minimum wage workers. However, instead of focusing on very specific and narrow groups, as is often done in the literature, we used machine-learning tools to statistically predict likely minimum wage workers using all available demographic information, including age, education, race, gender, immigration status, rural versus urban status, and more. Our broadest group successfully predicted around three-quarters of all minimum wage workers, making our estimates highly informative for understanding the policy's impact on the overall low-wage workforce. This time we studied 172 policy changes between 1979 and 2019 and found that the impact on the broad group of low-wage workers was again quite small, with an OWE of around +0.11, and ruling out any sizable job loss.

Stepping back, there are thirteen studies in our repository that provide an OWE estimate for an "overall" impact on low-wage jobs using American data. The median across these thirteen estimates for overall employment impact is 0.003, and remains the same across twenty-three studies that include international evidence. When considering the full set of quantitative evidence, the size of the effects on employment has been small. Or, as Alan Manning put it in his 2021 review, the evidence for substantial job loss from minimum wage increases has been "elusive."[45]

One explanation lies in the fact that the labor market doesn't conform to the ideal of perfect competition. As economic theory tells us, the impact of the minimum wage on jobs can be less pronounced or even favorable when employers wield monopsony power. Recent research supports this argument. Take, for instance, a 2024 study by José Azar and others, which reveals that in the retail sector, employment effects tend to be more positive when the local retail labor market exhibits higher concentration, meaning it has relatively fewer employers.[46]

Let's also recall the work of Justin Wiltshire from the previous chapter, where he uncovered more positive employment effects of minimum wages in local areas experiencing an increase in employer concentration, largely due to Walmart's expanding market share.[47] These findings shed light on at least one reason why the employment effects of minimum wages often appear elusive: because the labor market is often beset by monopsony power.

A Great Disturbance in the (Labor) Force, and Other Controversies

But even as the *overall* evidence points to a small impact on employment, some of the studies do seem to suggest larger job losses. Part of this variation can be attributed to the inherent noise in statistical analyses. However, it's not solely a matter of chance; sometimes, even when assessing the same policy changes with identical data, studies have arrived at disparate conclusions. As a result, policymakers have at times drawn quite different conclusions from the scholarly literature over recent decades. That's why it's essential to understand how recent research has resolved some long-standing puzzles, marking real progress toward accurately interpreting the historical evidence. Gaining clarity on these issues will also help us avoid making policies based on outdated findings.

A significant factor behind the differences in employment estimates lies in how researchers account for deviations in the assumption that the background employment trends are similar across states with and without minimum wage increases (i.e., the treatment and control groups).

A key insight from the 2019 study by Cengiz, Dube, Lindner, and Zipperer addresses several discrepancies in previous research. In this analysis, we divided states into two groups: the fifteen states that *did not* enact their own minimum wage laws between 1996 and 2016 and those that *did* at some point in this period. This lets us compare aggregate employment patterns between the two groups.

Because minimum wage policy directly affects a relatively small segment of the workforce, it isn't expected to move overall employment rates much. So, if aggregate employment trends in states with and without minimum wages look similar, it reassures us that comparing a state like New Jersey (which raised its minimum wage) to states like Pennsylvania (that didn't) is reasonable. Conversely, if we observed large differences in aggregate employment trends, that would call such comparisons into question.

Figure 6.8 tracks the evolution of the effective minimum wage (the higher of the state or federal rate) and aggregate employment rates for states that enacted their own minimums (dashed line) and those that did not (solid line). For most of the study period, employment trends for both groups moved closely together. Even after the mid-1990s, when state-level differences in minimum wages became more pronounced, employment rates continued to grow similarly in both groups, whether the minimum wage gaps were large or small. So far, so good.

However, a different pattern emerges in the late 1980s and early to mid-1990s, before state-level minimum wage variations became pronounced. During this period, states that would later adopt their own minimums experienced a sharper boom-and-bust cycle than states that did not—what I refer to as the "eighties–nineties disturbance." This matters because a study that compares minimum wage and employment between 1990 and 2019 could reach misleading conclusions if it doesn't account for this disturbance.

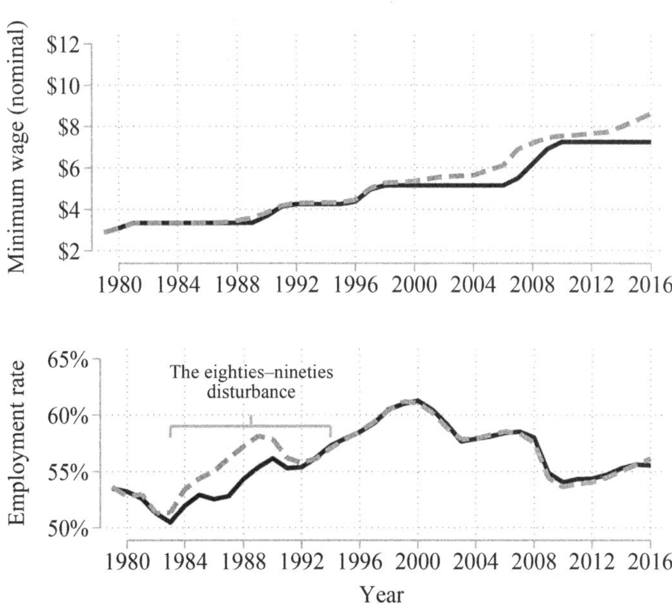

FIGURE 6.8 **MINIMUM WAGE AND TOTAL EMPLOYMENT RATE OVER TIME: STATES WITH AND WITHOUT THEIR OWN MINIMUM WAGE LAWS**[48]

Recognizing the eighties–nineties disturbance helps clarify the debate over teen and restaurant employment estimates. Studies that applied more aggressive controls for background trends in this period tended to find more positive (or less negative) employment effects as compared to studies that didn't.[49] However, this discrepancy largely disappears in data from the late 1990s onward, when most minimum wage changes occurred. From that point forward, employment estimates became less sensitive to statistical methods and generally suggested minimal job impacts.

The lesson here is that some commonly used statistical methods, which compare data across very different periods, can amplify hidden biases. A more reliable approach is to focus on clear treatment-control comparisons, identifying specific minimum wage increases and comparing changes between "treatment" and "control" states over defined periods. This approach mitigates many biases, including those from the eighties–nineties disturbance.[50]

By identifying the sources of bias in earlier studies and showing how they can be addressed, our 2019 study resolved some long-standing controversies in the minimum wage literature.

Jobless in Seattle?

More recently, some high-profile studies have offered different conclusions when examining citywide minimum wages. Beginning in 2015 with Seattle, numerous cities across America implemented substantial minimum wage hikes, often reaching $15 per hour. At first glance, these wage levels seem high, but it's important to consider the context. Cities like Seattle, San Francisco, New York, and Chicago are high-wage, high-cost-of-living areas, which means that a $15 minimum wage in these cities may not be all that different from more moderate minimum wage increases in other parts of America. For example, Seattle's $15 wage was actually somewhat below 50 percent of the city's median wage, making it comparable to minimum wage hikes studied in the broader literature.

A well-known study from the University of Washington by Ekaterina Jardim and coauthors estimated the impact of Seattle raising its minimum wage to $13 per hour.[51] The study was published in 2022 but made a major splash as early as 2017 when the original working paper was released. The authors found a significant decrease in the total number of low-wage jobs paying $19 per hour or lower in Seattle compared to their control group, which was based on other areas in the state of Washington. They interpreted this as indicative of widespread job losses and reduction in hours, and reported an OWE of approximately –2.8, making it one of the most negative estimates in our database summarizing the literature.[52] Taken literally, the implied job losses were nearly three times as large as wage gains, suggesting that the Seattle minimum wage was highly ineffective in helping low-wage workers. "A 'Very Credible' New Study on Seattle's $15 Minimum Has Bad News for Liberals," read the title of a story in *The Washington Post*.[53]

That conclusion, however, was premature, as there were some serious concerns about interpreting these findings. The exceptionally high overall wage growth in Seattle, compared to other areas in Washington State during this period, may have led to fewer low-paid jobs not because those jobs were eliminated but because many people received raises. In fact, over the same period under study, there was a substantial increase in the number of people being paid more than $19 per hour in Seattle as compared to the control group. This raises the possibility that Jardim and her coauthors' findings of job losses may be attributed to strong wage growth, not actual job destruction.

In the final (peer-reviewed) version of the paper, the authors also provided another estimate using a very different approach, where they evaluated the impact of the policy by following a group of low-wage Seattle workers who were initially earning below the new minimum wage. Following the minimum wage increase, the authors compared the evolution of this group's employment retention to that of similar workers outside of Seattle. In this case, their findings indicated a negligible impact on employment and a modest reduction in hours. Accounting for both jobs and hours, the OWE implied by these estimates was around –0.19, similar to the overall median in our database. This estimate suggests a very successful Seattle minimum wage policy and a far cry from the original estimate of –2.8.

One interpretation of these two divergent estimates is that their initial finding suggesting a substantial job loss was mistakenly capturing fewer jobs paying below $19 in Seattle due to the city's robust wage growth. Some other studies of the Seattle minimum wage arrived at a similar conclusion.[54]

Attila Lindner and I explored this issue further in our 2021 evaluation of citywide minimum wage policies, where we pooled data from twenty-one citywide increases, including Seattle, San Francisco, and other metropolitan areas.[55] Given the very different dynamics in some of these cities, as had become clear from the Seattle experience, we strived to compare these cities to other similar cities based on industry and demographic structure before the policy change. For the overall low-wage workforce, we observed significant wage increases but minimal impact on jobs paying below $20 per hour; the OWE of −0.12 wasn't distinguishable from zero. However, similar to the study by Jardim and colleagues, when we did not match these major cities to other similar metro areas, we found the same type of misleading suggestion of job loss due to strong wage growth.

While individual studies report negative effects of specific city policies or small positive impacts, and variations exist depending on the methodology used, the aggregate evidence from citywide minimum wage increases points to overall effects that are close to zero. This is despite substantial wage increases at the lower end of the wage distribution. When viewed in total, the data suggests that these city policies have not significantly affected employment levels, even as they have successfully raised wages for low-income workers.

Across the Pond

Since the introduction of its national minimum wage in 1998, and through several significant increases between 2014 and 2023, the United Kingdom has become a valuable case study for researchers examining the effectiveness of minimum wage policies. Remarkably, there is a broad consensus on the evidence and policy regarding the minimum wage in the UK. Both the Conservative and Labor Parties currently support a high minimum wage policy, which, in 2024, stood at around two-thirds of the country's median wage, ranking among the highest globally.[56]

Among the eight published UK studies, the median own-wage elasticity is approximately –0.12, in line with the American evidence of limited employment impact. This consistency persists when we focus on studies that assess the impact on low-wage workers broadly, as opposed to narrower subgroups. Within this subset of four studies, the median elasticity estimate is 0.16. The most comprehensive and sophisticated UK study to date was authored by Giulia Giupponi and her colleagues in 2023. It adopts a methodology similar to our 2019 paper, counting the impact on the total number of low-wage jobs.[57] But since there is only a single National Living Wage (NLW)—as the policy is known in the UK—it is infeasible to compare across regions with different statutory minimums, unlike, say New Jersey and Pennsylvania. Instead, the authors leverage the geographic variation that comes from the difference in bite of the NLW across different areas.

Imagine café baristas in the relatively high-wage Reading area already earning above the new NLW, so its introduction didn't affect them. In contrast, baristas in the lower-wage Bristol saw their pay rise when the NLW was implemented. The authors use this regional variation to compare barista job growth across the two areas and isolate the causal impact of a higher wage floor. In practice, they don't just look at baristas, but rather consider the full suite of low-wage jobs between 2015 and 2019 and pool comparisons across all UK regions.

Giupponi and her coauthors found that the NLW raised wages for workers up to the 20th percentile, leading to a significant reduction in wage inequality at the bottom. Despite these substantial pay increases, the employment effects were minimal, with an OWE of around −0.2, and not statistically different from a zero. In other words, the NLW effectively boosted wages and reduced inequality without causing major job losses, showing that wage increases can be achieved without a significant negative impact on employment.

What sets the UK apart from the United States and many other places is the presence of its Low Pay Commission (LPC), which annually issues recommendations for minimum wage policy. The LPC operates as an evidence-driven entity, meticulously examining data, commissioning reports, and releasing annual evidence reviews. In their 2022 report, the LPC succinctly summarized their findings: "Both our descriptive and econometric analysis find little evidence that recent NMW and NLW rises had harmed employment, either in the lowest-paying parts of the country or among the groups of workers most likely to be paid the minimum wage."[58]

In recent years, Germany has become another valuable source of high-quality evidence on the effects of minimum wages. To understand the significance of this evidence, it's important to place it in the context of Germany's wage landscape, where wage inequality rose after 1980. While the increase in inequality was less severe than in the United States or the UK, it continued into the twenty-first century. However, a turning point occurred after 2010, when wage inequality in Germany began to decline, eventually returning to its 2000 levels.[59] Did the introduction of a minimum wage contribute to this reversal? Researchers have examined German data to address this question. Before diving into their findings, let's briefly review Germany's wage-setting history.

It might come as a surprise that Germany didn't have a formal minimum wage until 2015. Historically, wages were set through sector-wide collective bargaining, and even low-wage jobs were typically covered by these agreements. Collective bargaining plays a key role in shaping wage standards, even without an official minimum wage, as we explore in the next chapter. Unlike some European countries such as Finland and Norway, Germany does not (typically) legally mandate that these collective agreements apply to all workplaces in an industry. Instead, major employers have often voluntarily followed the negotiated wage standards.

This system began to unravel following the reunification of East and West Germany, regions with very different wage structures. Over time, low-wage employers, such as supermarket chains, started withdrawing from sector-wide agreements.[60] As a result, wage standards eroded, particularly at the lower end of the wage distribution—similar to the current situation in some American states like Texas.

Despite rising wage inequality in Germany, policymakers and unions initially hesitated to push for a national minimum wage, partly due to concerns that it could undermine collective bargaining institutions. But as it became clear that union coverage in low-wage sectors like retail was unlikely to recover, the government shifted course. To address growing inequality and stagnant wages, Germany introduced its first statutory national minimum wage in 2015. At that time, nearly 15 percent of the workforce earned below the new minimum wage—a substantial portion.[61] By 2023, Germany's minimum wage had risen to €12 per hour (about $13), equivalent to around 57 percent of the median wage.[62]

Before the minimum wage was introduced, several analyses made grim forecasts, suggesting substantial job losses of 800,000 or more out of the roughly 4 million jobs impacted by the policy. These predictions were based on highly pessimistic assumptions, typically implying an own-wage elasticity of around −0.75.[63]

Since the implementation of the minimum wage, numerous high-quality studies have assessed its impact. Similar to the UK experience, the lack of geographic variation in the statutory minimum wage led researchers to focus on how different groups were affected by the national policy change. Despite variations in data and methodologies, the studies consistently showed that initial fears were largely unfounded, with the effect on jobs being minimal. The median OWE across the major studies in Germany was −0.24, indicating only a limited effect on employment, contrary to earlier concerns.

The most comprehensive evidence comes from a 2022 study by Christian Dustmann and colleagues. This study used both geographic variation in the policy's impact and a comparison between low-wage workers and those unaffected by the policy. Their findings showed an overall negligible impact on low-wage employment, with an OWE of 0.03, along with a significant wage increase resulting from the policy.[64]

What about wage inequality? After nearly two decades of rising inequality, Germany experienced a notable reversal after 2010. By 2017, wage inequality had returned to the same level as in the year 2000. Did the 2015 introduction of the national minimum wage help drive this turnaround? According to a compelling 2023 study by Mario Bossler, the answer is yes. Bossler found that the substantial wage increases at the lower end of the pay distribution, achieved with minimal job losses, contributed directly to reducing inequality. Remarkably, the introduction of the minimum wage alone accounted for half of the total decline in wage inequality observed between 2010 and 2017—a significant policy achievement.[65]

The Three P's

So, the employment response to minimum wage increases has been small. But how do employers actually adjust to a higher minimum wage? Let's break it down into what I call the three P's: productivity, prices, and profits.[66]

If a minimum wage hike boosts the productivity of low-wage workers, it can reduce the pressure on companies to cut jobs. One way this happens is through lower employee turnover, a concept we have encountered before. When the minimum wage rises, jobs become more attractive, reducing the rate at which workers quit to take other jobs. This means businesses spend less on advertising job openings, hiring, and training new employees. As a result, the overall increase in labor costs is often smaller than the wage hike itself. This prediction is strongly supported by evidence: Nearly all studies examining this find that minimum wage increases reduce worker turnover.[67]

Higher wages can also directly drive increased productivity. The best evidence comes from a 2022 study by Decio Coviello, Erika Deserranno, and Nicola Persico, who examined a group of workers from a major U.S. retailer with outlets across numerous states.[68] The authors compared stores that are located on opposite sides of borders with different minimum wage policies. They found that higher minimum wages led to more enhanced productivity among workers—likely due to greater motivation and effort from workers who now valued the jobs more. This effect was particularly pronounced for the least productive workers, who were at risk of losing their jobs prior to the minimum wage increase. While the study identified clear impacts on wages and store-level productivity, it failed to discern any notable effect on employment, consistent with the broader research literature. Similar findings have been observed in sectors like nursing homes and childcare, where wage increases led to better service quality.[69] This evidence on wages and improved worker performance has broader relevance for understanding how a higher wage standard (beyond the minimum wage) would be absorbed in the economy.

Minimum wages can also affect overall productivity by shifting employment within a market. Higher minimum wages might cause some job loss at low-wage, low-productivity businesses that can no longer compete while paying higher wages. However, as these employers reduce hiring or exit the market, higher-wage, more productive firms may step in to fill the gap. This reallocation could help explain why higher minimum wages don't necessarily reduce total employment, but instead shift jobs to more productive businesses. It's similar to what we saw in chapter 3, where the tight labor market in

2021 and 2022 led to a shift away from low-productivity employers toward higher-productivity ones. The difference here is that this shift is driven by wage-setting policies rather than increased competition in a tight labor market. Minimum wages could—in theory—block the "low road" and pave the "high road" when it comes to company wage policies.

But does the evidence back up this theory? Insights from Germany suggest that the introduction of the minimum wage led to work shifting toward larger, more productive enterprises.[70] There is also evidence from the United States showing that employment reallocated toward chain restaurants (which tend to be larger and more productive) in response to minimum wage changes, and away from low-quality restaurants with poor Yelp ratings.[71] Most directly, new research by Nirupama Rao and Max Risch offers compelling evidence of this reallocation using U.S. tax records for businesses and state minimum wage changes after 2010. They find that in the restaurant sector, a higher minimum wage leads to fewer low-productivity companies to enter the market, but existing higher-productivity restaurants expand their operations. As a result, the overall employment effect is small, but there is a significant shift in the composition toward higher-productivity businesses.[72]

Another channel for absorbing the impact of a minimum wage hike involves increases in product prices. Here, the evidence is clear: Price pass-throughs serve as a crucial mechanism of adjustment, especially in restaurants and grocery stores. Most memorably, studying over 80 percent of all McDonald's locations in America, Orley Ashenfelter and Štěpán Jurajda found that a 10 percent increase in the minimum wage usually raises the price of a Big Mac by 1.4 percent.[73] To put this in dollars and cents, if the New York minimum wage were to rise by 10 percent from the 2023 value of $14.20 to $15.62, the average price of a Big Mac in the Empire State could be expected to rise from around $5.30 to $5.37. This would constitute a noticeable but modest bump from most customers' perspectives. More broadly, Daniel Aaronson and coauthors found that a 10 percent increase in minimum wage raised overall restaurant prices by around 0.7 percent, or about half as much as the Big Mac.[74] This finding has been corroborated by additional work studying more recent citywide minimum wage increases using online menu price data.[75]

Turning to the retail sector, Tobias Renkin, Claire Montialoux, and Michael Siegenthaler used scanner data to examine how minimum wages affect supermarket prices, and they also observed clear pass-through effects. They found that a 10 percent higher minimum wage led to a 1 percent increase in average wages for grocery workers, no discernible impact on grocery jobs, and a 0.4 percent rise in grocery prices.[76] Other recent studies of the retail sector have found similar results.[77] Notice that the proportionate increase in grocery store prices is quite a bit less than at fast-food joints because minimum wage workers are a smaller share of overall grocery costs.

The extent of price pass-through depends on how sensitive product demand is to price changes. In high-income countries like the United States, most minimum wage workers are employed in the service sector, like retail and restaurants. It's relatively easier for businesses in these sectors to adjust prices in response to minimum wage hikes, as most customers are unlikely to travel to a neighboring state just to get a cheaper burger or a more affordable carton of eggs. Consequently, employers in these sectors can more readily adjust their prices in response to the minimum wage hikes. These adjustments reduce the need to cut jobs due to higher labor costs. In contrast, industries producing tradable goods, like manufacturing, may experience more notable job losses because they can't easily adjust prices at the local level. Based on the existing studies, there is more evidence of job loss in such tradable sectors, but they constitute a very small share of minimum wage workers in high-income economies.[78]

In summary, price adjustments represent an important way for businesses to manage the increased costs associated with minimum wage hikes. While prices in a few specific sectors may rise noticeably, the overall price level (e.g., the Consumer Price Index) is unlikely to be significantly affected because minimum wage jobs make up only a small portion of the overall economy. Importantly, these price adjustments do not negate the benefits of minimum wage policies. Instead, they act as a form of income redistribution from higher-income consumers to low-wage workers. This aligns with public sentiment. For example, a 2022 YouGov survey found that 54 percent of American voters believed that raising the minimum wage would lead to higher prices of goods and services, while only 21 percent disagreed. Yet, 77 percent of respondents felt the federal minimum wage was too low, with the median voter supporting a wage of around $15 per hour.[79]

The final "P" is for profits, and while data on profits are limited, international and domestic evidence suggests that lower profits may account for a portion of the additional labor costs from minimum wages. The most in-depth evidence comes from a study by Péter Harasztosi and Attila Lindner, who examined a substantial minimum wage increase in Hungary using high-quality data. They found that lower profits may have accounted for approximately a quarter of the additional labor costs resulting from minimum wages. Similar evidence of profit reduction has emerged from the UK and Israel.[80] Recent research using American data also indicates that profits in low-wage sectors decline in response to higher minimum wages. In his analysis, Damián Vergara found that a 10 percent increase in the minimum wage reduced profits in "exposed services" like retail or restaurants by around 5 percent, while increasing affected blue-collar wages by roughly 1.5 percent, with little impact on employment.[81] At the same time, our understanding of the size of the profits adjustment is still evolving, and more evidence will be helpful in pinning down the magnitudes.

In summary, the three P's—productivity, prices, and profits—offer valuable insights into how businesses adapt to higher wage standards. They do so through a combination of increased prices, lower profits, and enhanced productivity. Moreover, some of this productivity increase stems from reallocating work to more productive establishments, providing an added benefit of a higher minimum wage. The benefits of minimum wages accrue to low-wage workers and their family members, while the costs are borne by both business owners and consumers at large.

How High Is Too High?

This brings us to a crucial question: When setting minimum wages, how high is too high? If a $15 minimum wage is reasonable, would $30 also be sensible? Does the impact on employment become greater as the minimum wage approaches the median wage? These questions have practical significance as states and countries are increasingly adopting more ambitious minimum wage policies.

My 2019 study with Cengiz, Lindner, and Zipperer, "The Effect of Minimum Wages on Low-Wage Jobs," offers some clues. In our analysis, we examined cases where the minimum wage ranged between about 37 and 59 percent of the median wage for all workers—equivalent to hourly rates of between $8.86 and $14.13 in 2023 dollars. Encouragingly, even when the minimum wage reached 59 percent of the median wage (close to $15 per hour), we found little evidence of significant job losses.

To gain further perspective, it's helpful to look back to a period when the federal minimum wage was much higher than it is today. Two recent studies—one by Martha Bailey and coauthors, and another by Ellora Derenoncourt and Claire Montialoux—examined the late 1960s, when the federal minimum wage reached its historical peak.[82] At the time, it stood at 61 percent of the median wage, which would translate to about $14.60 in 2023. Similar to studies of minimum wage policies in countries like the UK and Germany, both papers used variation across U.S. states to compare places where the federal minimum wage was more binding to those where it had less bite.

Remarkably, both studies found that while the high minimum wage substantially impacted wages, its overall effect on employment was minimal. The estimates of the own-wage elasticities from these two studies ranged between 0.06 and −0.14.

Returning to the present, the weight of evidence from recent citywide minimum wage implementations also offers encouraging results. These city minimums were often set at a higher share of the median wage compared to most state policies, with 57 percent being the norm. Even at these elevated levels, our 2021 review of employment evidence from these cities revealed small overall impacts.[83]

Another approach to assessing the potential effects of high minimum wages is to focus on low-wage areas and gauge their impact there. Since the same minimum wage can have a much more significant impact in low-wage areas, these regions can serve as early indicators of what might happen when higher minimums are more widely implemented. Anna Godoey and Michael Reich analyzed data from low-wage counties, where the policy's impact is more substantial, and compared wage and employment trends for those without a college degree in states that raised the minimum wage versus those that did not between 2004 and 2017.[84] In some of these local areas, the minimum wage reached as high as 82 percent of the median wage. Their findings indicated a clear increase in average wages following the policy's implementation, but employment changes were close to zero. For their entire sample, the employment elasticity (OWE) was 0.12, suggesting little impact. Importantly, even in local areas where the minimum wage exceeded 60 percent of the median wage, the employment effect was not any more negative. This provides an encouraging preview of how further increases in the minimum wage could affect jobs.

A somewhat different conclusion emerges from a study by Jeffrey

Clemens and Michael Strain, who examined minimum wage changes between 2013 and 2019.[85] They focused on "young" workers and "low-skilled" workers (ages sixteen to twenty-five without a high school degree). On average, across all minimum wage increases during this period, they observed a modest employment effect, with an OWE of approximately −0.25. This finding isn't significantly different from the overall evidence base. However, for six states that raised the minimum wage by more than $2.50, their average OWE of −0.71 was larger in magnitude, though this mostly arose from their "low-skilled" group. It's worth noting that this conclusion is based on a limited number of cases and on specific methodological choices. My own evaluation from 2019, which I conducted for the UK Treasury, investigated seven larger state-level increases and found little overall impact on low-wage jobs during the same period.[86] In separate recent work with Attila Lindner, we also found that while bigger minimum wage hikes through 2019 led to higher wages, they were not associated with significant job losses for low-wage workers overall.[87] Finally, Justin Wiltshire and coauthors specifically evaluated the effects of a $15 minimum wage in California and New York separately by local areas and found no indication of a negative employment effect through 2023.[88]

Stepping back to consider the bigger picture, as states experiment with higher minimums, we may see clearer evidence of more substantial job losses, especially for specific subgroups. However, it's essential to remember that the goal isn't to entirely prevent job losses—an unrealistic objective for minimum wage policies. Instead, the aim is to balance any potential job losses with wage gains for workers at the bottom. Have some states already reached that point? It's possible, but there are also reasons to believe that more can be done when it comes to state action.

One reason that higher state minimum wages, like California's 2023 floor of $15.50 per hour, are less constraining than expected is due to rapid growth in nominal wages and prices in recent years.[89]

For instance, between 2019 and 2023, the average minimum wage across thirty states increased from $10.03 to $13.04. However, as a share of the median wage, it barely increased, going from 48 percent to 50 percent. Similarly, the proportion of workers earning within 10 percent of the minimum wage fell slightly, indicating that wage growth outpaced minimum wage increases. The significant post-pandemic wage gains, especially for lower-wage workers (remember the "unexpected compression"?) meant that in some cases, minimum wage laws didn't keep up with market wages. This suggests there is room to explore higher minimum wages than those currently set by most states.

So, what's a strong yet reasonable state-level target for the minimum wage given our current evidence base? A sensible benchmark is two-thirds of each state's median wage for all workers, which is slightly above the OECD average of 61 percent. As figure 6.9 shows, applied to 2023 data, this rule yields minimum wages from $12.73 in Mississippi) to $22.64 in Maryland, with a median across states of $15.92.

How do current minimum wages measure up to the two-thirds median wage rule? As of 2023, no state met it, though some were not too far off. Maine came the closest, with a minimum equal to 60 percent of its median wage. Interestingly, states with some of the highest minimums—California, Massachusetts, and New York ($14.20–$15.50)—still fell short: Their minimums amounted to 45 to 57 percent of the median wage. To hit the two-thirds benchmark in 2023, they would have needed minimums in the $18 to $22 range.

Of course, any threshold like the two-thirds median wage rule is somewhat arbitrary. It's meant as a guidepost, offering a comparison to other high-income countries that have adopted similar standards without experiencing major job losses. The UK, for instance, has already successfully raised its National Living Wage to two-thirds of the median, and other European countries may follow. The key point is this: Based on peer experience and available evidence, there's ample room for further experimentation, perhaps significantly so. Just as we saw with the Fed's interest rate experimentation in the 1990s, this is a classic *multi-armed bandit* problem: We can't make reliable, evidence-based policy without taking steps to create the evidence through real-world experimentation.

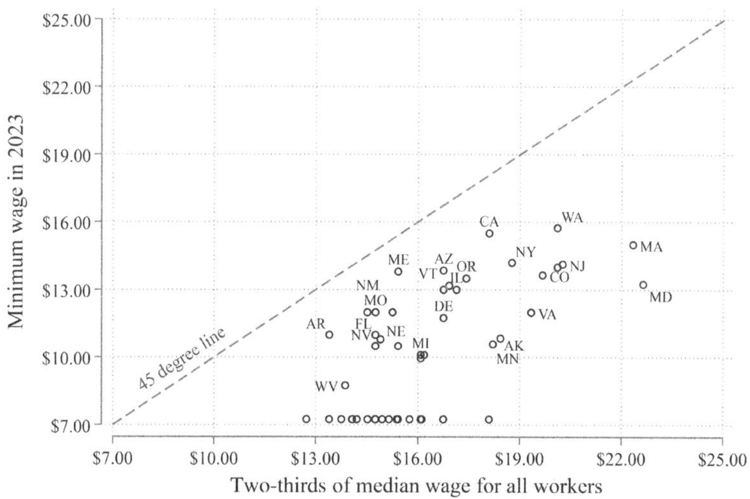

FIGURE 6.9 ACTUAL MINIMUM WAGES IN COMPARISON TO A TWO-THIRDS MEDIAN WAGE RULE[90]

It's important to note that this discussion about current state minimum wages and benchmarks overlooks the situation in the twenty states, such as Texas, that rely solely on the federal minimum wage. In these states, where the federal minimum ranges between 27 and 38 percent of median wages in 2023, it has become entirely inconsequential because it is so low. Setting the federal minimum at two-thirds of the national median would come to about $16 in 2023. Raising the federal wage floor is essential, but citizens in states without robust minimum wage policies can also advocate for state-level increases, often through ballot initiatives. Between 1980 and 2024, state minimum wage increases have appeared on ballots thirty-four times, passing thirty of those times. In more recent cases, 61 percent of Florida voters in 2020 and 59 percent of Nebraska voters in 2022 backed raising their state minimum wages to $15 per hour by 2026, while 58 percent of Missouri and Alaska voters followed suit in the 2024 election.[91] This demonstrates that a strong minimum wage is not just popular in blue states but in purple and red states as well.

Clearly, there is still much work to be done in establishing a strong wage floor in America. At the same time, we must recognize the limits of solely relying on an ambitious minimum wage to rebuild the wage standard. After all, the minimum wage probably shouldn't be set above the median wage, as this would require an extraordinary compression of wages, even for roles that demand vastly different training and skills, and place substantial pressure on prices.

Fortunately, we have other tools at our disposal to set standards across various parts of the pay scale, which we will explore in the next chapter.

CHAPTER 7

More Than the Minimum

Rebuilding the Middle Class

On September 15, 2023, members of the United Auto Workers began a strike that simultaneously stopped work at the Big Three American automakers: General Motors, Ford, and Stellantis (formerly Chrysler). The UAW called this a "stand-up strike" in an obvious reference to their historic "sit-down strike" at General Motors in 1937. The key to the stand-up strike was that it was happening simultaneously at all three manufacturers (first time in the union's history) and it was also ratcheting up pressure on the employers over time. The UAW struck a small number of highly profitable operations at first, which was designed to inflict maximum harm on the companies' bottom lines while making it relatively less costly on workers by minimizing the number of workers on strike and the length of time they were out of work. In addition, if workers were laid off from other plants by the employers, they could collect unemployment benefits. As the strike dragged on, UAW incrementally added other highly profitable operations to the list of struck establishments, dialing up the costs facing the struck employers.

This game plan caught employers by surprise, who were unfamiliar with this style of ratcheting. It was a smart play by the union. After forty-six days of the strike, employers agreed to many of the unions' key demands.[1] Ford was first to arrive at an agreement; Stellantis and

GM followed suit. The raises were at least 25 percent over the four-year contract, including an immediate 11 percent raise. Other gains included cost-of-living adjustment and getting rid of many tiers, allowing workers to climb up the ladder faster. In many ways, the 2023 contract clawed back losses that autoworkers suffered in their 2011 contract, which marked a low point for the workers.

The stand-up strike was a remarkable feat, aided by a resurgent leadership as exemplified by the union's president, Shawn Fain; by a tight labor market; and by change in political winds where the public and the Biden administration strongly supported the union's aims. Biden became the first sitting president to join striking workers at the picket line.

But perhaps even more noteworthy was what happened following the strike. It is important to recognize that three automakers combined employ only around half of all autoworkers in America. This may suggest that the outcome of the strike was of limited significance. In fact, if the UAW gains put the unionized Big Three at a cost disadvantage, it could even be self-defeating. However, within days of the announcement of the tentative contract, nonunion employers in the auto sector, including Toyota, Honda, Hyundai, Subaru, Nissan, and Volkswagen, announced wage increases very similar to those that the UAW negotiated for its members. For example, Honda and Volkswagen announced an immediate 11 percent raise, while Hyundai matched the headline 25 percent gain by 2028. Immediate raises of 10 percent at Nissan and 9 percent at Toyota were very close to the level secured by the UAW.[2]

What's remarkable here is the *sectoral* nature of the strike and its spillover effects on nonunion employers. This is reminiscent of the Treaty of Detroit era "pattern bargaining," where a deal struck with one of the Big Three automakers would often set the standard for negotiations with other car manufacturers and parts suppliers working with the UAW. Notably, this pattern frequently extended to nonunion employers as well.

The current case mirrors this dynamic: Union-won wage hikes quickly spilled over into wage increases for nonunion workers in the same sector. This echoes the broader evidence we've discussed previously, showing how union-negotiated gains often benefit nonunion workers. What makes this instance stand out is the scale, scope, and speed of the spillover. Nonunion employers across the sector moved swiftly to match key elements of the union-negotiated raises, leaving little doubt about the broader impact of the union's success.

The UAW strike was not the only 2023 labor action that showed how sector-wide changes can happen. The Writers Guild of America (WGA), representing nearly twelve thousand screenwriters, went on strike for 148 days between May and September 2023. At the heart of the strike was how the profit from streaming media ("residuals" in the industry parlance) was shared with the writers, and whether use of large language models (LLMs like ChatGPT) would be a tool to help the writers' scriptwriting, or to replace them. The strike was highly successful and led to increased pay, health and pension contributions, new streaming residuals and viewership-based bonuses, along with assurances against AI-based replacement.[3] Now, in general, not all contractual terms negotiated by the WGA would apply to writers who are not union members. However, the WGA "Minimum Basic Agreement" is negotiated with the employer association (Alliance of Motion Picture and Television Producers) and serves as a floor for the terms of employment of all jobs in the industry, whether performed by a union member or not. Again, the outcome of the strike affected a broader group of workers outside of union members.

These two examples suggest an intriguing possibility. What if sector-level agreements were used as a compensation floor for *all* jobs in that industry across the economy?

If this sounds like a radical idea, you might be surprised to learn that in much of the developed world, sector-wide standards set the basic terms of employment for many—if not most—jobs across the economy. In countries like the Netherlands, France, and Switzerland, national-level collective bargaining establishes the floor for wages and working conditions by industry and occupation. These standards are then extended to cover most jobs, regardless of whether they are unionized. While individual firms can choose to pay above the standard, they cannot go below it. In countries like Australia, sector-wide standards are set by a national commission. In many ways, the United States—along with Canada and the United Kingdom—is an outlier in its lack of such broad-based wage-setting mechanisms.

How do these sectoral standards work? Do they lead to overly rigid labor markets? Have they led to widespread unemployment or uncontrolled inflation? Or have they helped mitigate pay inequality in these countries as compared to here in America? Even more intriguingly, could we think of ways to use sectoral standards to raise wages for middle-income American workers, and not just those at the bottom through minimum wage?

In this chapter, we will dive into the data regarding sectoral standards from continental Europe, where they are typically based on national-level collective bargaining. Since our current labor laws don't mandate this kind of sector-based approach, we'll also explore other models—such as sectoral wage boards in Australia—that could be put in place in America. We will also examine how this can be done at the state level, and use data to show what the labor market would look like with such standards in place. Most excitingly, we will see that this process has already started, with several states experimenting with sectoral standards that can help raise pay for those in the middle of the income spectrum.

Union Membership Versus Union Coverage

As we saw in chapter 4, overall union membership reached a height of around 35 percent of the workforce in the mid-1950s. Since then, it has steadily declined, with membership in 2024 hovering around 10 percent, and 6 percent in the private sector.

The impact of a falling union *membership* has been particularly acute due to the enterprise-level bargaining structure in America (and other countries like the UK and Canada). This structure differs greatly from countries like France, Germany, and Italy, where collective bargaining *coverage*—share of jobs covered by collectively bargained contracts—is much greater than the union *membership* rates. In the United States, in contrast, coverage in 2024 was about 11 percent overall and roughly 7 percent in the private sector—very close to membership rates.[4]

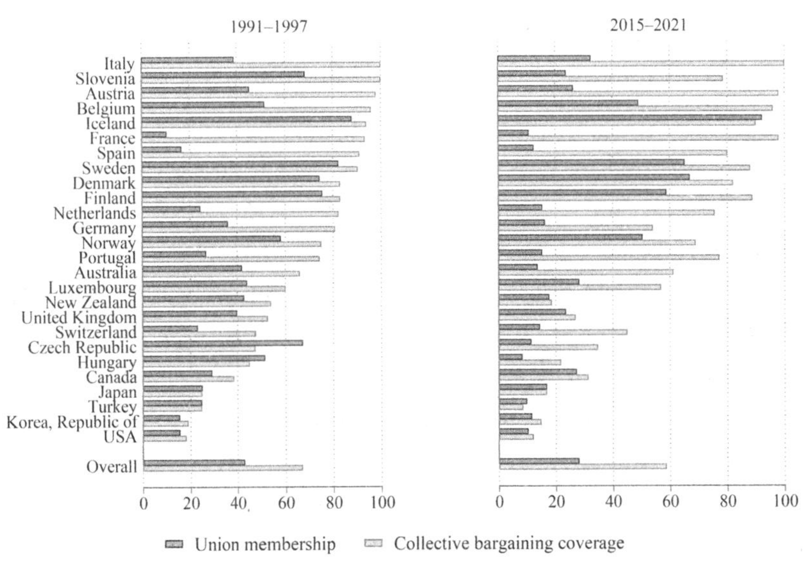

FIGURE 7.1 **UNION MEMBERSHIP AND COVERAGE**[5]

Figure 7.1 shows union coverage for major economies in the OECD, which generally far exceed union membership rates. To take one example, union membership in France was only 11 percent in 2016, but union coverage stood at 98 percent. How is this possible? In countries like France, much of the workforce operates under sectoral or national bargaining agreements, much like the Writers Guild model we discussed. Unions, while representing only a fraction of workers, negotiate agreements with employer associations that set the terms for all jobs in the sector, whether the individual worker is a union member or not. These collective bargaining agreements (CBAs) are then extended to cover the entire industry, ensuring that even nonunion workers benefit from the negotiated standards.

In some countries, the extension of CBAs is widespread. This includes Austria, Belgium, France, the Netherlands, Spain, Switzerland, and the Scandinavian countries. The mechanism of CBA extensions also differs somewhat across countries. Sometimes, the extensions are automatic. In other cases, extensions are subject to some thresholds: For example, in the Netherlands, a contract is extended throughout the industry when the share of workers represented in the original CBA is at least 55 percent.[6] But in most high-income countries, some form of sectoral-based wage standard is common, as shown by the gap in membership and coverage in figure 7.1.

While collective bargaining rates have declined across much of the developed world over the past several decades, the details have varied a lot depending on the country. In some places, both union membership and coverage rates have stayed relatively high—like in Denmark and Sweden, where the "Ghent system" incentivizes union membership by linking it to unemployment insurance.[7] Then there are countries like France, where the extension of collective bargaining agreements has kept coverage rates high, even though membership has dropped. And finally, there are countries like the United States, where both union membership and coverage have fallen sharply due to enterprise-level bargaining.

De-unionization's impact on inequality that we uncovered in chapter 5 might have been much less severe if membership and coverage weren't so tightly linked in this country. If union-negotiated standards continued to cover the same share of jobs, even as union membership declined, workers in the middle of the pay scale likely wouldn't have faced as much downward pressure on their wages. This suggests that sectoral standards could be a promising solution for helping middle-income workers.

So, the question is: How does sectoral bargaining actually work when it comes to wages, inequality, and economic performance?

Evidence on Sectoral Standards in Europe

Sectoral pay standards have a powerful effect on wages and inequality. Take, for example, the work of economists David Card and Ana Rute Cardoso, who used high-quality administrative data from Portugal to paint one of the clearest pictures of how these standards play out in practice.[8] The Portuguese system of collective bargaining is quite similar to those in Spain, Italy, Belgium, the Netherlands, and France. Even the Scandinavian systems have comparable elements. This makes the lessons from their study relevant to a much broader context.

The authors use administrative data from the Quadros de Pessoal (QP) to link individual workers to the collective bargaining agreements that govern their jobs. This unique data allows them to examine how the minimum wage, sectoral CBAs, and employer decisions to set wages interact together to determine the actual wages paid to a worker.

Card and Cardoso find that nearly 90 percent of all workers are at jobs that are covered by collective bargaining, and around 70 percent are specifically bound by sectoral CBAs, meaning their wages have to be at least as high as the floor. The authors' analysis reveals that sectoral wage floors play a significant role in setting wages in Portugal. Around a third of workers earn a wage exactly at the floor set by the sectoral agreement for that type of job. This is much higher than the share earning exactly the minimum wage, which is under 10 percent. Importantly, women are much more likely to be exactly at the sectoral floor (39 percent) than men (27 percent). This reflects the fact that women are more likely to earn lower wages even within a particular job type, and hence more likely to be swept up by sectoral standards. So, having wage floors by type of job helps reduce the gender pay gap.

The wage floor does not affect just the workers who are exactly bound by it; it also affects the nearly 60 percent of workers who earn a premium above the floor. For the typical worker, this premium is around 20 percent, meaning if the floor were around €15 per hour, the typical worker earns around €18.

One key takeaway is that many workers see their wages rise in tandem when the wage floor is negotiated upward. In other words, there are significant spillover effects when the floor is raised, as Card and Cardoso's research highlights. They find that the overall wage gains from raising the floor are typically about 45 percent larger than what you'd expect if only those earning below the new minimum got a raise. Put differently, the higher floor also lifts wages for those already earning above it, though not by a one-for-one margin. The further a worker's pay is from the new floor, the smaller their relative gains.

There are two important takeaways from these findings. First, setting a wage floor raises pay not only for those at the very bottom but also for workers earning somewhat above it, broadening the reach of sectoral wage-setting. Second, the floor delivers larger gains for those on the lower rungs within a job group, reducing pay disparities and narrowing inequality even within the group.

While sectoral bargaining has substantial impact on the pay distribution, Card and Cardoso also find that it leaves plenty of flexibility in the system, which is important for a well-functioning market. One concern is whether workers are being allocated to the best employers. In general, companies with higher productivity pay more, which allows them to recruit and retain more workers. If the sectoral wage-setting is overly rigid and reduces the pay gap across companies too much, perhaps it would impede the beneficial reallocation of workers toward higher-productivity employers, harming the overall dynamism of the economy. Card and Cardoso find that this is not the case. Indeed, higher-productivity employers still pay a higher premium, and the relationship between firm productivity and pay is only modestly reduced from the presence of sectoral floors. Classifying firms into deciles of average value added per worker, the average wages at top decile firms are about 50 percent higher than the average wages at bottom decile firms in the same sectoral agreement. And when there is an increase in firm-specific productivity, those firms see very strong growth in employment, as is the case in countries without sectoral bargaining like the United States and the United Kingdom. In other words, the wage compression and reduction in inequality from having a floor does not meaningfully impede the ability of higher-quality employers from being able to grow their workforce.

A related concern is whether the sectoral wage standards lead to reduced employment. This is similar to concerns about any wage floor, like a national or local minimum wage. We've already seen the evidence from minimum wages suggest that any impact from wage floors are likely modest, but perhaps there are differences higher up in the distribution.

Card and Cardoso find that when the sectoral floor is raised by 10 percent, overall wages in the job group rise by around 5.3 percent. At the same time, employment *increases* by around 1.7 percent, although statistically it cannot be distinguished from a zero effect. Dividing the employment effect (1.7) by the wage effect (5.3) suggests an own-wage elasticity of employment of around 0.3. You may recall that OWE of –1 would imply that the raise is self-defeating, while something more positive than –0.4 could be considered small. Factoring in the statistical margin of error rules out an OWE more negative than –0.36 from sector-based floors. In other words, the types of increases in sectoral wage standards enacted do not appear to have a measurable harmful effect on job growth.

A final concern is how the floors are set and adjusted. One worry is that floors could be pegged to the productivity of top-performing firms, squeezing out less productive competitors and thinning the market. In practice, however, the best predictor of increases in negotiated floors is growth in *average* sector-wide productivity: Within each sector the various floors tend to move together. In short, sectoral bargaining seems to tie bottom pay in a sector to overall sectoral productivity—pushing against the grain of inequality by tying most wages to the overall productivity growth.

This doesn't mean everyone in the same job group earns the same. Most workers receive a premium above the floor based on their own skills and capabilities as well as their employer's productivity. But by anchoring the bottom to sector-wide productivity, a sectoral system can deliver more broadly shared prosperity than the current American model.

Reforming Labor Law in the United States

Given some of the attractive aspects of a sectoral bargaining system, could we shift gears toward it here in America? While our current labor law framework doesn't readily accommodate such a shift, the idea isn't entirely out of reach. In theory, if unions wielded enough collective strength, they could exert pressure on employers to collaborate at an industry level, in a manner similar to the recent achievements of writers' and actors' guilds.

However, this theory quickly collides with reality. As we saw in 2024, the private-sector union membership rate in America stood at a mere 6 percent, even lower in some states. Reviving the labor movement and ushering in sectoral bargaining seem daunting given this backdrop.

To turn this vision into reality, we could push labor law reforms that make organizing easier. Over the years, there have been numerous efforts to boost unionization through labor law reform including the Employee Free Choice Act. Yet, none of these attempts actually led to successful change in the legislative arena. The most recent hope emerged with administrative rule changes by the National Labor Relations Board during the Biden administration, streamlining union elections and imposing stricter penalties for employer violations. Despite these changes, the surge in new union organizing has been relatively modest.

Take the Starbucks story, for example. Starting with an initial triumph in Buffalo, New York, in 2021, Starbucks Workers United has organized around six hundred locations. Public support for unions has soared, and the pro-worker NLRB under the Biden administration helped. On top of that, given the historically tight labor market of 2021–2023, workers had less to fear from getting fired by their bosses for their union organizing. After all, they could quickly get another job if necessary. When Tori Tambellini, a twenty-three-year-old union organizer at a Starbucks in Pittsburgh, was fired during the organizing drive, almost immediately she was able to get another job at a neighboring pizza place.[9] Yet, even with these tailwinds, organizing store by store remains an uphill battle, with less than 10 percent of Starbucks stores unionized so far. Other high-profile organizing efforts like Amazon and Trader Joe's have yielded at most a handful of organizing victories. Moreover, winning a union election is no guarantee that the union will be able to negotiate a collective bargaining agreement. Many newly organized establishments never get a CBA; this is especially likely when union presence is isolated at a small share of workplaces. For example, at the time of this writing, none of the high-profile organizing mentioned above had led to a successful contract.

This is not to say that these efforts are unimportant or that they will not yield any benefits. Even the threat of unionization often leads employers to improve working conditions, and it is certainly possible that at least at Starbucks, workers will eventually have a collectively bargained contract. However, given the current state of affairs, the math behind enterprise bargaining paints a less-than-rosy picture for a union resurgence, let alone one necessary to push employers to bargain at a sectoral level. Starting from a mere 10 percent union membership rate (or 6 percent in the private sector), even with a substantial increase in organizing, it would take decades to rebuild union strength to anywhere near its postwar peak.

Employers, too, fiercely resist unionization efforts, launching legal and other battles against workers' organizing drives. Starbucks, for instance, faced over one hundred NLRB cases in response to unionization efforts, highlighting the extent of employer opposition. Other corporate giants like Walmart and Amazon have also vehemently opposed unionizing campaigns. As John Logan, a labor relations expert, put it, while the NLRA's aim was to let workers choose freely whether to opt for union representation, in practice employer behavior has "turned it into a choice by the companies, not the workers."[10] Importantly, this employer resistance is partly due to the American enterprise-level bargaining system itself, which can put individual employers at a competitive disadvantage compared to sectoral bargaining.[11]

Given these challenges and the constraints of enterprise bargaining, it might seem sensible to push for labor law reform that favors sectoral bargaining. Reforming the National Labor Relations Act to encourage or require industry-level negotiations (perhaps once the union density is above a threshold) is certainly a worthy goal in the long run. However, we must also recognize the reality that labor law reform, even in small steps, has proven elusive. Therefore, perhaps we should consider alternative paths forward.

So, if resurrecting the labor movement on a grand scale remains a distant dream in America, is there still hope for establishing wage standards without embarking on the daunting quest of federal labor law reform? The answer is a resounding yes.

Lessons from Down Under: A Wage Board Approach

An alternative to European-style sectoral bargaining is to create sectoral councils (wage boards) that set multiple minimum pay standards by sector and occupation, ideally in consultation with business and worker representatives. This approach can lift not only the very lowest paid but also workers toward the middle of the ladder, much like sectoral bargaining. Consider nursing assistants: their wages are generally low, with a nationwide median of about $19 per hour in 2024.[12] Yet even in relatively high-minimum-wage states, more than 90 percent of nursing assistants earn above the statutory floor. As a result, raising a single, economy-wide minimum does little—unless it's set so high that many workers across the labor market with very different qualifications bunch at it. A wage-board model can instead set wage floors by job type that reach these low, but not lowest, rungs. Countries with sectoral bargaining accomplish this through collective agreements; a statutory system can do it by setting multiple minimum pay levels.

This sounds intriguing, but you may be wondering: Is this feasible in practice? For inspiration, we can travel to Down Under, where wage boards have been used to set standards for over a century. Australia's "Modern Awards" system provides a model. Australia has a combination of (1) national minimum wage, (2) the Modern Awards (hereafter Awards) system of industry- and occupation-specific minimums set by its Fair Work Commission (FWC), and (3) enterprise-level collective bargaining. Australia has a moderately high share of jobs covered by collective bargaining contracts (36 percent). However, like the United States, but different from continental Europe, most collective bargaining occurs at the enterprise level, especially since the 1990s. However, different from the United States, it has the system of wage standards set at the sectoral level through the Awards system. This makes it a particularly compelling example for us to learn from.

Let's start with the basics. The Award floors are set by the FWC, which is a federal tribunal whose members are appointed by the government to serve until the age of sixty-five. Most of these Awards are by industry, although some (e.g., nurses and pilots) are by occupation. There are 122 such Awards, and within each there are a host of wage rates based on skill requirements or experience; there may be anywhere from a handful to several dozen pay grades specified in each agreement. So, there are perhaps around one thousand different floors as part of the Awards system.

How many workers' pay are set by these Awards? As of 2018, around 22 percent of workers were earning wages matching exactly these floors. The share of jobs whose wages are directly set by Awards varies considerably. The share is above 40 percent in Accommodation and Food Services and Administrative Support Services, and between 30 and 40 percent in Retail, Healthcare, and Other Services sectors. In contrast, less than 10 percent of workers' wages are directly set by Awards floors in the high-end Finance and Professional Services sectors.[13]

However, there are many other workers whose wages are affected indirectly through wage spillovers. Employer surveys–based evidence suggests another 8 percent of workers are indirectly influenced by the Award floors, bringing the directly and indirectly affected to around 30 percent. This is a bit lower than what we saw under European-style sectoral bargaining, but it is still quite substantial.

As a practical matter, the annual wage increases are largely similar each year for most awards and pay grades. This is like what we saw in the European sectoral bargaining system. For example, in 2018, most Award pay standards were increased by 3.5 percent in low-wage sectors like Retail and Hospitality, the same amount as the baseline minimum wage increase. In some years or particular cases, there may be some additional adjustment to wages to further boost pay in the lowest categories of work to achieve greater pay compression.

While it's difficult to definitively quantify the impact of Australia's system of labor standards, we can start by looking at broad measures of inequality and labor market performance—and these paint a generally favorable picture. Take disposable household income, for instance. Inequality in Australia is noticeably lower than in the United States. According to OECD data, in 2018 (the last year before the pandemic), households at the 90th percentile in Australia earned 4.3 times as much as those at the 10th percentile. In the United States, the ratio was 6.3.[14]

Of course, household income captures more than just wages. To focus more directly on labor market outcomes, we can compare earnings inequality: In 2019, earnings at the 9th decile were 5 times those at the 1st decile in America, compared with 3.4 times in Australia—still unequal, but significantly more compressed.[15] While earnings inequality has risen in both countries over time, the difference between the United States and Australia remains substantial. This comparative evidence supports the view that labor market institutions—such as Australia's Awards system—have played a meaningful role in fostering more broadly shared prosperity and limiting wage inequality, particularly when contrasted with the American experience.

At the same time, the more muted inequality is not associated with any obvious differences in labor market performance. In 2023, Australia had an unemployment rate of 3.7 percent, while the unemployment rate in America was 3.6 percent. In general, unemployment in Australia has tended to be more stable over time, while in the United States it has been more cyclical during both the financial crisis and the Covid-19 recession. Over the past ten years (2014–2023), however, the two countries have had similar average unemployment rates: 5.3 percent in Australia and 4.9 percent in the United States. Focusing on younger or less-educated workers does not yield very different conclusions.

While these comparisons are informative in assessing overall performance, there are many other differences between the Australian and American labor markets. So, it is difficult to assess the causal role played by sectoral standards on labor market performance, including on job growth. Ideally, we would take advantage of natural experiments to see how the changes in wage floors in the Award system affect the performance of the system, similar to the work by Card and Cardoso on sectoral bargaining, or the voluminous work on minimum wages across many countries. Here the best work on the topic was done by the economist James Bishop, whose 2018 study investigated the impact of changes in the Awards rates. Bishop leverages the fact that often the wage changes are a flat dollar amount, but this means a relatively larger percent change in wages in job groups where the level is lower. This allows him to compare job groups where the floor rose more proportionately to groups where it rose less, using a *difference-in-differences* style research design that we have encountered before.[16]

So how did wages, hours, and employment probability react to a relatively larger change in the floor? Bishop finds that there are strong effects on actual wages when the floor rises more, as expected. This is consistent with the hypothesis that the floors compressed the wage distribution, lowering inequality. At the same time, he found no evidence of reduced hours or any increase in the probability that the employer got rid of the position in response to the higher pay hike from the sectoral wage floor. If anything, job destruction rate seems to fall in the job groups with the large wage gains in relative terms, though the estimates are not statistically different from zero. He is careful to note that these are incremental changes in the floor, so we should be cautious when extrapolating to much larger increases. However, the careful analysis of these hikes in the Awards floors lends more confidence to the notion that employment prospects are not substantially diminished from the sectoral standards.

Overall, the Australian evidence is broadly consistent with the perspective that judiciously applied wage-setting using a wage board system can help mitigate wage inequality without causing any serious harm to the labor market.

What Would Sectoral Wage Standards Look Like in the United States?

To institute sectoral wage bargaining at the national level in the United States, federal law would need to be changed. However, states are free to institute sectoral wage standards with statutory law or using sectoral councils. Indeed, some states (Arizona, Colorado, California, New Jersey, and New York) already have legislation on the books that allows for constituting sectoral councils (or wage boards) by industry or occupations.

Historically, these boards have been used infrequently. They were used to raise the overall minimum wages in California in the 1990s and more recently to establish a fast-food minimum wage in New York and California. However, there has been little effort to use the wage boards mechanism to target wages for the middle of the distribution. And as we will see, recently states like California and Minnesota have been moving forward with experimentation with sectoral wage-setting. While formal collective bargaining between worker and employer representatives is preempted by federal law (except for workers not covered by the National Labor Relations Act, like workers in agriculture or state employees), sectoral councils with stakeholder representation are free to make recommendations that lead to administrative or legislative action. The legal and institutional basis of wage boards has been studied extensively by scholars, including Kate Andrias and David Madland.[17]

State experimentation with sectoral standards higher up in the wage distribution—as in the Australian case—could play a possibly useful role in mitigating wage suppression and inequality. But what would such a system look like? Here, we can get a sense of this by looking at the data and simulating state-level policies. For this exercise, I use individual-level wage information from the main government data collected from households, the Current Population Survey. I start by taking the actual real wages data from 2021 through

2023, and then ask how pay would change at different parts of the distribution if we were to impose sectoral standards.

While details can vary, a state-level sectoral wage standard would set minimum pay floors by industry and occupation. As an illustration, I simulate the effect of a sectoral board by imposing state-specific standards across twenty sectors (as defined by the North American Industry Classification System). These include Retail Trade; Construction; Real Estate, Rental and Leasing; Manufacturing; Accommodation and Food Services; Health Care and Social Assistance; Educational Services; and thirteen other industries. Within each state-sector combination, I further consider six broad occupational categories: managerial and professional; technical, sales, and administrative; service; production, craft, and repair; operatives and laborers; and farming, forestry, and fishing. In principle, this produces 50 states by 20 sectors by 6 occupational categories, or 6,000 job groups. Of course, in reality, not every combination is a meaningful job group: For instance, there are few workers in "Farming/Fishing/Forestry" occupations in the Health Care sector! Once we restrict attention to combinations with a meaningful count of jobs in the data, it yields around 3,700 usable job groups.[18] For each of these job groups, I set a wage floor.

The choice of where exactly to set the floor is important; just as when setting a national or state minimum wage, we want to balance the equalizing benefits of a wage standard against unintended consequences, which includes potential for job losses. A related concern is "over-compression" of wages, where jobs with very different qualifications or skills are paid the same or very similarly, which can make it difficult for employers to provide incentives. For example, pay differentials within these broad job groupings may reflect higher pay for workers with more experience. If the floor is set so high as to greatly diminish any remaining differences in pay across jobs within the job group, it might inhibit the employer's ability to provide career advancement incentives to workers, possibly harming effort and productivity. In addition, as Card and Cardoso argue in the context of

Europe, the fact that many workers earn above the floor offers a premium through which economic shocks can be absorbed without too much rigidity.

For these reasons, I consider wage standards that are set below the current median wage in these job groups, namely at two-thirds of the median. To be clear, there is nothing special about this exact cutoff, but it is a reasonable starting place. Recall that two-thirds of the *overall* median wage is what several countries (including the United Kingdom) have chosen as the level to set their national minimum wage. Sectoral standards are somewhat distinct from minimum wages because they change wages within job groups. However, as we will see, there are a number of similarities as well.

Most important, around 14 percent of workers at present earn below two-thirds of the median wage in their job group. These are the directly affected workers who will get a bump in wages from a sectoral wage standard. This is comparable to the proportion of workers who are at the national minimum wage floor in many countries; in California (which has one of the highest minimum wages in the United States), the share is around 13 percent. So, one way to think about it is that the scale of intervention (i.e., share of the workforce whose wage is being directly set by the floor) under this proposed sectoral wage floor would be quite similar to many existing minimum wage policies, including here in America. However, different from a minimum wage, a sectoral standard can strongly influence pay for not only workers at the bottom of the scale but also those toward the middle.

For another comparison, in Australia, around 22 percent of workers' wages are set by the Modern Awards system. And in Portugal, around 33 percent of the workers are at the floor; but if we consider only sectoral floors that are not close to the national minimum wage, the share falls to around a quarter. Taking stock, the overall bite of the proposed sectoral wage standard here (as measured by the share of workers directly affected) is broadly comparable to, though somewhat lower than, other existing sectoral regimes. If anything, a two-thirds standard may be on the cautious side, and a higher target could be feasible.

If we set the floor at two-thirds of the median wage within each job group, how would that affect pay across the distribution? Figure 7.2 plots the change in wage by percentile. The dashed line shows the "direct effects," with the assumption that everyone below the floor is lifted to it, while those above see no change in wages. The biggest proportional wage gains are still at the bottom: The direct effects of instituting this sectoral standard would raise wages by almost 10 percent at the very bottom. However, there is also considerable wage growth toward the middle of the distribution, with a 4 percent pay bump at the median—around $25 per hour in 2023—and positive effects extending roughly to the 80th percentile.

These are the *direct* effects of raising everyone below the wage floor to exactly that level. But, as studies of minimum wages and sectoral bargaining show, workers above the floor often receive raises, too. I model these *spillovers* to be moderate-size based on the existing evidence from minimum wages as well as from collective bargaining, allowing them to extend up to the median wage within the job groups.[19] Allowing for these spillovers increases the wage gains, both because now more workers are affected and because some workers earning below the new sectoral floor may actually see their new wage rise above it. Factoring in spillovers, the wage boost from the standards is expected to be around 13 percent at the bottom of the distribution, 8 percent at the median, and around 2.5 percent at the 80th percentile before tapering off. In short, spillovers add a substantial boost around the middle: Roughly half of the overall wage gains come from spillovers and half from the direct effects of the floor.[20]

Interestingly, for the bottom fifth of the wage distribution, these gains from sectoral standards are broadly similar to what you'd expect from a strong minimum wage increase. Where they differ is in the middle—roughly the 25th to 75th percentiles—where, once spillovers are factored in, wages rise by about 6.5 percent. Long story

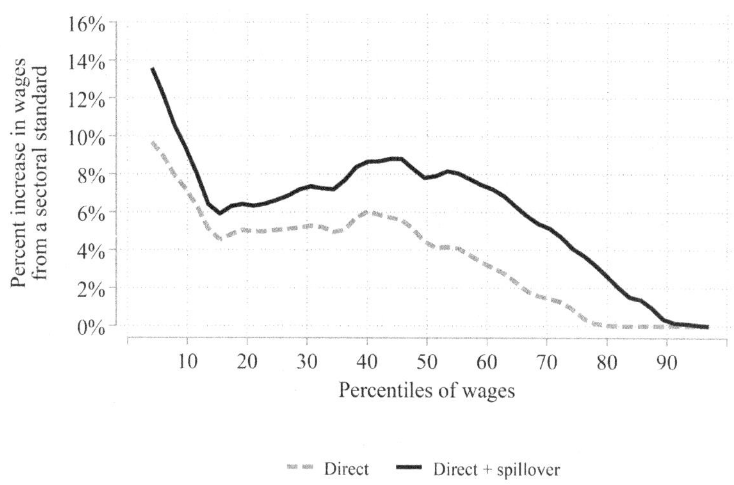

FIGURE 7.2 **EFFECT OF HYPOTHETICAL SECTORAL WAGE STANDARDS ON PAY**[21]

short, wage boards are far better positioned to deliver gains to middle-wage jobs than a single pay floor.

To contextualize the impact of sectoral wage standards on wage disparities, let's compare how such a standard could reduce inequality today relative to its rise since 1980. The 90–10 ratio, capturing overall wage inequality, increased by around 29 percent between 1980 and 2013. Between 2013 and 2024, about a third of this increase (around 10 percent) was undone—driven largely by the post-pandemic compression discussed in chapter 2.[22] Introducing a sectoral wage standard could reduce the 90–10 ratio by an additional 9 percent. In other words, a moderately designed wage board—setting the wage floor at two-thirds of the median within each job group—could erase roughly half of the remaining increase in overall wage inequality since 1980. That's a big deal.

It's also useful to examine how this reduction plays out across different parts of the wage distribution. The 90–50 ratio, which captures inequality in the upper half of the distribution, increased by about 22 percent between 1980 and 2019; unlike the 90–10 ratio, it showed little post-pandemic decline. Implementing the sectoral wage standard would reduce this ratio by 8 percent, reversing over a third of the post-1980 increase.

This reinforces a key feature of wage boards: When compared with a tightness-driven compression or a single minimum wage, they more strongly push up the *median wage* and narrow the gap between the middle and the top of the pay scale. In short, sectoral wage standards have a uniquely powerful effect in strengthening the *middle class*—more than most other policy tools available. In doing so, they can play a role similar to, and complementary with, labor unions.

Differences across States

These calculations give us a sense of how wages would change across the country with the introduction of state-based sectoral wage standards, averaging the effects across all fifty states. However, the impact would differ significantly between states with and without their own minimum wage laws.

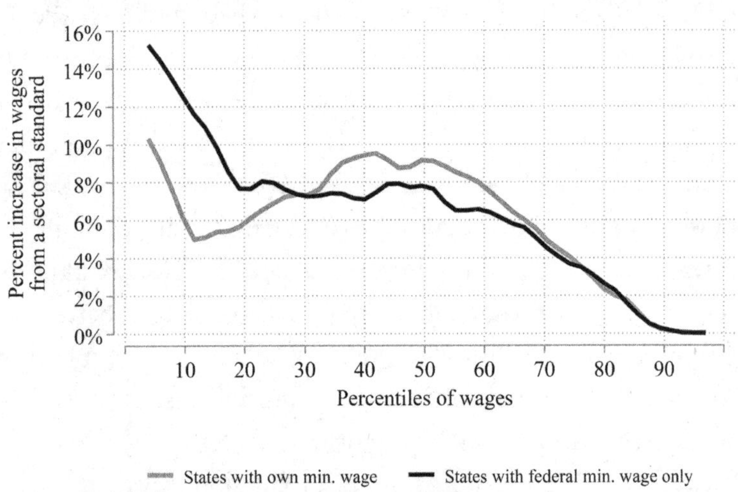

FIGURE 7.3 EFFECT OF HYPOTHETICAL SECTORAL WAGE STANDARDS ON PAY IN STATES WITH AND WITHOUT MINIMUM WAGES[23]

In the twenty states that currently lack state-level minimum wages—like Texas and Alabama—we would expect to see a more pronounced wage increase at the bottom of the pay scale, with gains of around 15 percent, tapering off to about 6 to 8 percent for workers between the 20th and 60th percentiles. This makes sense because, in these states, sectoral standards for workers in industries like fast food and retail would make up for the absence of a meaningful minimum wage (since the federal minimum wage is effectively nonbinding in these states today because it is set so low).

The picture looks different in the thirty states—such as California, Florida, Arizona, and New York—that do have state-level minimum wages (see figure 7.3). In these states, wage gains in the bottom fifth of the distribution would be more modest, as the existing minimum wage has already done some of the work the wage board would do. But sectoral standards would provide a bigger boost to middle-wage jobs in these states compared to the twenty states without minimum wage laws. Why? One reason is that many of these states—particularly coastal, Democratic-leaning ones—tend to have higher average wages, but also greater wage inequality. As a result, sectoral standards would be more effective at narrowing wage disparities in middle-income jobs.

Unintended Consequences?

If a wage board system leads to substantial wage increases, it's reasonable to worry about unintended consequences. After all, any significant shift in wage structures brings uncertainties. Two obvious concerns would be impact on jobs and potential price hikes. The combined evidence of sectoral bargaining in Europe, award floors in Australia, and minimum wages in general tell us that carefully chosen sectoral wage standards are unlikely to jeopardize job growth here in America. However, as with any new policy, there are always unknowns. This is why it makes sense to structure any changes incrementally, allowing time to learn from pilot programs.

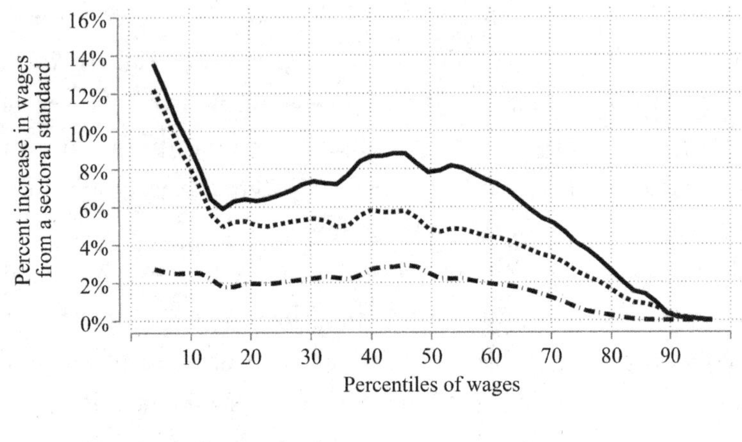

FIGURE 7.4 **EFFECT OF HYPOTHETICAL SECTORAL WAGE STANDARDS ON PAY, LIMITED TO NON-MANAGERIAL WORKERS, AND BY SECTOR**[24]

What might such steps look like? First, piloting wage standards in specific sectors—ideally those targeting wages at the lower and middle ends of the income distribution—would be a smart starting point. For example, we could begin by focusing on non-managerial occupations and then further narrow our focus to the health and education sectors. These sectors are also locally rooted and less exposed to global competition: Demand is tied to residents and public budgets, not international markets. As we saw with minimum wages, such *non-tradable* sectors tend to be more effective arenas for trying out higher standards.

As figure 7.4 shows, limiting the policy to non-managerial does not change the picture for lower-wage workers, though it would mean somewhat smaller wage gains in the middle. Now, if we further narrow our focus to health and education sectors, the results are quite striking. For workers outside the bottom fifth of the distribution, *about half of the wage gains from sectoral standards come from these two industries alone.* This includes a wide range of roles, from nurses and home-care workers to childcare providers, teachers, and cafeteria staff in schools. Together, these sectors employ a significant number of workers in the middle of the pay scale who could benefit substantially from the establishment of sectoral wage standards. In other words, the health and education sectors are prime candidates for piloting wage boards.

A second concern might be price increases and inflation. It's important to note, though, that in the long run, there's no inherent reason why sectoral wage standards would lead to a permanently higher inflation rate. As we've seen in both European and Australian contexts, most annual wage increases tied to sectoral standards are modest and tend to track productivity growth. This helps ensure that wages rise in a sustainable way, keeping the overall pace of wage growth aligned with economic fundamentals.

However, the introduction of sectoral wage standards is likely to have some impact on prices. Goods and services that rely more heavily on low- and middle-wage workers would likely become more expensive relative to those produced by higher-wage workers. This mirrors what we observe with minimum wage increases, where some wage costs get passed through as higher prices. As a result, shifting to sectoral standards would raise wages and likely produce a one-time bump in the overall price level, roughly 2 to 3 percent.[25] This makes it crucial to implement these wage hikes gradually, especially when scaling up sectoral standards across multiple sectors. Gradual increases help avoid sharp price spikes, easing the transition.

At a national level, any price pressure (even temporary) is closely monitored by the Federal Reserve. A fully implemented wage board system is most effective when wage boards and monetary authorities work together to maintain stable wage and price growth, with periodic adjustments to manage wage compression. The experiences in Australia and other countries with national-level sectoral bargaining demonstrate that this kind of coordination is not only feasible but can also be highly effective.

Sectoral Councils in Practice

The concept of sectoral wage-setting may seem conceptually appealing, but are there practical examples in America? Recently, there have been some shifts toward more systematic use of sectoral mechanisms. Let's dig into these developments.

California Healthcare Sectoral Standard

In October 2023, California enacted a transformative law that substantially affects the wages of hundreds of thousands of healthcare workers, including medical technicians, nursing assistants, custodians, and other support staff. Governor Gavin Newsom's legislation introduced a gradual wage increase, aiming for a $25-per-hour minimum wage. This shift, affecting around half a million workers, or 3 percent of the state's workforce, has had important implications for middle-wage Californians.

A significant factor in this development was the historic 2023 strike by Kaiser Permanente healthcare workers, marking the largest healthcare worker strike in American history. This strike, involving over seventy-five thousand workers, led to a tentative agreement that included a 21 percent wage increase over four years, starting with a 6 percent raise in October 2023. The contract set a $25 minimum wage for Kaiser workers in California by 2026, a standard that the new law extends to all healthcare employers in the state. This contract also addressed issues like performance bonuses and evening-shift incentives, reflecting the workers' concerns about staffing shortages and working conditions.

The law's enactment was the result of a unique collaboration between unions, particularly those representing Kaiser's lower-paid employees, healthcare providers, and the hospital lobby. These stakeholders reached a consensus that ultimately led to this legislative victory, with healthcare employers agreeing to wage increases and unions committing to a moratorium on local ballot measures for pay raises.[26]

This initiative marks a significant milestone for California's healthcare workforce, demonstrating the power of collective action and setting a precedent for sectoral wage standards in the healthcare industry.

California Fast Food Council

Healthcare isn't the only sector in California adopting sectoral standards. In September 2023, Governor Newsom signed AB 257, a law establishing a "Fast Food Council" within the Department of Industrial Relations. This council has the authority to set binding standards on wages, working hours, and conditions impacting the health, safety, and welfare of fast-food workers at "National Fast Food Chains"—defined as those with more than sixty establishments nationwide.

The formation of the council came after extensive negotiations between industry and labor representatives, facilitated by the governor's office. Its purpose goes beyond wages, addressing working conditions such as health and safety, workplace security, and protections against discrimination and harassment. The council is composed of nine voting members representing various stakeholders in the fast-food industry, including employees, franchisees, and advocates. This structure aims to ensure that decision-making reflects the interests of all parties involved.

Starting on April 1, 2024, the law sets a new minimum wage of $20 per hour for fast-food-chain employees, with the council having the authority to adjust this rate annually from 2025. Any wage increases are capped at the annual inflation rate or 3.5 percent, whichever is lower.[27]

Does California's fast-food law pose challenges? When a high fast-food minimum wage is applied only to major chains and statutory employees (excluding gig workers), while the rest of the restaurant industry operates under a much lower minimum, some risks emerge. There is a case for expecting larger, more productive firms to pay more, and many already do. But this type of partial coverage can encourage evasion, such as reclassifying workers as subcontractors or gig workers, undermining the policy's reach. Going forward, it will be important to monitor these risks and, if needed, recalibrate the policy to maximize benefits for workers. Finally, there's an open question whether a low-wage sector like fast food, already governed by a general minimum wage, is the best place to pilot sectoral standards, as opposed to sectors like healthcare.

That said, early evidence from California is broadly encouraging: Fast-food pay rose about 8 percent on average (a big increase!), with limited employment effects so far. In baseline *difference-in-differences* comparisons of California fast-food employment with other states, one study found a small-to-medium-sized negative effect, while another that adjusts for population-growth differences found effects near zero. Taken together, even with the nation's highest wage floor in this sector, the early evidence—subject to revision as more data arrive—suggests California's fast-food workforce has come out ahead.[28]

Minnesota's Nursing Home Workforce Standards Board

The Minnesota Nursing Home Workforce Standards Board Act, signed into law by Governor Tim Walz in 2023, marks another significant milestone in setting wage standards in the healthcare sector. Minnesota, facing a serious nursing home worker shortage, has seen its care system stretched to the limit, particularly during the pandemic. The core problem lies in a vicious cycle of low wages and harsh working conditions, leading to burnout and high turnover rates. In response, the new act establishes a sectoral council that brings together workers, employers, and government officials, all tasked with setting and enforcing standards that focus on compensation, working conditions, and healthcare safety.

With the legal authority to set industry-wide rules, the board has the power to enact meaningful reforms. It will focus on worker health and safety alongside compensation—areas long neglected in the industry. The board's unique makeup, drawing from all corners of the sector, represents a well-rounded approach.[29] In April 2024, the board took a historic step by voting to raise the average pay floor in nursing homes to $23.49 by 2027. This includes a $24 floor for certified nursing assistants, $28.50 for licensed practical nurses, and $20.50 for other workers, including subcontracted employees—creating a path toward establishing middle-class wage standards in the industry.[30]

Of course, this initiative isn't without its challenges. Some nursing home advocates have raised concerns about how feasible it will be to meet these standards without further legislative backing. However, efforts in the Minnesota legislature have shown a commitment to supporting the industry.

A Path Forward on Sectoral Standards

The adoption of sectoral wage standards in America, inspired by models in Australia and Europe, presents a promising path to address wage inequality and pay suppression. State-level experiments, like those in California and Minnesota, pave the way for broader implementation.

Going forward, it's important to carefully consider where sectoral standards make the most sense, especially when designing pilots: Poorly chosen initial experiments can sour the public for further trials. Healthcare is a strong candidate: It's a large sector with a public-service mission and many occupations that earn above the level typically covered by minimum wage laws. Sectoral standards can lift pay in parts of the healthcare workforce that would otherwise be out of reach for a standard minimum wage. Another promising venue is the gig economy, where app-based drivers are not covered by national labor law or minimum wage regulations. Massachusetts has paired a statewide earnings floor for Uber and Lyft drivers—$32.50 per engaged hour in 2024, and indexed annually—with a voter-approved, state-supervised bargaining model that gives these drivers a path to unionize and negotiate sector-wide standards. It's the first framework of its kind in a U.S. state and is now being implemented.[31]

If designed well, sectoral wage standards could fundamentally reshape how wages are set, benefiting a wide range of workers and fostering a more inclusive economy. The raise that so many American workers deserve could finally become a reality.

CHAPTER 8

The Politics of Possibility

A Wage Standard for the Twenty-First Century

On July 8, 2015, George Osborne, then chancellor of the exchequer of the United Kingdom, made a major policy announcement that shook the political landscape: the introduction of the National Living Wage, a wage floor that went above the existing UK minimum wage for workers age twenty-five and over. The announcement came at a time when wage stagnation and growing income inequality were hot topics in the UK. Following the 2007 financial crisis, many workers had seen their real wages decline, and the economic recovery was slow and uneven. Income inequality was rising, with low-wage workers being hit particularly hard. The Conservative government, under Prime Minister David Cameron, faced heavy criticism for austerity measures that seemed to exacerbate these trends. Against this backdrop, Osborne's introduction of the NLW was unexpected—a bold and strategic shift in policy.

Osborne's delivery of this announcement during his Summer Budget speech was both theatrical and consequential. He declared that, starting in April 2016, workers age twenty-five and over would see the wage floor rise from £6.70 ($9.05) to £7.20 ($9.72) per hour, with a planned increase to more than £9 ($12.15) by 2020 (all nominal, using the 2016 exchange rate). He cast this roughly 34 percent lift in the floor by 2020 as a shift toward a higher-wage, lower-welfare, lower-tax society, positioning the Conservatives as the party of the working people. This was a calculated appeal to low-income workers, traditionally not the Conservatives' base.

The introduction of the National Living Wage triggered a wave of experimentation and evaluation, including another surprise in 2019, when then Chancellor Philip Hammond announced plans to further raise the NLW. The goal was to push the NLW up to two-thirds of the median wage for adult workers if the evidence on its past impacts supported the increase. I was asked by the chancellor to evaluate the evidence, which I did, and in 2019, my review found that the NLW had been highly successful in raising pay for low-wage workers without causing noticeable job losses. As I have discussed in this book, subsequent evidence upheld this assessment. By 2022, the UK had significantly advanced toward Hammond's vision of reducing low-wage work. According to the OECD's definition—jobs paying less than two-thirds of the median wage—the share of UK workers in low-paid jobs had fallen from around 21 percent in 2015 to 13 percent in 2022. This achievement marked a return to the low levels of low-paid work seen in 1975, reversing decades of rising low-wage employment in the UK through the 1980s and 1990s, all without substantially harming employment prospects for low-wage workers.[1]

As it turns out, America, too, has seen a sharp reduction in low-wage work over the recent period, with some similarities to the UK, but also some differences. Defining "low-wage jobs" as those paying less than two-thirds of a state's median wage, the share of workers in such jobs rose from 21 percent to 25 percent in the early 1980s, a pattern strikingly similar to that seen in the UK.[2] While there were ebbs and flows, the share remained elevated over the following decades, reaching a peak of 25 percent in 2013. Then, spurred by the Fight for $15 movement, many states raised their minimum wage between 2013 and 2018, which reduced the share of low-paid workers in roughly half the country. In the other half, where state minimums stayed flat, the share of low-paid workers remained near its historic high. Then, propelled by a tight labor market in 2019, and especially during the aftermath of the pandemic in 2021–2023, low-paid workers saw historic gains across the country. The average share of American workers in low-paid positions dropped from 25 percent in 2013 to about 20 percent in 2023, dipping below its 1980 level for the first time.

The broad arc looks similar in Britain and the United States, though the mechanisms differ: Minimum wage policy played a role in both, but in the U.S. full-employment policy did more of the lifting, spanning the Trump and Biden administrations through fiscal and monetary support. Getting the low-paid share down to 20 percent isn't "mission accomplished," but it is real progress.

These outcomes were also not predictable: Not too many observers were predicting a sharp decline in wage inequality when the pandemic hit in 2020. And that's OK: Predictions, as the saying goes, are hard, especially about the future! What matters is recognizing positive developments when they occur and understanding why they happened.

As it turns out, this is often a problem because there is a myriad of forces at play in our current society that privilege more negative narratives. Our brains are wired for negativity bias, a well-documented cognitive quirk where negative information holds more weight than positive. This bias significantly impacts our perception of the economy, often leading to a skewed view dominated by anxieties and pessimism. Research by Roy Baumeister and colleagues in 2001 established the concept of *negativity dominance*, demonstrating how negative events carry a stronger emotional punch than positive ones.[3] This translates to economic news, where stories of recessions, job losses, a rise in the inflation rate, or market crashes hold our attention far longer than reports of stable growth, rising wages, or moderating prices.

For example, economic mood in America soured considerably in the aftermath of the pandemic. Some of this was surely understandable: After all, the pandemic was a hugely disruptive and painful episode, and the growing pains during the recovery—especially the sharp rise in inflation during 2021–2023 along with high interest rates—left a bad taste in the mouth for many families. At the same time, dissatisfaction can turn to negativity, where we tend to tune out good news and become increasingly pessimistic, discounting the possibility of positive developments, including ones that already happened.

Consider a particularly striking example: In early 2024, YouGov polled two thousand U.S. adults, asking which decades they believed had the best or worst outcomes across a range of social and economic measures.[4]

When it came to the economy, the most common response for the *worst* decade—by a wide margin—was the present one. About 32 percent of respondents said the 2020s had the worst economy, surpassing even the 1930s. Only 23 percent named the decade of the Great Depression as the worst, and no other decade from the past century was chosen by more than 6 percent of respondents.

This bleak view of the 2020s persisted despite strong economic indicators. The unemployment rate remained below 4 percent between February 2022 and April 2024—the longest such stretch since the 1960s. Despite the burst of inflation following the pandemic, real wages also rose broadly, with the largest gains going to lower-wage workers—marking a sharp contrast with much of the past fifty years, when real wage growth was often weak for most. For example, between 2023 and 2024, the median wage grew by an annual 1.2 percent after adjusting for inflation. Between 1980 and 2019, the annual growth had been only 0.5 percent.[5]

This poll was not an isolated example: A 2023 survey by Bankrate found that the majority of respondents thought the American economy was in a recession in 2023, despite a high growth rate and historically low unemployment.[6] Interestingly, according to annual surveys conducted by the Federal Reserve, from 2019 to 2023 the share of Americans who felt pessimistic about their *personal* financial situation remained fairly steady. Yet over the same period, perceptions of the *national* economy worsened dramatically—more so than perceptions of the *local* economy.[7] To be sure, the sharp price increases of 2021 and 2022 understandably dampened consumer sentiment. But these inflationary shocks seemed to trigger a broader sense of economic malaise—one that diverged significantly from the actual economic conditions.

In an ideal world, hard information from reliable media sources would help break the doom loop. In the real world, the media can amplify bad news. Work by Ben Harris and Aaron Sojourner shows that economic news has become increasingly more negative in recent years than what we would expect based on economic fundamentals, especially after the pandemic.[8] In other words, instead of providing a corrective, the media seemed to validate—or worse, amplify—the *Vibecession* of 2022–2023, a term coined by Kyla Scanlon.[9] And one key reason why the media (especially social media) accentuates the negative: Bad news gets more clicks. Compelling evidence comes from a 2023 study by Claire Robertson and coauthors, based on randomized control trials conducted by a media website (Upworthy) that used viral techniques to promote news pieces in social media.[10] Headlines had a randomized assortment of negative or positive words. The authors found that each additional negative word in the headline increased the rate of click-through by 2.3 percent. As they note, these findings justify the newsroom phrase "If it bleeds, it leads."

But before we get too upset at reporters or media organizations, we should note that journalists have often focused on exposing problems, which can be seen as righteously addressing injustices. There are plenty of ways in which the American economy did not deliver broad-based prosperity over the course of the last forty-five years, as this book has documented! However, just as it is vital to isolate trouble spots in the economy, it is also critical to recognize successes if we want to make progress. That requires being able to discern positive change and chart out a path forward. In that spirit, peering into the future, let me offer some reasons for hope for advancing shared prosperity. I do not mean these to be forecasts: The future depends on what we do as a society and a polity. However, these are possibilities that I think we should take seriously—possibilities that should give us hope. There are economic fundamentals and political dynamics that *can* provide a helping hand in rebuilding the wage standard.

I see three broad reasons for optimism about building a wage standard and inclusive prosperity. First—perhaps surprisingly—there are some tailwinds from economic fundamentals, including technological change that can work with, rather than undercut, institutional reforms. Second, today there is greater cross-partisan support for shaping the distribution of market income, including a renewed focus on full employment and other steps to improve job quality. Third, worker organizing and public pressure are rising at the workplace and sector levels (micro and meso), laying the groundwork for institutions that strengthen the working and middle class.

Let me be clear. A lot can go wrong. A lot can change for the worse. But we're living through historical changes we can build on to realign the American economy toward shared prosperity. And it begins with crafting a hopeful, evidence-grounded narrative about why meaningful change is possible.

The Headwinds and Tailwinds of Technology

This book has focused on the role of employer choices and labor market institutions in shaping the trajectory of wages and inequality. As I have said, this is not because I think technological change—often the key postulated driver of these changes—is unimportant. Rather, it is because I think too often observers have interpreted technological change in a fatalistic light, relegating it as destiny. The story in this book is one where the wage standard is set by social forces and economic policies. After all, we saw that even as high-income countries experienced similar forces of automation and information revolution in the eighties and nineties, the growth in wage inequality varied greatly across countries as well as time periods based on protective labor market institutions, macroeconomic policies, and more. At the same time, economic fundamentals, including technological change, can make our jobs either easier or harder when it comes to inclusive growth. Here I think there are reasons to believe that while technological change mostly worked against blue-collar workers during the eighties, nineties, and the aughts, that may be changing.

The digital revolution brought about a profound transformation in the way information is processed and utilized, significantly reducing the cost of calculations and expanding access to vast amounts of data. As computers became integral to the workplace starting in the eighties, the demand for workers capable of harnessing this digital throughput surged. These roles required individuals to provide highly technical and detailed instructions to computers, enabling them to execute tasks with incredible speed and precision. This shift created a burgeoning demand not only for computer programmers but also for professionals in various fields such as architecture, engineering, and social sciences who could effectively interface with the digital realm.

The adoption of computers and specialized software necessitated considerable training, leading to a concentration of control and decision-making among elite experts who possessed the requisite skills. This development contributed to a growing divide between those who could leverage technology to enhance productivity and those whose jobs were more susceptible to automation. As computers automated a wide spectrum of routine tasks—including clerical work, administrative support, and production operations—the jobs that had once formed the backbone of the middle class began to disappear.[11] This hollowing out of middle-paying jobs was a direct consequence of the digital revolution, as automation replaced human labor in tasks that could be codified into a set of repeatable instructions.

In some cases, technology played a role in augmenting the fortunes of a select few, particularly in industries where the digital revolution enabled the low-cost proliferation of products and services. A notable example is the music industry, where technology expanded economies of scale, allowing new talent to achieve unprecedented global success. This "superstar effect," where success begets further success, has been observed in many other fields, from finance to academia. The digital revolution created environments where the combination of skill and luck could propel individuals to the top, reinforcing existing inequalities.[12]

Importantly, the extent of wage stagnation and inequality in America was not an inevitable outcome of technological change. While the forces driving the superstar effect impacted many countries, the United States experienced a much greater increase in top income concentration. Some economists have argued that these effects explain the dramatic rise in executive compensation in America.[13] However, as we saw, the historical evidence from the Great Compression of the 1940s showed that top CEO pay was sharply curtailed through the presence of unions. In contrast to the United States, countries where unions have remained stronger have not seen the same rise in CEO pay, suggesting that institutional factors play a significant role in mediating the impact of technological change.

Recent work by economists Daron Acemoglu and Pascual Restrepo, who have written extensively about the impact of automation on inequality, has shown that automation not only reduced the average wages of blue-collar workers but particularly lowered wages at "good jobs" within this demographic that tended to pay an above-market premium.[14] This phenomenon aligns with the broader argument of this book, which contends that when guardrails against wage suppression were weakened—due to a declining labor movement and the emergence of a new cohort of companies with different wage norms—employers found it particularly attractive to adopt new technologies and organizational forms that reduced pay at traditionally "good jobs." After all, that is where the costs savings were the greatest. This dynamic was evident in practices such as outsourcing cafeteria workers at high-end firms that paid premiums to in-house employees, as well as automating away unionized manufacturing jobs.

The institutional reality that allowed for significant wage declines at "bad jobs" raised the relative costs to employers of providing "good jobs." In contrast, in many continental European economies, sectoral wage standards likely mitigated the incentive for employers to cut wage standards at better jobs. The presence of wage floors meant that the possibility of lowering wages substantially through outsourcing or automation was reduced from the outset.

Furthermore, the impact of automation on the overall demand for blue-collar workers was closely linked to the strength of the labor market. In periods of relatively slack labor markets, such as during the 1980s, the first half of the 1990s, and much of the first fifteen years of this century, there were greater disparities in pay between "bad" and "good" jobs, and the latter were scarce. The disappearance of good blue-collar jobs was particularly costly in such an environment, as there was no economic pressure to improve jobs generally. In contrast, in a tight labor market—perhaps due to more aggressive macroeconomic policies—these workers might have been more likely to find other "good" jobs instead of filling vacancies at low-paid positions, which would have better safeguarded wages for workers without college degrees.

This analysis underscores the broader point that technology is not destiny; the choices we make as a society can shape the future. For example, had we pursued more expansionary policies after the 2007–2008 recession or managed the globalization process more effectively to avoid a sharp decline in manufacturing jobs, we might have had a more favorable outcome for American workers. Better macroeconomic management focused on full employment, coupled with smart industrial policies, may have offered partial protection against the adverse effects of technological changes.

Nonetheless, while technology is not destiny, the job of protective institutions is easier when we have technological tailwinds instead of headwinds. Although pronouncements about the impact of generative artificial intelligence (AI) on the labor market is often apocalyptic, the reality is more complicated. Unlike earlier waves of automation and computerization, which tended to exacerbate inequality, generative AI has the *potential* to go in a different direction. For instance, the introduction of large language models allows us to communicate with computers with far less technical training, reducing the pressure to bid up pay for those with greater capabilities and credentials.

In a sense, AI could play the role of the superstar effect in reverse. A number of experiments have shown that the adoption of AI tends to help "normies" catch up to "star" performers, acting as a force multiplier for regular workers.[15] This could help partially erase some of the advantages that accrue to the highly skilled or the fortunate, promoting a more equitable distribution of benefits from technological advancements. Echoing these sentiments, the economist David Autor wrote: "AI, if used well, can assist with restoring the middle-skill, middle-class heart of the U.S. labor market that has been hollowed out by automation and globalization."[16]

To be sure, it is important not to be overly optimistic about AI, given the early stages of its development. Researchers have diverse and nuanced views on the potential impact of AI, with some, like Autor's MIT colleague Daron Acemoglu, adopting a skeptical stance about the extent of productivity gains.[17] The risks are real: Firms may cut back on hiring on the assumption that AI will quickly boost efficiency; or an exuberant investment boom could overshoot and end in a correction with broader macroeconomic fallout. And as with any disruptive technology, there will be winners and losers in the labor market. Even so, it is reasonable to suggest that the inequality-promoting technological headwinds, however strong they have been, may be calming in the near term. At least in *relative* terms, technological change may not keep nudging demand away from blue-collar roles.

But none of this guarantees that workers, as a whole, will automatically share in whatever productivity gains AI delivers. Without countervailing institutions, a larger share of the gains can flow to the owners of capital and dominant platforms. As Acemoglu and Simon Johnson put it, "Wages are unlikely to rise when workers cannot push for their share of productivity growth. Today, artificial intelligence may boost average productivity, but . . . the impact of automation on workers today is more complex than an automatic linkage from higher productivity to better wages."[18] That's why the kind of institutional changes I argue for in this book, like sectoral standards, matter in the age of AI: They help translate productivity growth into broadly shared wage gains, rather than letting the benefits pool at the top.

A Focus on Pre-Distribution

Between 1980 and the 2007 financial crisis, American policymakers, and their economic advisers, often tried to avoid direct intervention in market outcomes. The prevailing belief was that markets should be left to operate freely unless there were clear external harms, such as pollution, that required regulation. When markets produced excessive inequality or low wages, the proposed remedy—though not always enacted—was typically to address these issues through targeted transfers and the tax system, such as the Earned Income Tax Credit. This emphasis on after-the-fact redistribution reflected a deeper assumption: that markets were fundamentally competitive and governed by supply and demand, leaving little room for structural imbalances or social influences on wages.

As it turns out, many Americans favor *pre-distribution* policies—those that shape market outcomes directly—over purely redistributive approaches. Research by Ilyana Kuziemko and colleagues shows that a clear majority of voters support policies that boost pay at the outset, such as raising the minimum wage, guaranteeing jobs, and adopting trade policies that protect domestic employment. In contrast, policies aimed at compensating the losers from globalization or institutional change—typically through welfare spending—attract support from only about a third of voters. This preference for pre-distribution is especially strong among those without a college degree, while higher-income college graduates are more likely to back tax-and-transfer solutions. Notably, the Democratic Party's shift in the 1980s away from pre-distribution and toward redistribution appears to have contributed to the erosion of support among non-college-educated voters.[19]

The idea of "let markets work, and redistribute as necessary" may be unpopular among lower- and middle-income Americans, but is it flawed? This approach aligns with the view that markets are highly competitive and largely self-regulating, leaving little room for power imbalances, norms, or other social forces to influence outcomes. However, in the real world, where markets are often imperfect and riddled with power dynamics, this view can lead to ineffective or misguided policies.

The changing consensus on minimum wages illustrates how better evidence and a deeper understanding of labor market dynamics have shifted perspectives. The Great Financial Crisis of 2007–2009 and the ensuing economic downturn further highlighted the vulnerabilities of markets, particularly how they can break down and cause widespread harm when left unchecked. This experience underscored the importance of countercyclical policies, fiscal stimulus, and prudential regulation of the financial sector. Yet, the measures implemented in response to the Great Financial Crisis, such as the countercyclical fiscal stimulus of the 2009 American Recovery and Reinvestment Act, were often too modest, resulting in prolonged high unemployment, a weakened job ladder, and a less competitive labor market. As a result, workers were too often stuck in low-paying jobs, unable to quit and move to better-paying, higher-productivity positions.

However, the lessons from the Great Financial Crisis were learned, and during the pandemic, there was a much greater willingness to use countercyclical policies to mitigate economic harm. While the pandemic-era economic context was complicated by supply bottlenecks and a global burst of inflation during 2021–2023, America uniquely experienced substantial real wage gains among G7 countries. This experience clearly demonstrates the critical role of macroeconomic policies in fostering tight labor markets and broad-based prosperity. Going forward, it will be vital for us collectively to remember these valuable lessons and have the political will to enact policies to prevent unnecessary mass deprivation.

There is reason to believe that the pursuit of full employment *can* transcend partisan politics. Both Democrats and Republicans have recognized its benefits in recent years, at least at times. In 2021, President Joe Biden declared, "We are aiming for full employment, and that means keeping our pace on job growth, including for Black, Hispanic, and Asian workers." In 2024, vice presidential candidate Senator J. D. Vance echoed a similar sentiment, stating, "President Trump believes very strongly that the best way to promote raising Americans' wages is with tight labor markets—when an employer has to pay a good wage to attract the right people."[20] Despite their many differences, both sides of the political spectrum have, from time to time, shown an awareness of the value of a hot labor market. It will be enormously important to keep pushing on this, because full employment is a key pillar for strong wage growth for working and middle-class Americans. This is particularly true because the wage gains and compression associated with tight labor markets are not just egalitarian: They represent a more efficient allocation of labor, offering a double dividend.

And it is not just fiscal or monetary policy. The growing acceptance of targeted industrial policies—be it to achieve supply chain resilience, manage energy transition, or bolster national security—also reflects a broader recognition that globalization can have more nuanced and potentially harmful effects than was acknowledged in elite circles during the 1980s and 1990s. This broader rethinking of market governance now extends to wage policy itself. In 2025, Senator Josh Hawley (R-MO) became the first Republican senator in recent memory to back a significant increase in the federal minimum wage, co-sponsoring a bill to raise it to $15 by 2026. As he put it: "For decades, working Americans have seen their wages flatline. One major culprit of this is the failure of the federal minimum wage to keep up with the economic reality facing hard-working Americans every day."

While the increased political space for pre-distribution does not necessarily guarantee the implementation of policies that enhance middle- and working-class incomes, it does open the door for effective interventions. Let's be clear: Poorly designed market interventions—such as indiscriminate tariffs—can backfire and harm living standards, possibly reducing appetite for smarter interventions. But a broader willingness to shape market outcomes, including guiding technological change and being more attentive to the risks faced by middle- and low-income workers, including those stemming from trade, can help guard against policies that erode wages or undercut good jobs.

In sum, the focus on pre-distribution marks a shift toward influencing market outcomes directly, reflecting a broader understanding of the limitations of relying solely on redistribution after the fact. As economic realities and public preferences evolve, there is growing recognition of the need for proactive policies that address inequality and wage stagnation at their source. As we've seen, when unregulated markets are riddled with power imbalances and imperfections, interventions in the market motivated by distributive concerns can also end up improving market performance. In this sense, a predistributive approach can complement efforts to expand the economy's capacity to deliver broadly shared prosperity—or "abundance," as journalists Ezra Klein and Derek Thompson put it in their 2025 book of the same name, *Abundance*.[21]

Change for the Future

As we look ahead, it's clear that both economic headwinds and tailwinds will continue to shape the landscape of labor markets and wage standards. However, the path to ensuring shared prosperity lies not just in reacting to these forces but in proactively enacting institutional reforms that can provide long-term security and well-being for workers. One of the most promising avenues for such reform is the revision of our collective bargaining system. Moving toward sectoral bargaining, where contracts are negotiated at the industry level and extended across all firms in that sector, is a goal worth pursuing. This approach has historically provided better protection against economic shocks and helped maintain more equitable wage structures.

However, achieving such a fundamental change in the United States is politically challenging, particularly given the current legal and political landscape. A few voices on the political right—such as Oren Cass, founder of the think tank American Compass, and Sohrab Ahmari, author of *Tyranny, Inc.*, who has argued for curbing private power and rebuilding worker leverage—have voiced support for sectoral bargaining.[22] Still, reforming the National Labor Relations Act to make sectoral bargaining viable would require substantial political will and a broad consensus—a heavy lift. In the meantime, there are other paths we can take to build on recent successes. For example, the expansion of state-level minimum wages has proven effective in raising the wage floor for many workers, and there is growing interest in establishing wage boards to set sectoral standards for specific industries.

The care sector—encompassing healthcare, childcare, and education—is particularly well suited for pilot programs that set pay standards by job types. These sectors are essential to the functioning of society, yet they often suffer from low pay and inadequate working conditions.[23] By implementing sector-specific wage standards, coupled with training programs and supply-side reforms, we can begin to address these issues in a meaningful way. The success of such programs would not only improve the lives of workers in these sectors but could also serve as a model for broader application across other industries.

As we've seen, policies like minimum wage increases and unionization efforts can have positive productivity offsets. For example, higher wages can lead to lower turnover rates, increased worker morale, and better overall performance. Encouraging complementary institutions that facilitate these benefits can amplify the positive effects of wage policies. However, we also must be clear-eyed about their limitations. Policies that affect workers toward the middle of the pay scale can have a greater impact on overall production costs, particularly in sectors where a significant share of costs are absorbed as public expenditures. In these cases, higher taxes or price levels may be necessary to support fair wages, but this is a trade-off that many voters seem willing to accept in pursuit of greater equity.

In other words, while the opportunities ahead for rebuilding the labor market are significant, we must also acknowledge the limits of what any given reform can achieve. This is where openness to evidence and a willingness to experiment become crucial. As we develop and implement new policies—whether in monetary policy, sectoral standards, or national minimum wages—we should be guided by the best available evidence, knowing that not every policy will succeed as intended. This approach demands a commitment to continuous evaluation and adaptation, learning from both our successes and our failures.

Just as we need to guard against negativity bias—overlooking positive developments—we must also be wary of confirmation bias. Becoming too attached to a single approach can make it hard to recognize when it's not working, even as evidence mounts against it. In those moments, it's crucial to remember that in the pursuit of shared prosperity, we have many tools at our disposal. We should never hesitate to abandon what isn't effective, because holding on to failure only stands in the way of progress.

The key to long-term success lies in understanding that no single policy or approach will solve the complex challenges we face. Figure 8.1 lays out the big picture about how to think about the policy tools in our tool kit. Micro-level interventions—like improving wage policies within individual firms—can make an immediate and meaningful difference for workers on the ground, particularly those at the bottom of the pay scale, with some spillover benefits for middle-income earners. At the macro level, policies that prioritize full employment and promote wage growth have broad effects across the labor market, though they, too, tend to benefit lower-wage workers the most. Finally, at the meso level, minimum wage policies can create broader standards across industries, again providing crucial support to low-wage earners. Wage boards, however, offer a more powerful mechanism for raising pay among middle-income workers. In short, we must utilize all three levels—micro, macro, and meso—strategically and in concert, to build a truly inclusive and sustainable labor market. Relying on any one pillar alone will not be enough to get the job done.

The arc of the American economy has been complex. Amid incredible prosperity over the past century, we have experienced both significant challenges and great successes. Over the past half century, we've witnessed rising overall productivity, but wage growth has lagged too often and disparities have widened. And yet, in recent

	Low-wage	*Middle-wage*	*High-wage*
Voluntary minimum wage	Moderate	Weak	
Statutory minimum wage	Strong		
Sectoral standards	Moderate	Strong	
Tight labor market	Strong	Moderate	Weak

FIGURE 8.1 **EXPECTED IMPACT OF DIFFERENT APPROACHES TO REBUILDING THE WAGE STANDARD ON DIFFERENT GROUPS OF WORKERS**

years, we have made encouraging strides in rebuilding the wage standard—raising wages for low- and middle-income workers.

That is not a sign that our work is done. The vast amount of data we have amassed, and the evidence from a wide range of policies and institutions, give us the tools to keep moving forward; what matters is how effectively we use them. Some of the green shoots documented in this book—especially those tied to a tight labor market—remain fragile and at risk even now. The choices we make today will determine whether we build an economy that truly works for everyone.

Our future depends on it.

Acknowledgments

A book like this draws on conversations, collaborations, and acts of generosity that stretch over many years. Far more friends, colleagues, students, and mentors have shaped it than I can name here, but I hope each of you sees traces of your influence in these pages.

When I wrestle with an economic idea, I often ask how my doctoral adviser, Richard Freeman, would explain it. Richard, thank you for the guidance that still shapes how I think and write.

Five collaborators deserve special mention. Working with Ethan Kaplan, Attila Lindner, Suresh Naidu, Michael Reich, and Ben Zipperer has informed much of the research and ideas that anchor this book: I am grateful for your insight and support over the years.

Thanks to Margo Fleming, who kept nudging me to write for a broader audience, and to Cassidy Sachs, whose steady editorial guidance sharpened each draft. I also wish to recognize Akash Bhatt and Annie McGrew for their exceptional research assistance.

My deepest gratitude belongs to my family. To my partner, Kelly Turley: Your encouragement, wise counsel, and incisive comments turned many late nights into lighter ones. To my parents, Syamalima and Dipak Dube: Your enduring belief in this project—and the generous practical help that came with it—made finishing the book possible. To my sister and occasional coauthor, Oeindrila Dube: Our conversations and your insights continually pushed my thinking forward. And to my amazing children, Amaya and Kiran: You remind me every day why creating a fairer world of work matters. May your generation inherit workplaces that honor your talents with dignity.

This book is dedicated to the late Frank Morley, an outsourced janitor I met while visiting Harvard as a graduate student. He was also an invaluable member of the Harvard Living Wage Campaign. Frank's quiet persistence helped raise standards for more than a thousand workers on campus, and showed that change often begins with those who refuse to stay invisible.

To everyone mentioned—and to the many unnamed, but not forgotten—thank you.

APPENDIX A

Econ-Speak and Other Jargon, Decoded

Difference in Differences (DiD)

Difference in differences is a statistical method that compares the "before and after" changes in two groups, one exposed to a policy (or event) and one not exposed. By subtracting the change observed in the unaffected group from the change in the affected group, DiD helps filter out broader trends and pin down the specific impact of the policy or event, offering a clearer picture of cause and effect. Chapter 6 discussed use of DiD to quantify the effect of minimum wages on pay, jobs, and other outcomes.

Economic Rent

Economic rent is the extra benefit someone—like a worker or a company—gets from a situation compared to their next best alternative. For example, a company might earn unusually high profits because it has market power. Sometimes firms share these rents with workers (rent-sharing), which can raise wages—but if only some groups benefit, it can also deepen inequality. When powerful actors limit competition or lobby for special treatment to protect those gains, it's called rent-seeking.

Elasticity

Elasticity measures how responsive one variable is to changes in another in percentage terms. In labor economics, it is often used to describe how workers alter their labor supply, or how firms change their labor demand when wages shift. For example, a 10 percent wage increase that leads to a 15 percent drop in labor demanded implies a labor demand elasticity of –1.5. These sensitivities matter because they predict how quickly workers and employers will adjust to shifts in wages, policies, or economic conditions. Chapter 3 showed how the elasticity of quits to wages measures labor market power, and chapter 6 used the elasticity of employment with respect to wage hikes from minimum wages (*own-wage elasticity*) to quantify how the policy affects jobs.

Field Experiment

Field experiments are real-world randomized controlled trials that introduce a specific treatment or policy to actual people in everyday settings. Because they occur in natural conditions rather than labs, field experiments can more convincingly demonstrate cause-and-effect relationships in practical contexts. In chapter 3, we encountered such randomization of pay, which helped estimate monopsony power in the context of public sector hiring as well as in the gig economy.

Instrumental Variables (IV)

Instrumental variables help tease out cause-and-effect relationships when it's hard to tell what's really driving what. The key is to find an "instrument"—something that influences the factor you're interested in (like years of schooling or unionization) but doesn't directly affect the outcome (like wages or inequality), except through that channel. In chapter 4, we looked at how the IV method was used to study the effect of unionization on inequality, using things like wartime government spending—which somewhat randomly boosted union membership in some sectors and locations but not others—as an instrument.

Kaitz Index

The Kaitz index is calculated by dividing the minimum wage by a broader wage benchmark, like the median wage. As the Kaitz index gets closer to 1, it indicates that the minimum wage is probably raising pay more for low-wage workers—but if it's too high, it might harm hiring. So, this index is a quick way to gauge how "binding" the minimum wage is in a given labor market. In chapter 6, we saw that in high-income countries, the minimum wage is on average around 61 percent of the median wage (a Kaitz index of 0.61). The United States falls short of that standard—both nationally and in all states individually.

Marginal Product of Labor

The marginal product of labor shows how much additional output (or revenue) a firm gains by hiring one more worker or adding an extra hour of labor. Because firms generally pay wages based on the value of the output an additional worker can produce, this concept underlies wage determination. In a perfectly competitive labor market, the wage is equal to the marginal product. In contrast, in a market where employers have market power (*monopsony*), the wage is typically below the marginal product.

Marginal Tax Rate (MTR)

The marginal tax rate is the share of tax you pay on each additional dollar of income. For example, if your MTR is 25 percent, then for every extra $1, you keep 75 cents. This matters because it shapes decisions about whether to work extra hours, take a promotion, or negotiate for higher pay. It's different from the *average tax rate*, which is the total tax you pay divided by your total income. With progressive income taxation, a higher income tends to mean a higher MTR. So, most people's average tax rate is lower than their marginal tax rate because lower portions of their income are taxed at lower rates. The marginal rate is thought to influence behavior "at the margin," since it determines how much of the next dollar earned you actually keep.

Measures of Inequality: 90–10, 50–10, 90–50

These metrics track how wages or incomes are distributed across different segments of the population. The 90–10 ratio compares high earners (at the 90th percentile) to low earners (at the 10th percentile), offering a broad measure of overall inequality. The 50–10 ratio focuses on the lower half of the distribution by comparing the median wage to the bottom, while the 90–50 ratio captures inequality in the upper half by comparing top earners to the median. In some cases, depending on the data source, I report ratios of deciles—such as the 9th to 1st decile—which are closely related to percentile-based measures like the 90–10 ratio. Taken together, these indicators show who is pulling ahead, who is falling behind, and how these patterns shift over time. The Economic Policy Institute regularly updates U.S. data on inflation-adjusted wage percentiles and ratios here: https://data.epi.org/#wages. International comparisons from the OECD can be found by searching "Decile ratios of gross earnings" in https://data-explorer.oecd.org.

Monopsony Power

Monopsony power in labor markets refers to a situation where employers have significant power to set wages, as workers have limited alternatives. This can happen because markets are concentrated with a relatively few employers. It can also happen due to search frictions, which makes it difficult for workers to find better alternatives. Finally, monopsony power also arises from workers valuing the same job somewhat differently, which also makes it harder for some workers to change jobs. In such markets, employers can keep wages lower than they would be under full competition, since workers cannot easily switch to other firms. We reviewed the empirical evidence on monopsony power in chapter 2. We also saw how tight labor markets can reduce monopsony power in chapter 3. Finally, in chapter 6 we discussed how with monopsony power, a higher minimum wage could have positive effects on jobs by improving recruitment and retention, different from a simple supply/demand model.

Multi-Armed Bandit Problem

The multi-armed bandit is a classic decision problem in statistics and computer science about learning while doing. Picture a row of slot machines ("arms"), each with an unknown payout. You want to maximize total winnings over time, which means balancing two goals: *explore* (try different arms to learn their payouts) and *exploit* (pull the arm that currently looks best). Because information arrives sequentially, good strategies keep testing alternatives—just enough—while shifting play toward the better performers as confidence grows. For policy, this means setting measurable pilots (e.g., different minimum wage levels), monitoring outcomes, and ratcheting toward what works. Sometimes, this entails trying out (and then pulling back on) policies that end up not working, because accepting some short-term "regret" (foregone gains while experimenting) helps achieve better long-run results.

Natural Experiment

Natural experiments happen when external events—like a sudden policy shift or economic shock—impact one group but not another in a way that resembles a controlled experiment. For example, if one local area gets more federal government contracts than others, or if a large employer like Amazon or Walmart unexpectedly introduces a company-wide wage floor, or one state raises its minimum wage while another does not, researchers can estimate the impact by comparing outcomes across affected and unaffected groups. Because these changes aren't caused by the outcomes being studied, they offer a kind of accidental but powerful test of cause and effect in the real world.

Quit Elasticity

Quit elasticity measures how likely workers are to leave their current jobs in response to wage changes. If quit elasticity is high, workers quickly move to better-paying opportunities, prompting employers to raise wages to retain staff. A low quit elasticity implies workers are less responsive to wage differences, indicating that employers have considerable wage-setting (*monopsony*) power. We looked more deeply into the quit elasticity and reviewed the empirical estimates in chapter 2.

Real Wage

Real wages reflect the actual purchasing power of a worker's paycheck, accounting for how inflation affects the prices of goods and services. If prices rise but the nominal paycheck stays the same, a worker's real wage falls because that paycheck buys less. Tracking real wages helps us see whether people's living standards are genuinely improving or declining over time, beyond the raw dollar amount on their pay stubs.

To compare dollar amounts over time, I adjust for inflation using a version of the Consumer Price Index (CPI) that blends together four different series. The best option is the *chained CPI*, which does a better job than other variants in accounting for how people actually change their spending when prices shift; but it's only available from 2000 onward. For earlier years, I use the CPI-U-RS (1978–1999), which fixes some problems with how inflation was measured in the past; the CPI-U-X1 for 1967–1977; and the regular CPI-U for years before that. This "stitched together" measure is also used by the U.S. Census Bureau and maintained by the Economic Policy Institute: https://data.epi.org/#prices.

Tightness

Tightness describes how easy it is for workers to find a job. It's often measured by the ratio of job openings to unemployed people. When the labor market is tight—meaning there are lots of openings and fewer job seekers—workers have more leverage, which tends to raise wages and improve working conditions. Other useful measures of tightness include the unemployment rate and the quit rate, since high quit rates usually signal that workers have better options. In chapter 3, we saw how tight labor markets helped boost pay at the bottom and reduce inequality. A tighter labor market can also channel workers to more productive workplaces, improving the functioning of the economy.

Tradable Versus Non-Tradable Sectors

Tradable sectors produce goods and services that can be sold across regions or countries, like cars, electronics, or software. Non-tradable sectors are rooted locally—jobs in healthcare, education, retail, or restaurants can't *usually* be imported from elsewhere. This matters for wage policy because businesses in tradable sectors face global competition and have less room to raise prices when wages rise. In non-tradable sectors, firms can more easily pass on higher labor costs to local customers, making floors more sustainable. That's why minimum wages or sectoral standards often are most effective in locally anchored industries.

U-Star (U*)

U-star (often the "natural rate of unemployment") is the unemployment level at which inflation remains stable over the long run, reflecting structural aspects of the economy—like demographics, skill distributions, and technological factors—rather than short-term business cycles. Economists and policymakers watch U* to gauge whether the labor market is running "too hot" (potentially driving inflation up) or "too cold" (wasting potential labor resources).

Five Equations That Explain How Wages Are Set

Here are five key equations that economists use to describe how workers' wages are determined, how employers decide how many people to hire, and how policies or market conditions can shift these outcomes. We'll keep the math light and focus on the big picture.

1. The Mincer Earnings Function[1]

$$ln(Wage) = \alpha + \beta 1 \times (Years\ of\ Education) + \beta 2 \times (Work\ Experience) + e$$

What it means: This statistical model of earnings says that (the natural logarithm of) your wage depends on your years of education, work experience, and potentially other individual-level traits—such as training or test scores. Each additional year of education or experience is associated with a higher wage. The error term, *e*, captures everything else—some of it personal (like unmeasured skills) and some related to external factors (like the wage policies of your employer, as discussed in this book).

Why it matters: This is one of the most widely used equations in labor economics. It helps show how human capital—education and experience—affects earnings. But it also highlights what's missing, such as employer practices or broader labor market structures. In chapters 2 and 3, we used this framework to measure industry wage premiums—that is, the wage differences across industries after controlling for education, demographics, and location. It can be used to quantify job quality by holding worker characteristics constant.

2. Wage-Productivity Relationship under Competition

$$Wage = MRPL(L)$$

In words: In a perfectly competitive labor market, there is a going competitive market wage at which rate a firm can hire as many laborers (*L*) as it wishes. A profit-maximizing company will keep hiring labor at that wage as long as each new worker brings in (in extra revenue) at least as much as that worker costs in wages. *Marginal revenue product of labor* (*MRPL*) means how much extra revenue the next hire generates. As more workers are hired, each additional worker brings in incrementally lower revenue due to the law of diminishing returns—so *MRPL*(*L*) falls as more workers (*L*) are hired.

Why it matters: This is the basic principle of how employers decide the "right" number of employees to keep on the payroll in a competitive market, where there is a going market wage, *W*, at which employers can hire as many workers as they wish. When all employers do this, competition ensures that wages of all workers are equated to their contribution to the economy, i.e., the *MRPL*. This is the essence of what a competitive labor market looks like: Demand for labor is determined by the *MRPL* and is equated to the supply of labor at the market wage, which ensures supply/demand balance and that each worker is paid their marginal product.

3. Elasticity of Labor Supply to a Firm

$$\varepsilon_s = \frac{\%\Delta(\text{Labor Supply to a Firm})}{\%\Delta(Wage)}$$

In words: Under *monopsony*, employers do not face a single market wage. Instead, the higher the wage they offer, the more workers they can recruit and retain. The firm's labor-supply elasticity measures how responsive its workforce is to its wage. For example, if a 10 percent wage increase raises the number of workers (or hours supplied) by 20 percent, the elasticity is 2. This elasticity has two components: a recruitment elasticity (attracting new hires) and a quit or separation elasticity (improving retention). The total elasticity equals the sum of these two magnitudes (in absolute value). This total elasticity is sometimes approximated as roughly twice the magnitude of the quit elasticity.

Why it matters: If labor supply is very elastic (workers respond strongly to small wage changes), then small pay raises can bring in a lot of new workers. This means the labor market is highly competitive, and employers have very limited scope for determining wages. If it's inelastic (workers barely respond), then raising wages doesn't do much to attract people. This indicates a highly monopsonistic market, where employers have a lot of scope to set wages.

4. Monopsony Wage Markdown

$$Wage = MRPL \times \frac{\varepsilon_s}{1+\varepsilon_s}$$

In words: Under monopsonistic conditions, where employers have some scope to set wages, the employment-wage trade-off is captured by the elasticity of labor supply to the firm, ε_s. Given this elasticity, a profit-maximizing firm will now wish to set wages using this markdown formula, leading workers to get paid less than what they contribute in revenue—their *marginal revenue product of labor* (*MRPL*)—because the employer has monopsony power. For example, if $\varepsilon_s = 4$, the wage will be equal to 80 percent (⅘) of the *MRPL*. If $\varepsilon_s = 2$, then it will be 67 percent (⅔) of the *MRPL*.

Why it matters: In a competitive market, the wage equals the marginal revenue product of labor. But in a monopsonistic setting, the firm can "mark down" the wage, capturing some of the value that workers create.

5. Own-Wage Elasticity (from a Change in Minimum Wage)

$$OWE = \frac{\%\Delta E}{\%\Delta W}$$

In words: The *own-wage elasticity* (OWE) tells us how much employment for a group of workers changes when their wages go up due to a minimum wage hike. It's calculated by dividing the percentage change in employment caused by the minimum wage hike $\%\Delta E$ by the percentage change in average wages for the same group $\%\Delta W$.

Why it matters: This helps us understand the trade-off between higher wages and potential job loss. If OWE = –1, that means job losses completely cancel out the wage gains—so total earnings for the group don't change. But if OWE = –0.1, for example, total earnings still go up a lot: Workers lose a little in employment but gain much more in wages. More generally, if $OWE = e$, total earnings rise by $(1 + e) \times 100\%$ compared to a scenario with no job losses.

We focus on total earnings of all low-wage workers because it aligns closely with how individual workers experience wage changes. If wages rise by 10 percent while the number of jobs declines by 1 percent, most workers will spend about 1 percent more time unemployed but earn 10 percent more when employed—an overall 9 percent increase in their typical earnings.

Finally, although the exact thresholds are somewhat arbitrary, OWE values less negative than –0.4 should be seen as small, those between –0.4 and –0.8 as medium, and those more negative than

–0.8 as large. In chapter 6, we reviewed dozens of studies and found that the typical OWE is around –0.11—suggesting that minimum wage hikes usually lead to only modest job reductions. You can explore an up-to-date collection of OWE estimates from minimum wage studies here: https://economic.github.io/owe/.

Notes

Chapter 1: A Raise Deferred

1. Throughout the book, whenever I refer to how much something costs or how much someone earns, I'm using inflation-adjusted figures—in 2023 dollars—unless otherwise noted. This helps make comparisons across time clearer and reflects the real value of money. To adjust for inflation, I use the extended chained Consumer Price Index (CPI), which stitches together four CPI series for consistency over time. The primary index is the chained CPI, available from 2000 onward. For 1978 to 2000, I use the CPI-U-RS (with "RS" standing for "research series"), which corrects for methodological issues that had caused earlier versions of the CPI to overstate inflation. For earlier periods, I rely on the CPI-U-X1 (1967–1977) and the standard CPI (pre-1966). This blended CPI approach is also used by the U.S. Census Bureau in their historical income series, and the data is maintained and regularly updated by the Economic Policy Institute (EPI): https://data.epi.org/#prices.
2. In this book, I measure overall productivity growth using an inflation adjustment that makes it directly comparable to wage growth. Wages are typically adjusted using the Consumer Price Index, and I follow the same approach in *The Wage Standard*, specifically using the extended chained CPI described in the previous note. By contrast, the Bureau of Economic Analysis adjusts productivity using the GDP price deflator.

These two indices differ in how they weigh goods and services and how they account for consumer substitution during inflationary periods.

Between 1980 and 2019, the CPI rose by 181 percent, while the GDP deflator increased by 164 percent. This discrepancy affects estimates of real productivity growth: Using the GDP deflator, productivity rose by 84 percent over this period. However, because the wage and productivity measures rely on different inflation adjustments, it wouldn't be meaningful to compare them directly.

To make them comparable, I adjust the productivity estimate to reflect CPI-based inflation. Specifically, I scale the 84 percent productivity growth by the ratio of CPI to GDP deflator growth: 1.84 × (2.64 / 2.81) = 1.73. This implies a 73 percent increase in what we can call "consumable productivity," as shown in figure 1.1. This type of alignment—adjusting productivity growth to match the inflation basis used for wages—is now also used by the EPI in their comparisons of productivity and pay trends: https://www.epi.org/productivity-pay-gap/.

3. In 2023, GDP per capita after adjusting for cost-of-living differences was around $75,000 in America, while for Estonia and Poland it was $42,000 and $44,000, respectively. World Bank (2023)—with minor processing by Our World in Data. Retrieved June 11, 2025, from https://ourworldindata.org/grapher/gdp-per-capita-worldbank.
4. Here both productivity and wages are adjusted for inflation using the extended chained CPI.
5. Calculated using earnings data from the 1980 and 2019 Current Population Survey micro data for hourly workers in Retail Trade. Current Population Survey Extracts, Version 2025.5.8, Economic Policy Institute, May 8, 2025, https://microdata.epi.org.
6. Data on wages at the 10th, 50th, 90th, and 95th percentiles come from the Economic Policy Institute's State of Working America Data Library, which is based on Current Population Survey (CPS) Outgoing Rotation Group (ORG) data. Source: https://data.epi.org/#wages. "Productivity" refers to economy-wide hourly labor productivity, net of capital depreciation. It is calculated by dividing net domestic product (NDP) by total hours worked. While NDP and other output measures like GDP

are typically adjusted for inflation using the GDP deflator, here we use a "consumable productivity" measure that applies the same extended chained CPI used to deflate wages—ensuring a consistent, apples-to-apples comparison. https://www.epi.org/productivity-pay-gap/.

7. Calculated using earnings data from 1980 and 2019 CPS data micro data for all workers. Current Population Survey Extracts, Version 2025.5.8, Economic Policy Institute.
8. Lawrence Mishel, "Growing Inequalities, Reflecting Growing Employer Power, Have Generated a Productivity–Pay Gap Since 1979: Productivity Has Grown 3.5 Times as Much as Pay for the Typical Worker," *Working Economics Blog,* Economic Policy Institute, September 2, 2021, https://www.epi.org/blog/growing-inequalities-reflecting-growing-employer-power-have-generated-a-productivity-pay-gap-since-1979-productivity-has-grown-3-5-times-as-much-as-pay-for-the-typical-worker/.
9. According to the Economic Policy Institute's State of Working America Data Library, which uses CPS ORG data, the real average wage (2023 dollars) in 1980 was $22.04 and in 2019 was $31.34.
10. For example, the Personal Consumption Expenditures (PCE) index offers an alternative way to measure inflation compared to the chained Consumer Price Index (CPI), which is used throughout much of this book. The PCE assigns different weights to categories of consumer spending—for instance, it gives less weight to housing costs. In addition, the chained CPI only goes back to 2000. For earlier years, we rely on the CPI-U-RS series, which makes different assumptions than the PCE about how consumers respond to price changes. Each method has its advantages and limitations. Overall, the PCE shows lower inflation since the 1970s than the CPI does. Using the PCE to adjust for inflation, median real wages would have risen by about 30 percent between 1980 and 2019—more than the 23 percent increase suggested by the CPI. That may sound more encouraging, but it doesn't change the broader picture: The PCE also implies that consumable productivity rose by 83 percent over the same period, compared to 73 percent using the CPI. In both cases, median wages rose by only about one-third as much as productivity. However we measure

inflation, the conclusion remains the same: Typical workers' pay has not kept up with the growth in the American economy.

11. See the EPI's compilation of Social Security data at: https://data.epi.org/wages/annual_wage_ssa/line/year/national/real_annual_wage_ssa_2023/ssa_wage.

    Note that the *annual* earnings growth for the bottom 90 percent is somewhat larger than the *hourly* wage growth for the bottom 90 percent reported earlier. This reflects change in annual hours worked, a somewhat different composition of the bottom 90 percent in each category, as well as different data sources being used (CPS data for hourly wages versus Social Security data for annual earnings).
12. Data is from the Congressional Budget Office's November 2023 report on "The Distribution of Household Income in 2020," available at www.cbo.gov/publication/59509. While CBO adjusts income for inflation using the PCE price index, the estimates in this book are adjusted using the extended chained CPI price index.
13. The fact that household income growth at all percentiles exceeds hourly productivity growth may seem puzzling. The explanation is straightforward: Compared to 1980, households today work more hours in paid employment, largely because of increased labor force participation among women.
14. Gerald Auten and David Splinter, "Income Inequality in the United States: Using Tax Data to Measure Long-Term Trends," *Journal of Political Economy* 132, no. 7 (2024): 2179–227.
15. Thomas Piketty, Emmanuel Saez, and Gabriel Zucman, "Distributional National Accounts: Methods and Estimates for the United States," *Quarterly Journal of Economics* 133, no. 2 (2018): 553–609; Thomas Piketty, Emmanual Saez, and Gabriel Zucman, "Comment on Auten and Splinter (2023)," Technical Note No. 2023/09, World Inequality Lab, December 13, 2023.
16. Daron Acemoglu, "Clarifying America's Great Inequality Debate," Project Syndicate, January 3, 2024, https://www.project-syndicate.org/commentary/inequality-different-metrics-but-larger-trend-still-a-problem-by-daron-acemoglu-2024-01.
17. Paul Krugman, *The Conscience of a Liberal* (W. W. Norton, 2007).

18. Thomas Piketty and Emmanuel Saez, "Income Inequality in the United States, 1913–1998," *Quarterly Journal of Economics* 118, no. 1 (2003): 1–41. See also Matthew Smith, Danny Yagan, Owen Zidar, and Eric Zwick, "Capitalists in the Twenty-First Century," *Quarterly Journal of Economics* 134, no. 4 (2019): 1675–745.
19. Data on the ratio of the 9th and 1st wage deciles for different countries comes from OECD. I take the log of this ratio, and calculate differences across years. "Decile Ratios of Gross Earnings," OECD, https://data-explorer.oecd.org.
20. For productivity sources, see note 6 from this chapter. Data on median wages come from the Economic Policy Institute's State of Working America Data Library, which relies on Current Population Survey (CPS) Outgoing Rotation Group (ORG) data. For average non-managerial wages, we use the average wage of production and nonsupervisory workers starting in 1964. Prior to 1964, average wage data are only available for production and nonsupervisory workers in the manufacturing sector. To estimate average wages for all non-managerial workers before 1964, we calculate year-to-year wage growth for manufacturing workers and assume that overall non-managerial wages grew at the same rate. This method allows us to backfill average non-managerial wages from 1948 to 1963.

    Sources: U.S. Bureau of Labor Statistics, "Average Hourly Earnings of Production and Nonsupervisory Employees, Manufacturing (CES3000000008)," Federal Reserve Bank of St. Louis, accessed June 5, 2024, https://fred.stlouisfed.org/series/CES3000000008.

    U.S. Bureau of Labor Statistics, "Average Hourly Earnings of Production and Nonsupervisory Employees, Total Private (CEU0500000008)," Federal Reserve Bank of St. Louis, accessed June 5, 2024, https://fred.stlouisfed.org/series/CEU0500000008.

    Compensation estimates are from the EPI, which adjusts Bureau of Labor Statistics wage data using the ratio of compensation to wage-and-salary income reported in the Bureau of Economic Analysis's National Income and Product Accounts. https://www.epi.org/productivity-pay-gap/.
21. Between 1980 and 2019, real hourly compensation for non-managerial

workers grew by 27 percent, as compared to 22 percent growth in their wages. (See note 20 from this chapter for sources.) Wage data come from the Bureau of Labor Statistics, retrieved via FRED, Federal Reserve Bank of St. Louis, https://fred.stlouisfed.org/series/CES0500000006.

22. From 1951 to 1980, Social Security earnings grew 1.5 percent a year for the bottom 90 percent and 2.0 percent for the top 1 percent. From 1980 to 2019, growth slowed to 0.9 percent annually for the bottom 90 percent, while the top 1 percent rose 2.6 percent a year. Economic Policy Institute, State of Working America Data Library, "Annual wages for select wage groups - Average real annual wage (2023$)," 2025, https://data.epi.org/wages/annual_wage_ssa/line/year/national/real_annual_wage_ssa_2023/ssa_wage.
23. David H. Autor and David Dorn, "The Growth of Low-Skill Service Jobs and the Polarization of the U.S. Labor Market," *American Economic Review* 103, no. 5 (2013): 1553–97; Daron Acemoglu and Pascual Restrepo, "Robots and Jobs: Evidence from U.S. Labor Markets," *Journal of Political Economy* 128, no. 6 (2020): 2188–2244.
24. Claudia Dale Goldin and Lawrence F. Katz, *The Race between Education and Technology* (Harvard University Press, 2008).
25. For evidence on the China shock, see David H. Autor, David Dorn, and Gordon H. Hanson, "The China Shock: Learning from Labor-Market Adjustment to Large Changes in Trade," *Annual Review of Economics* 8, no. 1 (2016): 205–40. For evidence on NAFTA, see Jiwon Choi, Ilyana Kuziemko, Ebonya Washington, and Gavin Wright, "Local Economic and Political Effects of Trade Deals: Evidence from NAFTA," *American Economic Review* 114, no. 6 (2024): 1540–75.
26. For an early, insightful exposition of the disjuncture between America and Canada, see David Card and Richard B. Freeman, eds., *Small Differences That Matter: Labor Markets and Income Maintenance in Canada and the United States* (University of Chicago Press, 2009).
27. For more on the impact of Jack Welch and his disciples, see David Gelles, *The Man Who Broke Capitalism: How Jack Welch Gutted the Heartland and Crushed the Soul of Corporate America—and How to Undo His Legacy* (Simon & Schuster, 2022).

28. Interestingly, in 2020, public pressure led Apple to pay for its contract janitors during the lockdown period of the Covid-19 pandemic, instead of the workers getting laid off by Apple's contractors. See Malcolm Owen, "Apple Will Pay Contract Apple Park Workers, Including Janitors and Drivers," AppleInsider, March 31, 2020, https://appleinsider.com/articles/20/03/31/apple-will-pay-contract-apple-park-workers-including-janitors-and-drivers.

Chapter 2: Monopsony!

1. According to the Company Wage Tracker, revenue in 2021 for UPS was almost $84.6 billion and their employment was 543,000. I divide revenue by employment to get average revenue per worker of around $156,000. Revenue per worker at FedEx was $145,500. https://www.epi.org/company-wage-tracker/.
2. Adam Smith, *An Inquiry into the Nature and Causes of the Wealth of Nations* (London: W. Strahan and T. Cadell, 1776).
3. Sumner H. Slichter, "Notes on the Structure of Wages," *Review of Economics and Statistics* 32, no. 1 (1950): 80–91.
4. Peter B. Doeringer and Michael J. Piore, *Internal Labor Markets and Manpower Analysis* (Routledge, 2020); Michael Reich, David M. Gordon, and Richard C. Edwards, "A Theory of Labor Market Segmentation," *American Economic Review* 63, no. 2 (1973): 359–65.
5. Alan B. Krueger and Lawrence H. Summers, "Efficiency Wages and the Inter-Industry Wage Structure," *Econometrica: Journal of the Econometric Society* 56, no. 2 (1988): 259–293; Lawrence F. Katz and Lawrence H. Summers, "Can Interindustry Wage Differentials Justify Strategic Trade Policy?" in *Trade Policies for International Competitiveness*, ed. Robert C. Feenstra (University of Chicago Press, 1989), 85–124; Lawrence F. Katz et al., "Industry Rents: Evidence and Implications," *Brookings Papers on Economic Activity. Microeconomics* (1989): 209–90; William T. Dickens and Lawrence F. Katz, "Inter-Industry Wage Differences and Industry Characteristics," in *Unemployment and the Structure of Labor Markets*, eds. K. Lang and J. Leonard (Basil Blackwood, 1987), 48–89.
6. Robert Gibbons and Lawrence Katz, "Does Unmeasured Ability

Explain Inter-Industry Wage Differentials?," *Review of Economic Studies* 59, no. 3 (1992): 515–35.

7. Ihsaan Bassier, Arindrajit Dube, and Suresh Naidu, "Monopsony in Movers: The Elasticity of Labor Supply to Firm Wage Policies," *Journal of Human Resources* 57, no. S (2022): S50–S86.
8. This estimate for the share of wage gap due to company pay policy (20 percent) is for the "low-skill" workforce (in the sense of low "person effects" in statistical models), typically working in sectors such as retail. For the overall workforce, we found the share to be around 15 percent.
9. One common approach to decomposing the role of workplace versus other factors is to use a statistical model developed by John Abowd, Francis Kramarz, and David Margolis, or "AKM" (1999). This model recovers a pay premium by each company by looking at what happens when the same workers move across jobs between companies. This includes work by David Card and coauthors who used data from Germany and Portugal to study these questions, as well as the work by Jae Song and coauthors discussed in this chapter. In my 2021 research with Ihsaan Bassier and Suresh Naidu, we also showed results from this AKM model as one of the two approaches. However, we also developed the matched-mover model (e.g., Petra and Marta) to control for a rich set of history more granularly, which we show is especially important when analyzing the quits decisions. See John M. Abowd, Francis Kramarz, and David N. Margolis, "High Wage Workers and High Wage Firms," *Econometrica* 67, no. 2 (1999): 251–333; David Card, Ana Rute Cardoso, Joerg Heining, and Patrick Kline, "Firms and Labor Market Inequality: Evidence and Some Theory," *Journal of Labor Economics* 36, no. S1 (2018): S13–S70.
10. See Jae Song et al., "Firming Up Inequality," *Quarterly Journal of Economics* 134, no. 1 (2019): 1–50.
11. This reflects how much of the variation in wages can be explained by the firms people work for—either directly through firm-specific pay policies (the variance of firm fixed effects) or indirectly through the kinds of workers those firms tend to hire (the covariance between firm and worker fixed effects).
12. See Arindrajit Dube and Ethan Kaplan, "Does Outsourcing Reduce

Wages in the Low-Wage Service Occupations? Evidence from Janitors and Guards," *ILR Review* 63, no. 2 (2010): 287–306. For evidence from Germany, see Deborah Goldschmidt and Johannes F. Schmieder, "The Rise of Domestic Outsourcing and the Evolution of the German Wage Structure," *Quarterly Journal of Economics* 132, no. 3 (2017): 1165–1217. On the increasing occupational homogeneity in American companies, see Elizabeth Weber Handwerker, "Outsourcing, Occupationally Homogeneous Employers, and Wage Inequality in the United States," *Journal of Labor Economics* 41, no. S1 (2023): S173–S203.

13. Nathan Wilmer and Clem Aeppli, "Consolidated Advantage: New Organizational Dynamics of Wage Inequality," *American Sociological Review* 86, no. 6 (2021): 1100–30.
14. Till von Wachter, "The Persistent Effects of Initial Labor Market Conditions for Young Adults and Their Sources," *Journal of Economic Perspectives* 34, no. 4 (2020): 168–94.
15. Arindrajit Dube, Suresh Naidu, and Adam D. Reich, "Power and Dignity in the Low Wage Labor Market: Theory and Evidence from Wal-Mart Workers." Working Paper No. 30441 (National Bureau of Economic Research, 2022).
16. The same question is asked in the General Social Survey, fielded to a random sample of American adults. In 2016, the most recent year this question was asked, a minority of respondents (44 percent) said it would be "very easy" or "somewhat easy" to find another job as good as their current one. Data from: https://gssdataexplorer.norc.org/home.
17. For simplicity, these calculations assume that Target is like an average retail firm in Oregon during this period, which had a monthly separation rate of around 6.5 percent.
18. The figure plots the relationship between company component of log wage and workers' separation rate relative to the average separation rate in the sample. Adapted from figure 3 in Ihsaan Bassier, Arindrajit Dube, and Suresh Naidu, "Monopsony in Movers: The Elasticity of Labor Supply to Firm Wage Policies," *Journal of Human Resources* 57, no. S (2022): S50–S86. © 2022 by the Board of Regents of the University of Wisconsin System. Reprinted courtesy of the University of Wisconsin Press.

19. The quit elasticity was –2.2 in the Portland metro area, and –2.0 outside Portland.
20. You can't simply look at how a higher wage affects the number of new hires each month, since hiring may be lower at high-wage firms simply because fewer workers are quitting—meaning fewer positions need to be filled. Nor is it enough to examine how many applications a higher wage attracts, as a large applicant pool might include many unqualified or uncommitted candidates. To truly understand the recruitment margin, you need data on both the number of job vacancies and the rate at which those vacancies are filled.
21. Arindrajit Dube, Jeff Jacobs, Suresh Naidu, and Siddharth Suri, "Monopsony in Online Labor Markets," *American Economic Review: Insights* 2, no. 1 (2020): 33–46.
22. Our findings were not an outlier, either. It turns out, several researchers had randomized pay on MTurk and recorded the impact on task acceptance rate; however, they had not interpreted the resulting sensitivity as reflecting market power. Pooling across all that evidence produced an elasticity of labor supply to MTurk employers of around 0.13.
23. Sydnee Caldwell and Emily Oehlsen, "Gender, Outside Options, and Labor Supply: Experimental Evidence from the Gig Economy," Working Paper (University of California, Berkeley, September 2023).
24. Nikhil Datta, "The Measure of Monopsony: The Labour Supply Elasticity to the Firm and Its Constituents," CEP Discussion Paper No. 1930 (Centre for Economic Performance, London School of Economics and Political Science, 2023).
25. Ernesto Dal Bó, Frederico Finan, and Martín A. Rossi, "Strengthening State Capabilities: The Role of Financial Incentives in the Call to Public Service," *Quarterly Journal of Economics* 128, no. 3 (2013): 1169–1218.
26. Anna Sokolova and Todd Sorensen, "Monopsony in Labor Markets: A Meta-Analysis," *ILR Review* 74, no. 1 (2021): 27–55.
27. Matthew Gibson, "Employer Market Power in Silicon Valley," Working Paper No. 24-398 (Upjohn Institute, March 18, 2024).
28. Alan B. Krueger and Orley Ashenfelter, "Theory and Evidence on Employer Collusion in the Franchise Sector," *Journal of Human Resources* 57, no. S (2022): S324–S348.

29. Evan P. Starr, James J. Prescott, and Norman D. Bishara, "Noncompete Agreements in the US Labor Force," *Journal of Law and Economics* 64, no. 1 (2021): 53–84.
30. Natarajan Balasubramanian et al., "Locked In? The Enforceability of Covenants Not to Compete and the Careers of High-Tech Workers," *Journal of Human Resources* 57, no. S (2022): S349–S396; Michael Lipsitz and Evan Starr, "Low-Wage Workers and the Enforceability of Noncompete Agreements," *Management Science* 68, no. 1 (2022): 143–70.
31. Daniel Block, "How the Ski Business Got Too Big for Its Boots," *Atlantic* (blog), January 12, 2025, https://www.theatlantic.com/ideas/archive/2025/01/big-ski-snow-strike/681291/.
32. José Azar, Ioana Marinescu, and Marshall Steinbaum, "Labor Market Concentration," *Journal of Human Resources* 57, no. S (2022): S167–S199.
33. R. Jason Faberman, Andreas I. Mueller, Ayşegül Şahin, and Giorgio Topa, "Job Search Behavior among the Employed and Non-Employed," *Econometrica* 90, no. 4 (2022): 1743–79.
34. Simon Jäger, Christopher Roth, Nina Roussille, and Benjamin Schoefer, "Worker Beliefs about Outside Options," *Quarterly Journal of Economics* 139, no. 3 (2024): 1505–56.
35. Nikhil Datta, "Local Monopsony Power," CEP Discussion Paper No. 2012 (Centre for Economic Performance, London School of Economics and Political Science, June 2024).
36. If employers could pay each worker a different wage, the inefficiency from under-hiring in a monopsonistic labor market would disappear. That's because they could offer higher pay to attract new workers without having to raise wages for everyone. But this comes at a cost: It likely makes many workers worse off—especially those with few outside options—by pushing their wages down.

    In reality, employers often don't know exactly who's willing to accept lower pay and who would only work for more. And even if they did, paying different workers differently for doing the same job at the same workplace tends to violate basic notions of fairness. Research, and common sense, show that unequal pay for equal work leads to dissatisfaction and higher turnover. For more on fairness concerns and aversion to wage differences within a company, see Arindrajit Dube,

Laura Giuliano, and Jonathan Leonard, "Fairness and Frictions: The Impact of Unequal Raises on Quit Behavior," *American Economic Review* 109, no. 2 (2019): 620–63.

37. Danielle Wiener-Bronner, "'A Perfect Storm': These Restaurants Survived the Pandemic. Now They Can't Find Workers," CNN Business, April 21, 2021, https://www.cnn.com/2021/04/21/business/restaurant-labor-shortage.
38. In the early phase of the reopening after the Covid-19 lockdown, employers were often reluctant to raise wages across the board, which would mean paying more for their existing workers. Instead, they opted to raise pay for new hires using "sign-on bonuses." However, this did not work very well, as it fueled resentment due to fairness concerns, and eventually most low-wage employers raised base pay. For more on post-Covid sign-on bonuses, see Andrea Hsu, "A $500 Sign-On Bonus to Deliver Pizzas? Here's What to Know about Hiring Incentives," NPR, July 6, 2021, https://www.npr.org/2021/07/06/1012344023/heres-what-you-should-know-about-that-eye-popping-sign-on-bonus.

Chapter 3: Tales of Market Tightness

1. A. W. Phillips, "The Relationship between Unemployment and the Rate of Change of Money in the UK, 1861–1957," *Economica* 25 (1958): 283–99.
2. Data on the unemployment rate and U* downloaded from the Federal Reserve Economic Data (FRED). U.S. Congressional Budget Office, Noncyclical Rate of Unemployment [NROU], retrieved from FRED, Federal Reserve Bank of St. Louis, February 11, 2024, https://fred.stlouisfed.org/series/NROU; U.S. Bureau of Labor Statistics, Unemployment Rate [UNRATE], retrieved from Federal Reserve Bank of St. Louis, February 11, 2024, https://fred.stlouisfed.org/series/UNRATE.
3. As it turns out, Dale Mortensen's own research with Ken Burdett is the seminal paper on how job-to-job movements affect labor market competition. See Kenneth Burdett and Dale T. Mortensen, "Wage Differentials, Employer Size, and Unemployment," *International Economic Review* 39, no. 2 (1998): 257–73.

4. The job-to-job separations ("job-hopping") rate and poaching index are calculated as annual averages of quarterly data from the Job-to-Job Flows dataset, part of the Longitudinal Employer-Household Dynamics (LEHD) program published by the U.S. Census Bureau. The job-hopping rate is lagged because, in data collection, separations from the previous quarter are recorded as hires for the current quarter.
5. Ihsaan Bassier, Arindrajit Dube, and Suresh Naidu, "Monopsony in Movers: The Elasticity of Labor Supply to Firm Wage Policies," *Journal of Human Resources* 57, no. S (2022): S50–S86. This finding was also reported in work by Douglas A. Webber, "Labor Market Competition and Employment Adjustment over the Business Cycle," *Journal of Human Resources* 57, no. S (2022): S87–S110.
6. John C. Haltiwanger, Henry R. Hyatt, Lisa B. Kahn, and Erika McEntarfer, "Cyclical Job Ladders by Firm Size and Firm Wage," *American Economic Journal: Macroeconomics* 10, no. 2 (2018): 52–85.
7. After 1980 and before the pandemic, unemployment dipped to 4 percent or lower only in the late 1990s and the late 2010s. I chose these seven years from those periods, limiting the sample to years when unemployment was below the CBO's estimate of U* every month.
8. Wage percentiles are retrieved from Economic Policy Institute's State of Working America Data Library and are based on CPS data. They are adjusted for inflation using the extended chained CPI.
9. National Science Foundation, "Birth of the Commercial Internet," NSF Impacts, accessed September 15, 2025, https://www.nsf.gov/impacts/internet.
10. Jeff Fischer, "Why Pets.com Died," *The Motley Fool*, November 14, 2000.
11. Lawrence F. Katz, Alan B. Krueger, Gary Burtless, and William T. Dickens, "The High-Pressure U.S. Labor Market of the 1990s," *Brookings Papers on Economic Activity* 1999, no. 1 (1999): 1–87. Also see Dean Baker, and Jared Bernstein, "Getting Back to Full Employment," Center for Economic and Policy Research, March 12, 2014, https://cepr.net/publications/getting-back-to-full-employment/.
12. See Katz and Krueger, "The High-Pressure U.S. Labor Market of the 1990s."

13. See FOMC meeting notes: https://www.federalreserve.gov/monetarypolicy/files/FOMC19990203meeting.pdf.
14. Jared Bernstein and Dean Baker, *The Benefits of Full Employment: When Markets Work for People* (Washington, DC: Economic Policy Institute, 2003), https://www.epi.org/publication/books_full_employment/.
15. FOMC meeting notes by year can be accessed here: https://www.federalreserve.gov/monetarypolicy/fomc_historical_year.htm.
16. Federal Funds Rate downloaded from the Federal Reserve Economic Database (FRED). Board of Governors of the Federal Reserve System (US), Federal Funds Effective Rate [FEDFUNDS], retrieved on February 19, 2024, from Federal Reserve Bank of St. Louis, https://fred.stlouisfed.org/series/FEDFUNDS.
17. Paul Krugman, "Too Little of a Good Thing," *New York Times*, November 1, 2009, https://www.nytimes.com/2009/11/02/opinion/02krugman.html.
18. U.S. Bureau of Labor Statistics, Employment-Population Ratio—25–54 Yrs. [LNS12300060], retrieved on May 28, 2024, from FRED, Federal Reserve Bank of St. Louis, https://fred.stlouisfed.org/series/LNS12300060. Shaded bars represent recessions. Federal Reserve Bank of St. Louis, NBER-based Recession Indicators for the United States from the Period following the Peak through the Trough [USREC], retrieved on May 28, 2024, from FRED, Federal Reserve Bank of St. Louis, https://fred.stlouisfed.org/series/USREC.
19. John Haltiwanger, Stefano Scarpetta, and Helena Schweiger, "Assessing Job Flows Across Countries: The Role of Industry, Firm Size, and Regulations," NBER Working Paper w13920 (2008).
20. Hannes Schwandt and Till von Wachter, "Unlucky Cohorts: Estimating the Long-Term Effects of Entering the Labor Market in a Recession in Large Cross-Sectional Data Sets," *Journal of Labor Economics* 37, no. S1 (2019): S161–S198. The calculations in the text are reported in: Till von Wachter, "The Persistent Effects of Initial Labor Market Conditions for Young Adults and Their Sources," *Journal of Economic Perspectives* 34, no. 4 (2020): 168–94.
21. For a review of the evidence, see von Wachter, "The Persistent Effects of Initial Labor Market Conditions."

22. Gabriel Chodorow-Reich, "Geographic Cross-Sectional Fiscal Spending Multipliers: What Have We Learned?," *American Economic Journal: Economic Policy* 11, no. 2 (2019): 1–34.
23. See FOMC meeting notes: https://www.federalreserve.gov/monetarypolicy/fomcminutes 20180926.htm.
24. Jérémie Cohen-Setton, Egor Gornostay, and Colombe Ladreit de Lacharrière, "Impact of the Trump Fiscal Stimulus on US Economic Growth," Peterson Institute for International Economics, August 6, 2018, https://www.piie.com/blogs/realtime-economic-issues-watch/impact-trump-fiscal-stimulus-us-economic-growth.
25. Neel Kashkari, "Why I Dissented," *Medium* (blog), September 18, 2020, https://medium.com/@neelkashkari/why-i-dissented-feb698ae4d08.
26. Josh Bivens and Ben Zipperer, "The Importance of Locking in Full Employment for the Long Haul," Economic Policy Institute, August 21, 2018, https://www.epi.org/publication/the-importance-of-locking-in-full-employment-for-the-long-haul/. Several other studies have documented the greater responsiveness of pay at the bottom and the middle to unemployment rates than at the top.
27. The job-hopping rate for those without a high school diploma was 5.2 percent on average from 2001 to 2016 and 5.9 percent from 2017 to 2019. U.S. Census Bureau, Job-to-Job Flows data (2000–2023) Longitudinal-Employer Household Dynamics Program, version R2025Q1, accessed August 7, 2025, https://ledextract.ces.census.gov.
28. Katherine S. Newman and Elisabeth S. Jacobs, *Moving the Needle: What Tight Labor Markets Do for the Poor* (University of California Press, 2023).
29. Calculations using microdata from: IPUMS CPS, Version 12.0 [dataset] (IPUMS, University of Minnesota, 2024), https://doi.org/10.18128/D030.V12.0.
30. Wage percentiles are retrieved from the Economic Policy Institute's State of Working America Data Library and are based on CPS data. They are adjusted for inflation using the extended chained CPI.
31. David Autor, Arindrajit Dube, and Annie McGrew, "The Unexpected Compression: Competition at Work in the Low Wage Labor Market," NBER Working Paper w31010 (2024).

32. Reproduction of figure 3.7 from Autor, Dube, and McGrew, "The Unexpected Compression."
33. More precisely, the log of the 90–10 ratio *fell* by around 0.02 between 2013 and 2019, and then fell by 0.08 between 2019 and 2024, combining to 0.10. In contrast, the log of the 90–10 ratio had *risen* by 0.29 between 1980 and 2013. This means that the change since 2013 erased around one-third of the rise in the log 90–10 ratio between 1980 and 2013 (since 0.10 ÷ 0.29 = 0.34, or around one-third).
34. Monthly quit rates obtained from the Bureau of Labor Statistics' Job Openings and Labor Turnover Survey (JOLTS).
35. This quit elasticity of –0.8 for non-college-educated workers under forty is smaller in magnitude than the estimates based on cross-firm wage premia using matched employer-employee data—like the Marta and Petra evidence from Oregon in chapter 2. For lower-wage workers like Marta and Petra (who likely fall into the non-college-educated, under-forty group), we found a quit elasticity of about –1.4. This difference reflects several factors: the distinction between firm- and industry-level wage premia, and the fact that cross-sectional CPS data likely overstate wage premia. As a result, they tend to understate quit elasticities relative to administrative data, which track the same workers as they move across firms.
36. For workers as a whole, the quit elasticity at the average industry wage premium was around –1 in the 2015–2019 period. It remained stable in the 2021–2022 period, indicating little change in competition. This contrasts with low-wage workers for whom labor market competition rose sharply in 2021–2022.
37. Reproduction of figure 3.9 from Autor, Dube, and McGrew, "The Unexpected Compression."
38. Paul Krugman credited me for coining the term the "Great Reshuffling." While I cannot be entirely sure he is correct, I will go along with his version of the origin story. See Paul Krugman, "What Ever Happened to the Great Resignation?," *New York Times*, April 5, 2022, https://www.nytimes.com/2022/04/05/opinion/great-resignation-employment.html.
39. Autor, Dube, and McGrew, "The Unexpected Compression."

40. Peter Ganong et al., "Spending and Job-Finding Impacts of Expanded Unemployment Benefits: Evidence from Administrative Micro Data," *American Economic Review* 114, no. 9 (2024): 2898–939.
41. Simon Jäger, Christopher Roth, Nina Roussille, and Benjamin Schoefer, "Worker Beliefs about Outside Options," *Quarterly Journal of Economics* 139, no. 3 (2024): 1505–56.
42. Paul Krugman, "Wonking Out: Is the Great Resignation a Great Rethink?," *New York Times*, November 5, 2021, https://www.nytimes.com/2021/11/05/opinion/great-resignation-quit-job.html.
43. For proposals to reform UI benefits see Peter Ganong et al., "Lessons Learned from Expanded Unemployment Insurance during COVID-19," in *Recession Remedies: Lessons Learned from the U.S. Economic Policy Response to COVID-19*, eds. Wendy Edelberg, Louise Sheiner, and David Wessel (Brookings, 2022), 49–90; Arindrajit Dube, "A Plan to Reform the Unemployment Insurance System in the United States," *Hamilton Project Policy Proposal* 3, no. 2 (2021).
44. Peter Ganong et al., "Spending and Job-Finding Impacts of Expanded Unemployment Benefits: Evidence from Administrative Micro Data," *American Economic Review* 114, no. 9 (2024): 2898–939.
45. Arindrajit Dube et al., "Early Withdrawal of Pandemic Unemployment Insurance: Effects on Employment and Earnings," in *AEA Papers and Proceedings*, vol. 112 (American Economic Association, 2022), 85–90.
46. Paul Krugman, "Wonking Out: Discombobulation, Recombobulation and Disinflation," *New York Times,* July 21, 2023, https://www.nytimes.com/2023/07/21/opinion/inflation-federal-reserve.html.
47. Jordan Weissmann, "Why Larry Summers Thinks We Need Massive Unemployment to Beat Inflation," *Slate*, July 7, 2022, https://slate.com/business/2022/07/larry-summers-massive-unemployment-fed-inflation.html.
48. Andrea Cerrato and Giulia Gitti, "Inflation Since COVID: Demand or Supply," SSRN, last revised December 10, 2022, https://papers.ssrn.com/sol3/papers.cfm?abstract_id=4193594; Jonathon Hazell and Stephan Hobler, "Do Deficits Cause Inflation?: A High Frequency Narrative Approach," *Centre for Macroeconomics Discussion Papers 2439* (2024).

49. "The Purchasing Power of American Households," U.S. Department of the Treasury, February 8, 2025, https://home.treasury.gov/news/featured-stories/the-purchasing-power-of-american-households.
50. Justin Lahart, "The Era of Big Raises for Low-Paid Workers Is Over," *Wall Street Journal*, August 12, 2025, https://www.wsj.com/economy/jobs/low-wage-employees-pay-growth-cdf3cd36.

Chapter 4: The Treaty of Detroit

1. Nicholas Bloom et al., "The Disappearing Large-Firm Wage Premium," in *AEA Papers and Proceedings*, vol. 108 (American Economic Association, 2018), 317–22.
2. J. Adam Cobb and Ken-Hou Lin, "Growing Apart: The Changing Firm-Size Wage Premium and Its Inequality Consequences," *Organization Science* 28, no. 3 (2017): 429–46.
3. Research from Song et al., "Firming Up Inequality," was discussed in chapter 2 (see Song et al., "Firming Up Inequality," 1–50). Some of these findings echo prior research by Erling Barth, Alex Bryson, James C. Davis, and Richard Freeman, "It's Where You Work: Increases in the Dispersion of Earnings across Establishments and Individuals in the United States," *Journal of Labor Economics* 34, no. S2 (2016): S67–S97.
4. Paul A. David, "The Dynamo and the Computer: An Historical Perspective on the Modern Productivity Paradox," *American Economic Review* 80, no. 2 (1990): 355–61.
5. Robert J. Gordon, "The 1920s and the 1990s in Mutual Reflection," Working Paper No. 11778 (National Bureau of Economic Research, November 2005).
6. The figures reported in the last two paragraphs—growth in real income, productivity, and the stock market—come from Gordon, "The 1920s and the 1990s in Mutual Reflection." The estimates for population growth used to construct per capita income growth come from the World Inequality Database (WID), https://wid.world/country/usa/.
7. Valerie A. Ramey and Sarah Zubairy, "Government Spending Multipliers in Good Times and in Bad: Evidence from US Historical Data," *Journal of Political Economy* 126, no. 2 (2018): 850–901.

8. Lloyd Ulman, ed., *Challenges to Collective Bargaining* (Prentice-Hall, 1967).
9. Nelson Lichtenstein, *State of the Union: A Century of American Labor*, rev. and exp. ed. (Princeton University Press, 2013).
10. Ease of job finding can have contradictory effects on union organizing. On the one hand, when workers can easily leave a bad job, they may feel less inclined to push for change—such as by joining a union—because finding new employment is simpler than trying to improve conditions where they are. On the other hand, when jobs are plentiful, workers face less risk of retaliation—namely being fired for organizing—because they can more readily secure another job.
11. Richard B. Freeman, "Spurts in Union Growth: Defining Moments and Social Processes," in *The Defining Moment: The Great Depression and the American Economy in the Twentieth Century*, eds. Michael D. Bordo, Claudia Goldin, and Eugene N. White (University of Chicago Press, 1998), 265–96.
12. Figure 4.1 was reproduced from figure 1 in Henry S. Farber, Daniel Herbst, Ilyana Kuziemko, and Suresh Naidu, "Unions and Inequality over the Twentieth Century: New Evidence from Survey Data," *Quarterly Journal of Economics* 136, no. 3 (2021): 1325–85. By permission of Oxford University Press.
13. Gary Public Library and Jennifer Guiliano, "The Steel Strike of 1919 in Gary," Discover Indiana, accessed June 1, 2025, https://discoverindianahistory.org/items/show/603.
14. Lichtenstein, *State of the Union.*
15. Freeman, "Spurts in Union Growth."
16. Freeman, "Spurts in Union Growth."
17. "Work Stoppages Caused by Labor-Management Disputes in 1946," Bureau of Labor Statistics, accessed June 1, 2025, https://www.bls.gov/wsp/publications/annual-summaries/pdf/work-stoppages-1946.pdf; "The Importance of Locking in Full Employment for the Long Haul," Economic Policy Institute, accessed June 1, 2025, https://www.epi.org/publication/the-importance-of-locking-in-full-employment-for-the-long-haul/.
18. Lichtenstein, *State of the Union.*
19. Harold M. Levinson, "Pattern Bargaining: A Case Study of the

Automobile Workers," *Quarterly Journal of Economics* 74, no. 2 (1960): 296–317.

20. Claudia Goldin and Robert A. Margo, "The Great Compression: The Wage Structure in the United States at Mid-Century," *Quarterly Journal of Economics* 107, no. 1 (1992): 1–34.
21. Analysis of Census micro data from 1940 to 1950, retrieved from IPUMS. The sample includes eighteen- to sixty-four-year-old male workers, who worked for at least forty weeks in the year and had weekly earnings at least as much as would be obtained from a job paying half the hourly minimum wage in that year. IPUMS CPS, Version 12.0 [dataset] (Minneapolis: IPUMS, University of Minnesota, 2024), https://doi.org/10.18128/D030.V12.0.
22. The data on union density compiled by Richard Freeman discussed was based on national aggregate-level union membership and couldn't be broken down by geography or demographic groups.
23. Reproduced from Farber et al., "Unions and Inequality over the Twentieth Century." By permission of Oxford University Press.
24. For the statistically curious: The estimate of 1.4 percentage points comes from dividing the slope in the right panel of figure 4.3 (about 1.1) by the slope in the left panel (around 3.3), then multiplying by the 5-point increase in union density—yielding 1.1/3.6 × 5 = 1.4. This method is known as an instrumental variables approach, as explained in appendix A.
25. Carola Frydman and Raven Molloy, "Pay Cuts for the Boss: Executive Compensation in the 1940s," *Journal of Economic History* 72, no. 1 (2012): 225–51.
26. Chris Vickers and Nicolas L. Ziebarth, "The Effects of the National War Labor Board on Labor Income Inequality," unpublished manuscript, 2025.
27. Thomas Piketty, Emmanuel Saez, and Stefanie Stantcheva, "Optimal Taxation of Top Labor Incomes: A Tale of Three Elasticities," *American Economic Journal: Economic Policy* 6, no. 1 (2014): 230–71.
28. Marianne Bertrand and Sendhil Mullainathan, "Are CEOs Rewarded for Luck? The Ones without Principals Are," *Quarterly Journal of Economics* 116, no. 3 (2001): 901–32.
29. Most work tends to find a union pay premium between 10 and 20

percent. The premium also tends to be somewhat larger among those with less education and non-white workers (see Farber et al., "Unions and Inequality over the Twentieth Century").

30. Two other closely related works that document the overall impact of de-unionization on wages include Bruce Western and Jake Rosenfeld, "Unions, Norms, and the Rise in US Wage Inequality," *American Sociological Review* 76, no. 4 (2011): 513–37; as well as Farber et al., "Unions and Inequality over the Twentieth Century," mentioned above. Like Fortin and others, these two studies also use differential falls in state unionization to quantify spillovers. For a comprehensive review of the evidence on unionization and wages, see Simon Jäger, Suresh Naidu, and Benjamin Schoefer, "Collective Bargaining, Unions, and the Wage Structure: An International Perspective," Working Paper No. 33267 (National Bureau of Economic Research, December 2024).

Chapter 5: Corporate Pay Strategies

1. For evidence on salary benchmarking see Zoe B. Cullen, Shengwu Li, and Ricardo Perez-Truglia, "What's My Employee Worth? The Effects of Salary Benchmarking," Working Paper No. 30570 (National Bureau of Economic Research, rev. August 2024).
2. For a skeptical view on whether "high road" practices are profit neutral, see Paul Osterman, "In Search of the High Road: Meaning and Evidence," *ILR Review* 71, no. 1 (2018): 3–34.
3. The limited impact of wage changes on profits under monopsony power reflects a broader idea known as the "envelope theorem." Simply put, the envelope theorem says that when a firm—or any decision-maker—chooses the option that maximizes its goal (such as setting wages to maximize profits), small adjustments around that choice have only a minimal effect on the outcome. That's because the firm is already close to its best possible point. For example, slightly raising wages increases payroll costs, but also helps attract and retain workers; lowering wages saves money, but may make it harder to hire or keep staff. Near the optimal wage, these opposing effects mostly cancel out, leaving profits relatively unaffected by small changes in pay. For more on how monopsony power helps explain quirks in pay setting—such as

employers' tendency to pay round-numbered wages—see Arindrajit Dube, Alan Manning, and Suresh Naidu, "Monopsony and Employer Mis-Optimization Explain Why Wages Bunch at Round Numbers," *American Economic Review* 115, no. 8 (2025): 2689-721.

4. Daniel M. G. Raff and Lawrence H. Summers, "Did Henry Ford Pay Efficiency Wages?," *Journal of Labor Economics* 5, no. 4, pt. 2 (October 1987): S57–S86.
5. For more on the spread of Walmart, see Charles Fishman, *The Wal-Mart Effect: How the World's Most Powerful Company Really Works—and How It's Transforming the American Economy* (Penguin, 2006).
6. The data release was likely spurred by criticism of the company's pay policies and was coupled with the publication of a Walmart-funded study: *The Economic Impact of Wal-Mart* (Global Insight, 2005). For our study, see Arindrajit Dube and Steve Wertheim, "Wal-Mart and Job Quality—What Do We Know, and Should We Care?," UC Berkeley Center for Labor Research and Education, October 16, 2005, https://escholarship.org/uc/item/2s84b3fc.
7. Arindrajit Dube, T. William Lester, and Barry Eidlin, "Firm Entry and Wages: Impact of Wal-Mart Growth on Earnings throughout the Retail Sector," Working Paper No. iirwps-126-05 (Institute of Industrial Relations, August 7, 2007).
8. David Neumark, Junfu Zhang, and Stephen Ciccarella, "The Effects of Wal-Mart on Local Labor Markets," *Journal of Urban Economics* 63, no. 2 (2008): 405–30.
9. Neumark and his team's results found a reduction in total retail earnings, though not in earnings per worker.
10. Emek Basker, "The Causes and Consequences of Wal-Mart's Growth," *Journal of Economic Perspectives* 21, no. 3 (2007): 177–98.
11. Justin C. Wiltshire, "Walmart Supercenters and Monopsony Power: How a Large, Low-Wage Employer Impacts Local Labor Markets," unpublished manuscript, 2021.
12. This approach, known as "synthetic control," has become an increasingly popular, data-driven method for determining causal effects from nonexperimental data. See Alberto Abadie, Alexis Diamond, and Jens Hainmueller, "Synthetic Control Methods for Comparative Case

Studies: Estimating the Effect of California's Tobacco Control Program," *Journal of the American Statistical Association* 105, no. 490 (2010): 493–505.

13. For more on supply chain impacts, see Nathan Wilmers, "Wage Stagnation and Buyer Power: How Buyer-Supplier Relations Affect US Workers' Wages, 1978 to 2014," *American Sociological Review* 83, no. 2 (2018): 213–242; Paul N. Bloom and Vanessa G. Perry, "Retailer Power and Supplier Welfare: The Case of Wal-Mart," *Journal of Retailing* 77, no. 3 (2001): 379–96.
14. Nelson Lichtenstein, "The Return of Merchant Capitalism," *International Labor and Working-Class History* 81 (2012): 8–27.
15. Emek Basker and Michael Noel, "The Evolving Food Chain: Competitive Effects of Wal-Mart's Entry into the Supermarket Industry," *Journal of Economics & Management Strategy* 18, no. 4 (2009): 977–1009; Jerry Hausman and Ephraim Leibtag, "Consumer Benefits from Increased Competition in Shopping Outlets: Measuring the Effect of Wal-Mart," *Journal of Applied Econometrics* 22, no. 7 (2007): 1157–77.
16. Nathan Wilmers, "Solidarity within and across Workplaces: How Cross-Workplace Coordination Affects Earnings Inequality," *RSF: The Russell Sage Foundation Journal of the Social Sciences* 5, no. 4 (2019): 190–215.
17. Daron Acemoglu, Alex He, and Daniel le Maire, "Eclipse of Rent-Sharing: The Effects of Managers' Business Education on Wages and the Labor Share in the US and Denmark," Working Paper No. 29874 (National Bureau of Economic Research, March 2022).
18. Milton Friedman, "The Social Responsibility of Business Is to Increase Its Profits," in *Corporate Ethics and Corporate Governance*, eds. Walter Ch. Zimmerli, Klaus Richter, and Markus Holzinger (Springer, 2007), 173–78.
19. Michael C. Jensen and William H. Meckling, "Theory of the Firm: Managerial Behavior, Agency Costs and Ownership Structure," *Journal of Financial Economics* 3, no. 4 (1976): 305–60.
20. Examples of corporate finance textbooks arguing that managers should focus on shareholder value maximization include Richard A. Brealey, Stewart C. Myers, and Franklin Allen, *Principles of Corporate Finance* (McGraw-Hill, 1980). Also see Thomas E. Copeland, J. Fred

Weston, and Kuldeep Shastri, *Financial Theory and Corporate Policy* (Addison-Wesley, 1979).

21. William Lazonick and Mary O'Sullivan, "Maximizing Shareholder Value: A New Ideology for Corporate Governance," *Economy and Society* 29, no. 1 (2000): 13–35.
22. Maxim Massenkoff and Nathan Wilmers, "Wage Stagnation and the Decline of Standardized Pay Rates, 1974–1991," *American Economic Journal: Applied Economics* 15, no. 1 (2023): 474–507.
23. For research showing how workers respond to being treated unfairly along these lines, see Arindrajit Dube, Laura Giuliano, and Jonathan Leonard, "Fairness and Frictions: The Impact of Unequal Raises on Quit Behavior," *American Economic Review* 109, no. 2 (2019): 620–663. Also see Emily Breza, Supreet Kaur, and Yogita Shamdasani, "The Morale Effects of Pay Inequality," *Quarterly Journal of Economics* 133, no. 2 (2018): 611–63.
24. David Weil, *The Fissured Workplace* (Harvard University Press, 2014).
25. Steven Greenhouse, "Gap to Raise Minimum Hourly Pay," *New York Times,* February 2014, https://www.nytimes.com/2014/02/20/business/gap-to-raise-minimum-hourly-pay.html.
26. For a review of this movement's impact, see Yannet Lathrop, T. William Lester, and Matthew Wilson, "Quantifying the Impact of the Fight for $15: $150 Billion in Raises for 26 Million Workers, with $76 Billion Going to Workers of Color," National Employment Law Project, July 27, 2021.
27. Gavin Kelly, "SeaTac: The Small US Town That Sparked a New Movement against Low Wages," *Guardian*, February 22, 2014, https://www.theguardian.com/world/2014/feb/22/seatac-minimum-wage-increase-washington.
28. Jana Kasperkevic, "Target Joins Competitors in Raising Minimum Wage above Federal Standard," *Guardian*, March 19, 2015, https://www.theguardian.com/business/2015/mar/19/target-raises-minimum-wage.
29. The data on the voluntary minimum wage timing come from Ellora Derenoncourt and David Weil, "Voluntary Minimum Wages: The

Local Labor Market Effects of National Retailer Policies," *Quarterly Journal of Economics* 140, no. 3 (2025): 1901–58. Supplemented with my own research based on news articles.

30. Jordan Weissmann, "Amazon Raised Its Minimum Wage to $15 an Hour Thanks to Bernie Sanders (and Maybe Tucker Carlson)," *Slate*, October 2, 2018, https://slate.com/business/2018/10/amazon-15-an-hour-bernie-sanders.html.
31. Arindrajit Dube, Suresh Naidu, and Adam D. Reich, "Power and Dignity in the Low-Wage Labor Market: Theory and Evidence from Wal-Mart Workers," Working Paper No. 30441 (National Bureau of Economic Research, September 2022).
32. Reproduced from Dube, Naidu, and Reich, "Power and Dignity in the Low-Wage Labor Market."
33. Derenoncourt and Weil, "Voluntary Minimum Wages."
34. Reproduced from figure 2 in Derenoncourt and Weil, "Voluntary Minimum Wages." By permission of Oxford University Press.
35. Anna Hrushka, "Truist Bumps Minimum Hourly Wage to $22," *Banking Dive*, July 6, 2022, https://www.bankingdive.com/news/truist-bumps-minimum-hourly-wage-to-22/626646/; Katie Tabeling, "Bank of America Raises Minimum Wage to $24," *Delaware Business Times*, September 11, 2024, https://delawarebusinesstimes.com/news/bank-of-america-raises-minimum/.
36. Nathan Wilmers, Soohyun Roh, and Jiawei Tang, "Corporate Minimum Wages and Working Poverty," unpublished manuscript, 2025.
37. I estimate the large employer wage premium by averaging firm wage effects by firm size category. These firm effects come from an AKM model, which separates wages into worker and firm components.

    To calculate these effects, I use matched employer-employee data from Oregon (2000–2022) and run regressions of log hourly wages on worker and firm indicators: This produces a "fixed effect" estimate for each worker and firm. I estimate these estimates separately for 2000–2003, 2004–2007, 2008–2011, and then jointly for 2016–2022. In the figure, I define low-wage workers as those in the bottom quartile of worker fixed effects for each period. I then calculate the average firm effect for small firms (<100 employees) and large firms (2,500+

employees) separately for low-wage workers and for all other workers (top three quartiles). The large employer wage premium is the difference between these two averages for each worker group. I classify firms by their average size over the full period.

38. Jonathon Hazell, Christina Patterson, Heather Sarsons, and Bledi Taska, "National Wage Setting," Working Paper No. 30623 (National Bureau of Economic Research, November 2022).
39. Jonah Furman, "How Zoomers Organized the First Chipotle Union," Labor Notes, August 31, 2022, https://labornotes.org/2022/08/how-zoomers-organized-first-chipotle-union.
40. Chris Isidore, "These Baristas Are Leading a Nationwide Campaign to Unionize Starbucks. It Came at a Cost," CNN Business, November 2, 2022, https://www.cnn.com/2022/11/02/business/starbucks-union-organizers-risk-takers-22-ctrp.
41. Whether full employment can meaningfully alter the extent of organizing is a different question. Some recent evidence suggests that tight labor markets have not changed worker behavior when it comes to union organizing. See Chantal Pezold, Simon Jäger, and Patrick Nüss, "Labor Market Tightness and Union Activity," Working Paper No. 31988 (National Bureau of Economic Research, December 2023).
42. Zeynep Ton, *The Good Jobs Strategy: How the Smartest Companies Invest in Employees to Lower Costs and Boost Profits* (Houghton Mifflin Harcourt, 2014).
43. Natalia Emanuel and Emma Harrington, "Firm Frictions and the Payoffs of Higher Pay: Labor Supply and Productivity Responses to a Voluntary Firm Minimum Wage," unpublished manuscript, 2022.
44. Raff and Summers, "Did Henry Ford Pay Efficiency Wages?"

Chapter 6: The Minimal Cost of Higher Minimums

1. Based on regional price parities, in 2023, San Antonio and Tucson both had 6 percent lower overall cost of living than the country as a whole. The national median real wage in 2023 was $23.85. Wages are deflated using the chained CPI with 2023 as the base year. The wage calculations use the American Community Survey (ACS) micro data from IPUMS. IPUMS CPS, Version 12.0 [dataset] (IPUMS,

University of Minnesota, 2024), https://doi.org/10.18128/D030.V12.0.

2. ACS data from 2015 and 2019 from IPUMS. Wages are real in 2023 dollars and deflated using the chained CPI. Wages below $1 are censored and only individuals who reported working more than five weeks and usually working at least ten hours a week are included. I use fast-food or hospitality workers to describe the IPUMS industry category "Eating and Drinking Places."
3. This is calculated for a worker working fifty weeks in a year for forty hours per week.
4. According to the MIT Living Wage Calculator, typical expenses for food for a single adult were $3,644 for San Antonio–New Braunfels, Texas. Amy K. Glasmeier, "Living Wage Calculator," Massachusetts Institute of Technology, accessed February 14, 2024, https://livingwage.mit.edu/metros/41700 and https://livingwage.mit.edu /metros/46060.
5. My calculations using CPS ORG data, and information on minimum wage from Kavya Vaghul and Ben Zipperer, "Historical State and Sub-State Minimum Wages," Version 1.4.0, 2022, https://github.com/benzipperer/historicalminwage/releases/tag/v1.4.0.
6. Arindrajit Dube and Attila Lindner, "Minimum Wages in the 21st Century," in *Handbook of Labor Economics*, vol. 5, ed. Christian Dustmann and Thomas Lemieux (North Holland, 2024), 261–383.
7. Robert Pollin, *A Measure of Fairness: The Economics of Living Wages and Minimum Wages in the United States* (Cornell University Press, 2008).
8. Daniel Kahneman, Jack L. Knetsch, and Richard Thaler, "Fairness as a Constraint on Profit Seeking: Entitlements in the Market," *American Economic Review* 76, no. 4 (1986): 728–41; Ernst Fehr, Lorenz Goette, and Christian Zehnder, "A Behavioral Account of the Labor Market: The Role of Fairness Concerns," *Annual Review of Economics* 1, no. 1 (2009): 355–84; Ernst Fehr and Urs Fischbacher, "Third-Party Punishment and Social Norms," *Evolution and Human Behavior* 25, no. 2 (2004): 63–87.
9. Jasmine Payne-Patterson and Adewale A. Maye, "A History of the Federal Minimum Wage: 85 Years Later, the Minimum Wage Is Far from Equitable," *Working Economics Blog,* Economic Policy Institute,

August 31, 2023. https://www.epi.org/blog/a-history-of-the-federal-minimum-wage-85-years-later-the-minimum-wage-is-far-from-equitable/. I use the chained CPI to adjust for inflation, producing slightly different numbers than in the reference, which uses CPI-U-RS.

10. It's common to compare the minimum wage to the median wage, as we do later in the chapter. Unfortunately, there is no published annual series on median hourly wage in the United States stretching back before the 1970s. But the Bureau of Labor Statistics did publish the average wage of production and nonsupervisory ("non-managerial") workers going back to 1964; this group consists of around 80 percent of private-sector workers. (Reassuringly, the two series—median wage and the average wage of non-managerial workers—track each other over time fairly closely in the more recent period when these are both available, as we saw in figure 1.3.) Between 1947 and 1964, the average wage of non-managerial workers is available only for the goods-producing sector. In figure 6.2, I use the growth in the non-managerial wages for all workers after 1964, and for goods-producing workers only prior to that. Data on average hourly earnings of production and nonsupervisory workers overall and for manufacturing workers is from the Bureau of Labor Statistics, Current Employment Statistics.
11. In 2009, the real minimum wage was around $9.95 in 2023 dollars.
12. As described in chapter 1, hourly productivity grew by around 110 percent between 1968 and 2023. Multiplying the 1968 real minimum wage—$11.85 × 2.10—yields $24.89.
13. Median wage in 2023 calculated using CPS data downloaded from IPUMS.
14. The OECD provides a consistent cross-country comparison of minimum wages to median wages of full-time workers. See https://stats.oecd.org/index.aspx?DataSetCode=RMW#. Figure 6.3 displays this ratio (or the Kaitz index) for *all* workers averaged across OECD countries (grey line) and for the United States (black line). I adjust OECD data to reflect that median wages for full-time workers tend to be about 10 percent larger than median wages for all workers. The dashed line in figure 6.3 adjusts the U.S. ratio to account for state minimum wages by using a population-weighted average of state

minimum wages as the minimum wage measure to calculate the Kaitz index. Population counts used in the weighted average are obtained from CPS ORG data from NBER (1979–81) and IPUMS (1982–2022). State-level minimum wage dataset over time is obtained from Vaghul and Zipperer, "Historical State and Sub-State Minimum Wages."

15. "Minimum Wage Tracker," Economic Policy Institute, updated October 1, 2025, https://www.epi.org/minimum-wage-tracker/; "Workers' Rights Preemption in the U.S.: A Map of the Campaign to Suppress Workers' Rights in the States," Economic Policy Institute, updated February 2025, https://www.epi.org /preemption-map/; Arindrajit Dube Attila Lindner, "City Limits: What Do Local-Area Minimum Wages Do?," *Journal of Economic Perspectives* 35, no. 1 (2021): 27–50.
16. The demographic information and mobility statistics come from https://fivethirtyeight.com/features/its-getting-harder-to-move -beyond-a-minimum-wage-job/.
17. Evidence from the following papers suggests the importance of internal pay concerns: Arindrajit Dube, Laura Giuliano, and Jonathan Leonard, "Fairness and Frictions: The Impact of Unequal Raises on Quit Behavior," *American Economic Review* 109, no. 2 (2019): 620–63; Radhakrishnan Gopalan, Barton H. Hamilton, Ankit Kalda, and David Sovich, "State Minimum Wages, Employment, and Wage Spillovers: Evidence from Administrative Payroll Data," *Journal of Labor Economics* 39, no. 3 (2021): 673–707.
18. Tim Butcher, Richard Dickens, and Alan Manning, "Minimum Wages and Wage Inequality: Some Theory and an Application to the UK," CEP Discussion Paper No. 1177 (Centre for Economic Performance, London School of Economics and Political Science, November 2012).
19. "Wages by Percentile and Wage Ratios," State of Working America Data Library, Economic Policy Institute, 2024.
20. David S. Lee, "Wage Inequality in the United States during the 1980s: Rising Dispersion or Falling Minimum Wage?," *Quarterly Journal of Economics* 114, no. 3 (1999): 977–1023.
21. David H. Autor, Alan Manning, and Christopher L. Smith, "The

Contribution of the Minimum Wage to US Wage Inequality over Three Decades: A Reassessment," *American Economic Journal: Applied Economics* 8, no. 1 (2016): 58–99.

22. These moderate-sized wage spillovers from state-level policy changes were also found using a different research design in Doruk Cengiz, Arindrajit Dube, Attila Lindner, and Ben Zipperer, "The Effect of Minimum Wages on Low-Wage Jobs," *Quarterly Journal of Economics* 134, no. 3 (2019): 1405–454.
23. Nicole M. Fortin, Thomas Lemieux, and Neil Lloyd, "Labor Market Institutions and the Distribution of Wages: The Role of Spillover Effects," *Journal of Labor Economics* 39, no. S2 (2021): S369–S412.
24. Richard A. Lester, "Shortcomings of Marginal Analysis for Wage-Employment Problems," *American Economic Review* 36, no. 1 (1946): 63–82.
25. George J. Stigler, "The Economics of Minimum Wage Legislation," *American Economic Review* 36, no. 3 (1946): 358–65.
26. Fritz Machlup, "Marginal Analysis and Empirical Research," *American Economic Review* 36, no. 4 (1946): 519–54.
27. Charles Brown, Curtis Gilroy, and Andrew Kohen, "The Effect of the Minimum Wage on Employment and Unemployment," *Journal of Economic Literature* 20, no. 2 (June 1982): 487–528.
28. David Card and Alan B. Krueger, "Minimum Wages and Employment: A Case Study of the Fast-Food Industry in New Jersey and Pennsylvania," *American Economic Review* 84, no. 4 (1994): 772–93.
29. Reproduced from David Card and Alan B. Krueger, "Minimum Wages and Employment: A Case Study of the Fast-Food Industry in New Jersey and Pennsylvania: Reply," *American Economic Review* 90, no. 5 (2000): 1397–420. © American Economic Association. Used with permission.
30. David Card and Alan B. Krueger, *Myth and Measurement: The New Economics of the Minimum Wage* (Princeton University Press, 2016).
31. James Buchanan, "Commentary on the Minimum Wage," *Wall Street Journal*, April 25, 1996.
32. David Neumark and William Wascher, "Minimum Wages and Employment: A Case Study of the Fast-Food Industry in New Jersey

and Pennsylvania: Comment," *American Economic Review* 90, no. 5 (2000): 1362–396.

33. Card and Krueger, "Minimum Wages and Employment: A Case Study of the Fast-Food Industry in New Jersey and Pennsylvania: Reply."
34. Arindrajit Dube, T. William Lester, and Michael Reich, "Minimum Wage Effects across State Borders: Estimates Using Contiguous Counties," *Review of Economics and Statistics* 92, no. 4 (2010): 945–64.
35. Arindrajit Dube, Michael Reich, Akash Bhatt, and Denis Sosinskiy, "Restaurant Employment, Minimum Wages, and Border Discontinuities," Working Paper No. 32902 (National Bureau of Economic Research, September 2024).
36. In a recent paper, David Neumark and coauthors argued that using a different measure of local area (commuting zone) instead of county pairs, they find evidence of job loss, contrary to Dube, Lester, and Reich. Priyaranjan Jha, David Neumark, and Antonio Rodriguez-Lopez, "What's Across the Border? Re-Evaluating the Cross-Border Evidence on Minimum Wage Effects," Working Paper No. 32901 (National Bureau of Economic Research, September 2024). However, in follow-up work, we find that commuting zones are less effective and fall prey to the shocks from the 1980s and 1990s that I discuss in this chapter. Importantly, we also show that the findings in Dube, Lester, and Reich in "Minimum Wage Effects across State Borders" are reproduced with more recent data and updated statistical techniques for pooling individual state-level increases, whether one uses commuting zones or border county pairs. Dube, Reich, Bhatt, and Sosinskiy, "Restaurant Employment, Minimum Wages, and Border Discontinuities."
37. Reproduced from Dube, Reich, Bhatt, and Sosinskiy, "Restaurant Employment, Minimum Wages, and Border Discontinuities."
38. Arindrajit Dube and Ben Zipperer, *Minimum Wage Own-Wage Elasticity Repository*, Version 1.0.0, 2024, https://economic.github.io/owe.
39. Arindrajit Dube and Ben Zipperer, "Own-Wage Elasticity: Quantifying the Impact of Minimum Wages on Employment," Working Paper No. 32925 (National Bureau of Economic Research, September 2024).
40. David Card, "Using Regional Variation in Wages to Measure the Effects of the Federal Minimum Wage," *ILR Review* 46, no. 1 (1992):

22–37; David Neumark and William Wascher, "Employment Effects of Minimum and Subminimum Wages: Panel Data on State Minimum Wage Laws," *ILR Review* 46, no. 1 (1992): 55–81; David Card and Alan B. Krueger, *Myth and Measurement: The New Economics of the Minimum Wage* (Princeton University Press, 2016).

41. Alan Manning, "The Elusive Employment Effect of the Minimum Wage," *Journal of Economic Perspectives* 35, no. 1 (2021): 3–26.
42. Cengiz, Dube, Lindner, and Zipperer, "The Effect of Minimum Wages on Low-Wage Jobs."
43. Figure reproduced from figure 2 in Cengiz, Dube, Lindner, and Zipperer, "The Effect of Minimum Wages on Low-Wage Jobs." By permission of Oxford University Press.
44. Doruk Cengiz, Arindrajit Dube, Attila Lindner, and David Zentler-Munro, "Seeing beyond the Trees: Using Machine Learning to Estimate the Impact of Minimum Wages on Labor Market Outcomes," *Journal of Labor Economics* 40, no. S1 (2022): S203–S247.
45. Alan Manning, "The Elusive Employment Effect of the Minimum Wage," *Journal of Economic Perspectives* 35, no. 1 (2021): 3–26.
46. José Azar et al., "Minimum Wage Employment Effects and Labour Market Concentration," *Review of Economic Studies* 91, no. 4 (2024): 1843–83.
47. Justin C. Wiltshire, "Walmart Supercenters and Monopsony Power: How a Large, Low-Wage Employer Impacts Local Labor Markets," Working Paper, 2021.
48. Figure reproduced from figure G4 in Cengiz, Dube, Lindner, and Zipperer, "The Effect of Minimum Wages on Low-Wage Jobs." By permission of Oxford University Press.
49. For example, Sylvia Allegretto and coauthors (2017) advocated using more aggressive controls, while Neumark, Salas, and Wascher (2014) argued against it. See Sylvia Allegretto, Arindrajit Dube, Michael Reich, and Ben Zipperer, "Credible Research Designs for Minimum Wage Studies: A Response to Neumark, Salas, and Wascher," *ILR Review* 70, no. 3 (2017): 559–92; David Neumark, J. M. Ian Salas, and William Wascher, "Revisiting the Minimum Wage–Employment

Debate: Throwing Out the Baby with the Bathwater?," *ILR Review* 67, supplement no. 3 (2014): 608–48.

50. In my review of the literature with Attila Lindner, we highlight how biases can arise from a commonly used regression technique (the two-way fixed effects model) when applied to data from the 1980s and 1990s. In contrast, transparent event-study designs—featuring clear treatment and control comparisons within a defined time window around minimum wage changes—are better at guarding against such biases. Importantly, when we focus on the 1998–2019 period and pool data from all major state-level minimum wage increases, the evidence shows that restaurant and low-wage employment remained largely unchanged, even as earnings rose significantly. These findings hold up across virtually all major statistical techniques used in the minimum wage literature. See Dube and Lindner, "Minimum Wages in the 21st Century."
51. Ekaterina Jardim et al., "Minimum-Wage Increases and Low-Wage Employment: Evidence from Seattle," *American Economic Journal: Economic Policy* 14, no. 2 (2022): 263–314.
52. The OWE repository is designed to capture effects on headcount employment, and this estimate from the study by Jardim and coauthors is –1.75. Adding the hours reductions on top produces –2.8.
53. Max Ehrenfreund, "A 'Very Credible' New Study on Seattle's $15 Minimum Wage Has Bad News for Liberals," *Washington Post,* June 26, 2017, https://www.washingtonpost.com/news/wonk/wp/2017/06/26/new-study-casts-doubt-on-whether-a-15-minimum-wage-really-helps-workers/.
54. Carl Nadler, Sylvia A. Allegretto, Anna Godøy, and Michael Reich, "Are Local Minimum Wages Too High?," Working Paper No. 102-19 (Institute for Research on Labor and Employment Working Paper, April 2019).
55. Arindrajit Dube and Attila Lindner, "City Limits: What Do Local-Area Minimum Wages Do?," *Journal of Economic Perspectives* 35, no. 1 (2021): 27–50.
56. OECD provides data on minimum wages to median wages of full-time workers. See https://stats.oecd.org/index.aspx?DataSetCode=RMW#.

I report data for all workers by adjusting OECD data to reflect that median wages for full-time workers tend to be about 10 percent higher than median wages for all workers.

57. Giulia Giupponi et al., "The Employment and Distributional Impacts of Nationwide Minimum Wage Changes," *Journal of Labor Economics* 42, no. S1 (2024): S293–S333.
58. "Low Pay Commission Report 2022," GOV.UK, May 18, 2023, https://www.gov.uk/government/publications/low-pay-commission-report-2022.
59. Mario Bossler and Thorsten Schank, "Wage Inequality in Germany After the Minimum Wage Introduction," *Journal of Labor Economics* 41, no. 3 (2023): 813–57.
60. Thomas Haipeter and Sophie Rosenbohm, *Decentralisation of Collective Bargaining in Germany – Recent Trends and Challenges,* IAQ-Report no. 2023-03 (Duisburg: Institut Arbeit und Qualifikation [IAQ]), Universität Duisburg-Essen, 2023), https://doi.org/10.17185/duepublico/78287.
61. Christian Dustmann, Attila Lindner, Uta Schönberg, Matthias Umkehrer, and Philipp Vom Berge, "Reallocation Effects of the Minimum Wage," *Quarterly Journal of Economics* 137, no. 1 (2022): 267–328.
62. The OECD reports minimum-to-median wage ratios based on full-time workers. To present figures for all workers, I adjust the OECD data to account for the fact that median wages for full-time workers are typically about 10 percent higher than those for all workers. See https://stats.oecd.org/index.aspx?DataSetCode=RMW#.
63. Andreas Knabe and Ronnie Schöb, "Minimum Wage Incidence: The Case for Germany," *FinanzArchiv/Public Finance Analysis* 65, no. 4 (2009): 403–441; Joachim Ragnitz and Marcel Thum, "The Empirical Relevance of Minimum Wages for the Low-Wage Sector," *CESifo Forum* 8, no. 2 (2007): 35–37.
64. Dustmann, Lindner, Schönberg, and Vom Berge, "Reallocation Effects of the Minimum Wage."
65. Bossler and Schank, "Wage Inequality in Germany After the Minimum Wage Introduction."

66. For a comprehensive review of the evidence on these channels of adjustment to the minimum wage, as well as employment, see Dube and Lindner, "Minimum Wages in the 21st Century."
67. Pedro Portugal and Ana Rute Cardoso, "Disentangling the Minimum Wage Puzzle: An Analysis of Worker Accessions and Separations," *Journal of the European Economic Association* 4, no. 5 (2006): 988–1013; Pierre Brochu and David A. Green, "The Impact of Minimum Wages on Labour Market Transitions," *Economic Journal* 123, no. 573 (2013): 1203–35; Arindrajit Dube, T. William Lester, and Michael Reich, "Minimum Wage Shocks, Employment Flows, and Labor Market Frictions," *Journal of Labor Economics* 34, no. 3 (2016): 663–704.
68. Decio Coviello, Erika Deserranno, and Nicola Persico, "Minimum Wage and Individual Worker Productivity: Evidence from a Large US Retailer," *Journal of Political Economy* 130, no. 9 (2022): 2315–60.
69. Krista Ruffini, "Worker Earnings, Service Quality, and Firm Profitability: Evidence from Nursing Homes and Minimum Wage Reforms," *Review of Economics and Statistics* 106, no. 6 (2024): 1477–1494; Jessica H. Brown and Chris M. Herbst, "Minimum Wage, Worker Quality, and Consumer Well-Being: Evidence from the Child Care Market," IZA Discussion Paper No. 16257 (IZA Institute of Labor Economics, June 2023).
70. Christian Dustmann et al., "Reallocation Effects of the Minimum Wage," *Quarterly Journal of Economics* 137, no. 1 (2022): 267–328.
71. Daniel Aaronson, Eric French, Isaac Sorkin, and Ted To, "Industry Dynamics and the Minimum Wage: A Putty-Clay Approach," *International Economic Review* 59, no. 1 (2018): 51–84; Dara Lee Luca and Michael Luca, "Survival of the Fittest: The Impact of the Minimum Wage on Firm Exit," Working Paper No. 25806 (National Bureau of Economic Research, May 2019).
72. Nirupama Rao and Max Risch, "Who's Afraid of the Minimum Wage? Measuring the Impacts on Independent Businesses Using Matched US Tax Returns," *Quarterly Journal of Economics* (forthcoming).
73. Orley Ashenfelter and Štěpán Jurajda, "Minimum Wages, Wages, and

Price Pass-Through: The Case of McDonald's Restaurants," *Journal of Labor Economics* 40, no. S1 (2022): S179–S201.

74. Daniel Aaronson, Eric French, and James MacDonald, "The Minimum Wage, Restaurant Prices, and Labor Market Structure," *Journal of Human Resources* 43, no. 3 (2008): 688–720.
75. Sylvia Allegretto and Michael Reich, "Are Local Minimum Wages Absorbed by Price Increases? Estimates from Internet-Based Restaurant Menus," *ILR Review* 71, no. 1 (2018): 35–63.
76. Tobias Renkin, Claire Montialoux, and Michael Siegenthaler, "The Pass-Through of Minimum Wages into US Retail Prices: Evidence from Supermarket Scanner Data," *Review of Economics and Statistics* 104, no. 5 (2022): 890–908.
77. Justin H. Leung, "Minimum Wage and Real Wage Inequality: Evidence from Pass-Through to Retail Prices," *Review of Economics and Statistics* 103, no. 4 (2021): 754–69.
78. For evidence on employment effect in tradable sector, see Doruk Cengiz, Arindrajit Dube, Attila Lindner, and Ben Zipperer, "The Effect of Minimum Wages on Low-Wage Jobs," *Quarterly Journal of Economics* 134, no. 3 (2019): 1405–54; Peter Harasztosi and Attila Lindner, "Who Pays for the Minimum Wage?," *American Economic Review* 109, no. 8 (2019): 2693–2727; Radhakrishnan Gopalan, Barton H. Hamilton, Ankit Kalda, and David Sovich, "State Minimum Wages, Employment, and Wage Spillovers: Evidence from Administrative Payroll Data," *Journal of Labor Economics* 39, no. 3 (2021): 673–707.
79. Taylor Orth, "Three-Quarters of Americans Think the Federal Minimum Wage Is Too Low," YouGov, December 1, 2022, https://today.yougov.com/politics/articles/44610-most-americans-think-minimum-wage-is-too-low.
80. Mirko Draca, Stephen Machin, and John Van Reenen, "Minimum Wages and Firm Profitability," *American Economic Journal: Applied Economics* 3, no. 1 (2011): 129–51; Lev Drucker, Katya Mazirov, and David Neumark, "Who Pays for and Who Benefits from Minimum Wage Increases? Evidence from Israeli Tax Data on Business Owners and Workers," *Journal of Public Economics* 199 (2021): 104423.

81. Damián Vergara, "Minimum Wages and Optimal Redistribution," *arXiv* preprint arXiv:2202.00839 (2022).
82. Martha J. Bailey, John DiNardo, and Bryan A. Stuart, "The Economic Impact of a High National Minimum Wage: Evidence from the 1966 Fair Labor Standards Act," *Journal of Labor Economics* 39, no. S2 (2021): S329–S367; Ellora Derenoncourt and Claire Montialoux, "Minimum Wages and Racial Inequality," *Quarterly Journal of Economics* 136, no. 1 (2021): 169–228. The two studies did have somewhat divergent findings by demographic groups, though the differences were not very large.
83. Dube and Lindner, "City Limits: What Do Local-Area Minimum Wages Do?"
84. Anna Godoey and Michael Reich, "Are Minimum Wage Effects Greater in Low-Wage Areas?" *Industrial Relations: A Journal of Economy and Society* 60, no. 1 (2021): 36–83.
85. Jeffrey Clemens and Michael R. Strain, "The Heterogeneous Effects of Large and Small Minimum Wage Changes: Evidence Using a Partially Pre-Committed Analysis Plan," *Journal of Labor Economics* (forthcoming), https://doi.org/10.1086/736552.
86. Arindrajit Dube, "Impacts of Minimum Wages: Review of the International Evidence." Independent Report. UK Government Publication 268, no. 304 (2019): 1–65.
87. Dube and Lindner, "Minimum Wages in the 21st Century."
88. Justin Wiltshire, Carl McPherson, Michael Reich, and Denis Sosinskiy, "Minimum Wage Effects and Monopsony Explanations," *Journal of Labor Economics* (forthcoming), https://doi.org/10.1086/735551.
89. Even in states with automatic indexation, caps on annual increases, like 2.5 percent in Minnesota, mean that minimum wages sometimes did not fully keep up with cost-of-living increases.
90. Author's analysis of CPS ORG data downloaded from IPUMS.
91. These figures come from https://ballotpedia.org/Minimum_wage_on_the_ballot. Alaska voted to raise the minimum to $15 by 2027. Notably, California voters turned down a 2024 proposition to raise the state minimum wage to $18, but there were some peculiar circumstances surrounding that effort, including the absence of an

active campaign by advocates. See https://www.abc10.com/article/news/local/california/why-did-prop-32-fail/103-82a6aec4-e748-4890-854d-ea8e7a3b35ba.

Chapter 7: More Than the Minimum

1. Kristopher J. Brooks, "UAW Ends Historic Strike after Reaching Tentative Deals with Big 3 Automakers," CBS News, October 30, 2023, https://www.cbsnews.com/news/uaw-strike-update-gm-tentative-agreement/.
2. Reuters, "Automakers with Non-Union Workforce Race to Bump Pay after UAW's Record Deals," November 22, 2023, https://www.reuters.com/business/autos-transportation/automakers-with-non-union-workforce-race-bump-pay-after-uaws-record-deals-2023-11-21/.
3. Alissa Wilkinson and Emily Stewart, "The Hollywood Writers' Strike Is Over—and They Won Big," *Vox*, September 25, 2023, https://www.vox.com/culture/2023/9/24/23888673/wga-strike-end-sag-aftra-contract.
4. "Union Members—2024," News release USDL-25-0105, U.S. Bureau of Labor Statistics, January 28, 2025, https://www.bls.gov/news.release/pdf/union2.pdf.
5. The figure reports union density and coverage from the earliest year of available data after 1991, and the latest year available after 2015. In practice, the early years span 1991–1997 for different countries, while the later years span 2015–2021. Based on OECD data: https://www.oecd.org/en/data/datasets/oecdaias-ictwss-database.html.
6. Ernesto Adamopoulou Villanueva and Effrosyni Adamopoulou, "Employment and Wage Effects of Extending Collective Bargaining Agreements," IZA World of Labor, 2022; Thorsten Schulten, Line Eldring, and Reinhard Naumann, "The Role of Extension for the Strength and Stability of Collective Bargaining in Europe," in *Wage Bargaining under the New European Economic Governance: Alternative Strategies for Inclusive Growth,* ed. Guy van Gyes and Thorsten Schulten (Brussels: European Trade Union Institute, 2015), 361–400.
7. Under the Ghent system, unemployment insurance is administered by state-subsidized, union-linked unemployment funds. Workers typically

need to join a fund to receive benefits, creating a strong incentive for union membership and helping sustain high union density.

8. David Card and Ana Rute Cardoso, "Wage Flexibility under Sectoral Bargaining," *Journal of the European Economic Association* 20, no. 5 (2022): 2013–61.
9. Chris Isidore, "These Baristas Are Leading a Nationwide Campaign to Unionize Starbucks. It Came at a Cost," CNN Business, November 2, 2022, https://www.cnn.com/2022/11/02/business/starbucks-union-organizers-risk-takers-22-ctrp.
10. Steven Greenhouse, "Will Starbucks' Union-Busting Stifle a Union Rebirth in the US?," *Guardian*, August 28, 2023, https://www.theguardian.com/us-news/2023/aug/28/will-starbucks-union-busting-stifle-a-union-rebirth-in-the-us.
11. Another concern about incremental union organizing is that the impact on workers' conditions from isolated victories could be limited. Many unionized jobs in the private sector were organized decades ago under more favorable conditions. However, by the 1980s, employers had become less amenable to unions and more focused on cost cutting. Recent organizing efforts have revealed relatively modest compensation gains, often in the form of improved health and retirement benefits rather than wage increases. This underscores the limitations of incremental change under enterprise-level bargaining. See John DiNardo and David S. Lee, "Economic Impacts of New Unionization on Private Sector Employers: 1984–2001," *Quarterly Journal of Economics* 119, no. 4 (2004): 1383–441.
12. "Occupational Employment and Wage Statistics (OEWS) Query System, Industry: Cross-industry (000000)," U.S. Bureau of Labor Statistics, accessed August 15, 2025, https://data.bls.gov/oes/#/industry/000000.
13. James Bishop and Natasha Cassidy, "Wages Growth by Pay-Setting Method," *Reserve Bank of Australia Bulletin* (2019): 67–86.
14. From the OECD Income Distribution Database: https://www.oecd.org/en/data/datasets/income-and-wealth-distribution-database.html.
15. Data on the ratio of 9th and 1st wage deciles for the two countries

comes from OECD. Source: "Decile Ratios of Gross Earnings" in https://data-explorer.oecd.org.

16. James Bishop, "The Effect of Minimum Wage Increases on Wages, Hours Worked and Job Loss," Research Discussion Paper 2018-06 (Reserve Bank of Australia, May 2018).
17. Kate Andrias, "An American Approach to Social Democracy: The Forgotten Promise of the Fair Labor Standards Act," *The Yale Law Journal* 128, no. 3 (2019): 616–709; David Madland, "Wage Boards for American Workers." *Center for American Progress,* April 9, 2018, https://www.americanprogress.org/article/wage-boards-american-workers/.
18. I use CPS-ORG data from 2021 to 2023 (IPUMS extract) to simulate wage boards for each state-by-industry-by-occupation group, excluding Washington, DC. Wage board groups containing less than five observations are dropped, yielding 3,665 job groups.
19. I assume that the spillovers extend up to the median wage when the floor is set at two-thirds of the median. In other words, the "span of spillovers" is assumed to extend up to 1.5 times the value of the floor. For example, if the floor is $15, the span of spillover is assumed to extend up to $22.50. This is greater than the evidence suggests from minimum wage laws, where the span of spillover from a $15 floor is not likely to extend past $20. See Nicole M. Fortin, Thomas Lemieux, and Neil Lloyd, "Labor Market Institutions and the Distribution of Wages: The Role of Spillover Effects," *Journal of Labor Economics* 39, no. S2 (2021): S369–S412; and Doruk Cengiz, Arindrajit Dube, Attila Lindner, and Ben Zipperer, "The Effect of Minimum Wages on Low-Wage Jobs," *Quarterly Journal of Economics* 134, no. 3 (2019): 1405–54. At the same time, the span of spillover appears to be somewhat larger with European sectoral bargaining as found in Card and Cardoso. For this reason, I take a span of 1.5 times the floor to be a reasonable estimate of the span for a sectoral standard in America, especially since I am using coarser job categories than used in the European context.
20. Recall that Card and Cardoso found that if the floor rose by 1 percent, wages overall in the job group would rise by around 0.45 percent. To

compare how my estimates compare to those, I also additionally simulated a small (1 percent) change in the floors. I found that this raised overall wages by 0.15 percent. This captures my assumptions of spillovers that are somewhere between the Card and Cardoso estimates from Portugal and the minimum wage evidence and Australian evidence, which suggest smaller spillovers.

21. My calculations use CPS ORG data (IPUMS extract), imposing a standard of two-thirds median wage within job groups.
22. More precisely, these percentages are approximated by log point changes. The 90/10 ratio rose by 0.29 log points between 1980 and 2013, fell by 0.02 points between 2013 and 2019, and fell by an additional 0.08 points between 2019 and 2024, for a total reduction of 0.10 log points. The 90/10 ratio would fall by a further 0.09 log points from the introduction of the wage board. The 90/50 ratio, on the other hand, rose by around 0.22 log points between 1980 and 2019 and rose by a further 0.01 log point between 2019 and 2024. This ratio would fall by 0.08 log points from the wage board, erasing 35 percent of the total increase between 1980 and 2024.
23. Analysis using CPS data (IPUMS extract).
24. Analysis using CPS data (IPUMS extract).
25. Accounting for spillovers, I estimate that a full sectoral standard would raise the total wage bill by about 4.5 percent. With labor's share around 70 percent, full pass-through implies roughly a 3 percent increase in the price level. Likely offsets, from productivity gains and lower profits, put the net effect closer to 2 to 3 percent. This means most workers still come out ahead after prices adjust.
26. Ana B. Ibarra, "New California Law Raises Minimum Wage to $25 for Health Care Workers," CalMatters, October 13, 2023, http://calmatters.org/health/2023/10/california-minimum-wage-health-care-law/. Also see Kristen Hwang, "Kaiser Unions Went on Strike Twice in 12 Months. The Latest Walkout Led to a 'Historic' Deal," CalMatters, October 17, 2023, http://calmatters.org/health/2023/10/kaiser-permanente-union-strikes-california-contract/.
27. Danielle Wiener-Bronner, Natasha Chen, and Jack Hannah, "California Law Raises Minimum Wage for Fast Food Workers," CNN

Business, September 28, 2023, https://www.cnn.com/2023/09/28/business/california-fast-food-law.

28. Clemens, Edwards, and Meer use QCEW data, and their baseline DiD that California fast-food employment fell about 2.7 percent relative to other states after the $20 floor; paired with sector-wide wage gains of roughly 8 percent, this implies an OWE near −0.34 (with alternative specifications ranging from −0.29 to −0.49). Sosinskiy and Reich also use QCEW data, but adjust for population-growth differences, apply a different seasonal adjustment, and make other smaller changes; they find employment effects not statistically different from zero, with OWE estimates between −0.20 and 0.01 (their preferred estimate is −0.12). Taken together, these results imply employment effects ranging from none to moderately negative—even at this unusually high wage floor. See Jeffrey Clemens, Olivia Edwards, and Jonathan Meer, "Did California's Fast Food Minimum Wage Reduce Employment?," Working Paper No. 34033 (National Bureau of Economic Research, July 2025). Also see Denis Sosinskiy and Michael Reich, "A $20 Minimum Wage: Effects on Wages, Employment and Price." IRLE Working Paper No. 104-24 (Center on Wage and Employment Dynamics, September 2024).
29. David Madland, "Minnesota Is Transforming Its Nursing Home Industry with a Model That Empowers Workers," Minnesota Reformer, June 15, 2023, https://minnesotareformer.com/2023/06/15/minnesota-is-transforming-its-nursing-home-industry-with-a-model-that-empowers-workers/.
30. Max Nesterak, "Minnesota's New Labor Board Votes for Nearly $23.50 an Hour Minimum Wage for Nursing Home Workers," Minnesota Reformer, April 29, 2024, https://minnesotareformer.com/2024/04/29/minnesotas-new-labor-board-votes-for-20-an-hour-minimum-wage-for-nursing-home-workers/.
31. "Uber and Lyft Settlement Information and Frequently Asked Questions," Massachusetts Office of the Attorney General, last updated August 15, 2025, https://www.mass.gov/info-details/uber-and-lyft-settlement-information-and-frequently-asked-questions; David Madland, "State Rideshare Collective Bargaining Policies Hold Great

Promise," Center for American Progress, August 6, 2025, https://www.americanprogress.org/article/state-rideshare-collective-bargaining-policies-hold-great-promise/.

Chapter 8: The Politics of Possibility

1. Nye Cominetti, Rui Costa, Nikhil Datta, and Felicia Odamtten, "Low Pay Britain 2022: Low Pay and Insecurity in the UK Labour Market," Resolution Foundation, May 25, 2022.
2. David Autor, Arindrajit Dube, and Annie McGrew, "The Unexpected Compression: Competition at Work in the Low Wage Labor Market," Working Paper No. 31010 (National Bureau of Economic Research, May 2024).
3. Roy F. Baumeister, Ellen Bratslavsky, Catrin Finkenauer, and Kathleen D. Vohs, "Bad Is Stronger Than Good," *Review of General Psychology* 5, no. 4 (2001): 323–70.
4. Andrew Van Dam, "America's Best Decade, According to Data," *Washington Post*, May 24, 2024, https://www.washingtonpost.com/business/2024/05/24/when-america-was-great-according-data/. Underlying survey data: https://ygo-assets-websites-editorial-emea.yougov.net/documents/crosstabs_Best_and_Worst_Decades_20240523.pdf.
5. "Hourly Wage, Median—Median Real Hourly Wage (2024$)," State of Working America Data Library, Economic Policy Institute, 2025.
6. Sarah Foster, "The 'Silent Recession': Economists Say the Economy Is Strong, but Most Americans Feel Like They're Living in a Downturn," Bankrate, December 6, 2023, https://www.bankrate.com/banking/federal-reserve/americans-experiencing-silent-recession/.
7. "Economic Well-Being of U.S. Households in 2023," Board of Governors of the Federal Reserve Board, May 2024, https://www.federalreserve.gov/publications/files/2023-report-economic-well-being-us-households-202405.pdf.
8. Ben Harris and Aaron Sojourner, "Why Are Americans So Displeased with the Economy?," Brookings Institution, January 5, 2024, https://www.brookings.edu/articles/why-are-americans-so-displeased-with-the-economy/.

9. Kyla Scanlon, "The Vibecession: The Self-Fulfilling Prophecy," *Kyla's Newsletter* (Substack), June 30, 2022, https://kyla.substack.com/p/the-vibecession-the-self-fulfilling.
10. Claire E. Robertson et al., "Negativity Drives Online News Consumption," *Nature Human Behaviour* 7, no. 5 (2023): 812–22.
11. David H. Autor and David Dorn, "The Growth of Low-Skill Service Jobs and the Polarization of the US Labor Market," *American Economic Review* 103, no. 5 (2013): 1553–97.
12. Alan B. Krueger, *Rockonomics: A Backstage Tour of What the Music Industry Can Teach Us about Economics and Life* (Currency, 2019).
13. Xavier Gabaix and Augustin Landier, "Why Has CEO Pay Increased So Much?" *Quarterly Journal of Economics* 123, no. 1 (2008): 49–100.
14. Daron Acemoglu and Pascual Restrepo, "Automation and Rent Dissipation: Implications for Wages, Inequality, and Productivity," Working Paper No. 32536 (National Bureau of Economic Research, June 2024).
15. Zheyuan Kevin Cui et al., "The Effects of Generative AI on High Skilled Work: Evidence from Three Field Experiments with Software Developers," SSRN, last revised August 21, 2025, https://papers.ssrn.com/sol3/papers.cfm?abstract_id=4945566; Erik Brynjolfsson, Danielle Li, and Lindsey Raymond, "Generative AI at Work," *Quarterly Journal of Economics* 140, no. 2 (2025): 889–942; Shakked Noy and Whitney Zhang, "Experimental Evidence on the Productivity Effects of Generative AI," *Science* 381, no. 6654 (2023): 187–92.
16. David Autor, "Applying AI to Rebuild Middle Class Jobs," Working Paper No. 32140 (National Bureau of Economic Research, February 2024).
17. Daron Acemoglu, "The Simple Macroeconomics of AI," *Economic Policy* 40, no. 121 (2025): 13–58.
18. Daron Acemoglu and Simon Johnson, "Learning from Ricardo and Thompson: Machinery and Labor in the Early Industrial Revolution and in the Age of Artificial Intelligence," *Annual Review of Economics* 16, no. 1 (2024): 597–621.
19. Ilyana Kuziemko, Nicolas Longuet-Marx, and Suresh Naidu,

"'Compensate the Losers?' Economic Policy and Partisan Realignment in the US," Working Paper No. 31794 (National Bureau of Economic Research, October 2023).

20. Peter Hall and John Cole, "Trump and Vance Take Message of 'Vast New Prosperity' to Pennsylvania Voters," *Pennsylvania Capital-Star,* August 19, 2024, https://penncapital-star.com/election-2024/trump-and-vance-take-message-of-vast-new-prosperity-to-pennsylvania-voters/.
21. Ezra Klein and Derek Thompson, *Abundance* (Avid Reader Press, 2025).
22. Jane Coaston, "This Conservative Wants to Change the Way Republicans Think About Economics," *New York Times,* December 4, 2023, https://www.nytimes.com/2023/12/04/opinion/oren-cass-republicans-unions.html. Also see Sohrab Ahmari, *Tyranny, Inc.: How Private Power Crushed American Liberty—and What to Do About It* (Forum Books, 2023).
23. Paula England, Michelle Budig, and Nancy Folbre, "Wages of Virtue: The Relative Pay of Care Work," *Social Problems* 49, no. 4 (2002): 455–473.

Appendix B: Five Equations That Explain How Wages Are Set

1. Jacob A. Mincer, *Schooling, Experience, and Earnings* (National Bureau of Economic Research, 1974).

Index

Page numbers in *italics* refer to figures.

About the Author

ARINDRAJIT (ARIN) DUBE is Provost Professor of Economics at the University of Massachusetts Amherst, research associate at the National Bureau of Economic Research, and research fellow at the Institute for Labor in Germany. He has testified before Congress, consulted with the UK government, provided counsel to many state legislatures, and is invited to speak about his research around the world. Dube publishes consistently in top economics journals, such as *The Quarterly Journal of Economics*, *The American Economic Review*, *The Review of Economics and Statistics*, and *American Economic Journal*. He has written opinion pieces for *The New York Times* and *The Washington Post*, and has been interviewed extensively on radio and television, including NPR, MSNBC, CNBC, and Bloomberg TV.